GODDARD PARENTING GUIDES

Going to School

How to Help Your Child Succeed

A HANDBOOK FOR PARENTS
OF CHILDREN AGES 3–8

Sharon L. Ramey, Ph.D. • Craig T. Ramey, Ph.D.

GODDARD PRESS
380 MADISON AVENUE
NEW YORK, NY 10017

Book design by Stan Adler Associates.
Manufactured in the United States of America.

PUBLISHER'S CATALOGING-IN-PUBLICATION DATA

Ramey, Sharon L.
Going to school: how to help your child succeed: a handbook for parents of children ages 3 to 8/
Sharon L. Ramey, Craig T. Ramey
Includes bibliographical references. 1. Parenting. 2. Child care.
ISBN 0-9666397-3-1

1. Education, Preschool — United States. 2. Education, Preschool — Parent participation — United States.
3. Child development — United States. I. Ramey, Craig T. II. Title.
BF720.S44 P78 1999 99-61457
372.21—dc21 CIP

THE AUTHOR AND PUBLISHER GRATEFULLY ACKNOWLEDGE PERMISSION TO REPRINT MATERIAL FROM THE FOLLOWING WORKS AND INDIVIDUALS:

CHAPTER PHOTOGRAPHS: *Cover:* Telegraph Colour Library/FPG, Jim Craigmyle/Masterfile; *Chap. 1:* C/B Productions/The Stock Market; *Chap. 2:* Telegraph Colour Library/FPG; *Chap. 3:* Ed Taylor Studio/FPG; *Chap. 4:* Index Stock Photography, Inc.; *Chap. 5:* Arthur Tilley/FPG; *Chap. 6:* Telegraph Colour Library/FPG; *Chap. 7:* Family Stock; *Chap. 8:* Telegraph Colour Library/FPG; *Chap. 9:* Mark Gibson/Index Stock Photography; *Chap. 10:* Roy Gumpel/Liaison International; *Chap. 11:* Jack McConnell/McConnell McNamara & Co.; *Chap. 12:* Lucille Khornak Photography; *Chap. 13:* Erlanson Productions/The Image Bank

We dedicate this book to all the great teachers we've had

First, our parents
Jim and Belle Ramey
Gene and Ellie Landesman

Next, our talented public school teachers
in University City, Missouri
and Martinsburg, West Virginia

Then, the wonderful faculty at
West Virgina University, New College,
the University of Minnesota,
the University of Washington, and
the University of California at Berkeley

And all of the great thinkers and scientists who taught us
through their writings and many contributions to the fields
of child development and education

Finally, to our children
Samuel, Lee, Ann, and Jane,
from whom we have learned so much

We are truly indebted, beyond mere words, to all of you

ACKNOWLEDGMENTS

WE EXTEND HEARTFELT THANKS TO MANY WHO MADE WRITING THIS BOOK POSSIBLE AND A JOY, INCLUDING:

Anthony Martino, Chairman of the Goddard Schools for Early Childhood Development, for his vision in creating Goddard Press. Our tireless and talented Editor in Chief, Diane Lansing, who skillfully attended to details while keeping the big picture in mind and who contributed immensely through her queries, edits, and encouragement. Suzanne du Pont and Fran Ritter of the Goddard Schools for their leadership in this innovative publishing endeavor. Jay Poynor for sound advice and continuous support for our efforts to share research findings with families, as well as excellent editorial input from Kathy Doane and Nancy Booth.

Our family, who has been patient, generous with suggestions, and supportive as always: our mothers — Eleanor Landesman and Belle Ramey — continue to be our teachers and cheerleaders. Our grown daughters — Jane Dwyer, Ann Andre, and Lee Ramey — are a source of great pride. Our seven-year-old son, Sam, is a great joy and was very patient as we wrote this book. He offered lots of good ideas for what parents and teachers can do to help children succeed in school. Thanks also to our siblings: Kathy and Jim Forget, Linda and David Landesman, and Barbara and Benjamin Landesman.

Our many colleagues, who have worked with us in studying young children and families, and especially the transition to school. Among those to whom we are indebted are: Donna Bryant, Frances Campbell, Joseph Sparling, Margaret (Peg) Burchinal, Barbara Wasik, Isabelle Lewis, Ron Haskins, Al Collier, Dale Farran, Jim Gallagher, Jim Sackett, Nancy Robinson, Molly Reid, Jim Jaccard, T.V. Kenley, Phil Dale, Martha Phillips, Robin Gaines Lanzi, Clancy Blair, Halldor Juliusson, Janice Rabkin, and Virgina Gunderson.

Our colleagues and advisors for the National Head Start–Public School Early Childhood Transition Demonstration Project, funded by the Administration on Children, Youth, and Families since 1991: The Commissioners (Wade Horn, Olivia Golden, Jim Harrell, and Patricia Montoya), our Federal Project Officers (Mary Bruce Webb, Pia Divine, Martha Moorehouse, and Michael Lopez), the head investigators at the 31 local sites (Martha Abbott-Shim, Annette Sibley, Ann Millard, Helen Barrett, Ray Fenton, Robert Abbott, John Hall, Ron Bramlett, Linda Wetzel, Richard Packard, Andrea Greene, Darryl Greenfield, Susan Gold, Gene Brody, Zolinda Stoneman, David Glassman, Kelly McCoy, Susan Hegland, Dania Clark-Lempers, Bryce Fifield, Carol J. Nelson, Margo Gottlieb, Sue Rasher, Mary Lewis, Harriet Talmage, Youli Mantzicopoulos, Lisanio Orlandi, Robert Mooney, Alice Stadhaus, David Robinson, Alice Galper, Carol Seefeldt, Thomas M. Reischl, Jeanette Gassaway, Daniel P. Mueller, Sue Vartuli, Donna Bryant, Frances Campbell, Gary Hoeltke, Helen Raikes, Gita Z. Wilder, Paul W. Speer, John R. Bergan, Jason Feld, Deborah Loesch-Griffin, JoAnn Everts, Carolyn Jarvis, Evelyn Luckey, Jan Jewett, Dean Arrasmith, Tim Speth, Joseph L. French, Michael Hoadley, Ray Thompson, Mark

Appelbaum, Jack Sellers, David Brown, Lin Moore, Marvin G. Cline, Frances Bridges-Cline, Joesph T. Lawton, Carole Vickers, Steve Banks, Robert Bickel, and Linda Spatig); key individuals in the Head Start Bureau (Michele Plutro, E. Dollie Wolverton, Esther Kresh); members of our National Research Advisory Panel (Karen Anderson, Margaret Burchinal, William Darity, III, Steve Forness, Nicholas Ialongo, Sharon Lynn Kagan, Luis Laosa, Ingram Olkin, Jack Pascoe, Nancy Robinson, William Rosenberg, Arnold J. Sameroff, Neal Schmitt, Diana Slaughter-Defore, and Richard A. Weinberg); and colleagues here at the University of Alabama at Birmingham (Clancy B. Blair, Carl Brezausek, Sandra Cluett, Betty Cotton, Robin Gaines Lanzi, Jay Hsu, Charles R. Katholi, Bette Keltner, Kathleen G. Nelon, Wanda Newell, Fran D. Perkins, Martha Phillips, Scott W. Snyder, and Joseph J. Sparling). This project has contributed immensely to the scientific understanding of how children, families, teachers, schools, and communities can collaborate to improve children's early school achievement and adjustment.

Many individuals at federal agencies who over the years have helped to further the research agenda and program development concerning the well-being and school adjustment of young children and their families, including those at the National Institute of Child Health and Human Development, the Department of Education, the Maternal and Child Health Bureau, and the Administration on Developmental Disabilities.

Key foundations that have supported our research and valuable conferences on children's school success, including the Ford Foundation, Robert Wood Johnson Foundation, MacArthur Foundation, Carnegie Corporation, Pew Charitable Trusts, W. T. Grant Foundation, Foundation for Child Development, Packard Foundation, and BellSouth Foundation.

The Civitan International Foundation for its remarkable vision in creating the Civitan International Research Center at the University of Alabama at Birmingham, which has brought together leading scientists from many disciplines to help further our understanding of the factors that lead to successful outcomes for children.

The A-Plus Education Foundation, especially its Executive Committee (Bill Smith, Caroline Novack, Cathy Gassenheimer, Ruth Ash, Jim Williams, Charles Mason, and Ted Kennedy), for its dedication to improving children's learning.

Individuals who provided timely and valuable information as we prepared this book, including Ruth Ash, Debi Strevy, Jeanne Box, Amanda Deeson, Bettye Caldwell, Nancy Robinson, Cathy Gassenheimer, M. Reid Lyon, Sarah Friedman, Janice Cotton, Margie Curry, Jack Fletcher, Justine Rynearson and Sharon Lynn Kagan. In addition, Zee Hildreth and Lori McClelland pitched in as needed.

Our son's remarkable teachers in his Waldorf School, the Redmont School (Sheila Rubin and Lynda Powell); his kindergarten teacher, Beth Miller, his first grade teacher, Christy Neely, and his principal, Mike Melvin, at Crestline School, along with Charles Mason, Superintendent of Mountain Brook Schools, and Kathy Person, who does lots for children and families. They have reminded us how much talent and effort go into providing a first-rate education in the early transition-to-school years. We are most indebted and grateful.

— Sharon and Craig Ramey, Birmingham, AL

Contents

INTRODUCTION

The world of school has changed dramatically in the last two generations. A host of reasons are at the root of this evolution: cultural and linguistic diversity; great changes in family lifestyles; wide disparities in funding for schools; the prevalence of preschool education; and new educational practices for children with disabilities. These are just some of the changes that have profoundly affected our schools and the ability of children to succeed in them.

Not many years ago, preparation for kindergarten consisted of a few pep talks and a visit to the school.

Not any more. Today we know from extensive research that *a successful transition to school is a multi-person, multi-year process*. The requirements go way beyond helping your child adjust to a new set of rules and expectations. Research also shows that *the family has as much impact as schools or teachers on a child's success in school*.

Fortunately, research also shows us many ways parents can leverage their impact to help their children make this transition successfully. In a nutshell, parents need to take an active role in their child's education from the start, and stick with it.

This book covers the period in a child's life from three to eight years of age. We chose this period because most parents begin to think seriously about schooling when their child is around three, and many parents enroll their children in preschool programs at this age. By the time a child is eight years old, most of the early opportunities and initial problems in schooling will have been encountered. However, we remind parents that early learning abilities, as well as language, social, and emotional skills, are being developed in profound ways right from birth and require great care and attention. And, of course, there are many transitions throughout a child's education — beyond age eight through the end of formal schooling.

Knowledge about how children learn and how adults can be effective teachers has expanded at a phenomenal rate in recent years. There are many unsettled issues and much debate about how to improve schools. But there are many valuable lessons to be learned from the recent experiences of children, families, and educators throughout our nation.

Going to School shares this valuable information — and proven results — with parents. It will serve as a guide, an up-to-date reference, and a source of ideas and encouragement to parents, as well as to grandparents, aunts and uncles, godparents, and teachers.

We have included many topics that range from the expected — such as how to encourage reading and what to do if your child does not like school — to the unexpected — such as why parents should expand their own learning and how family celebrations help children develop a sense of self and competency.

Although this book is about "going to school," it also is about promoting a lifelong love of learning and a sense of connection to others that has its roots in the experiences of early learning, sharing, struggling, and succeeding. After all, school is the primary institution in our society for instilling a love of accomplishment and encouraging lifelong learning — important for individual success and for the continuation of our democratic way of life.

School can be wonderful and terrifying, inviting and overwhelming, challenging and boring, predictable and changing, responsive and rigid. Since this is true regardless of how great the schools are, your child's school years will not be easy.

ORGANIZATION OF THE BOOK

The book is divided into twelve chapters. Each provides resources, activities, and a large body of information culled from scientific studies, theory, and practical experience.

There are many topics that address your child's changing needs from ages three to eight. Throughout we share compelling evidence to support three sweeping themes about going to school and being successful in life:

I. There is no *one* way that works best for everyone.

II. Children learn the most when they are happy and healthy.

III. As important as school is, it is only part of the learning experience.

As we gathered materials for this handbook, we found that everyone had vivid memories of school. Rarely did we encounter a grownup who didn't love to tell stories about the most awful school experience in kindergarten or first grade, or the most wonderful teacher, or the funniest thing that he or she did in class or on the playground. So we write this book with a special awareness that *school matters a lot*, and that parents can be instrumental in shaping the lifelong memories which help shape the child's future.

After family, school is the most influential institution in our society. Like family, school is a place that exists for the benefit of children and represents our collective hope for, and commitment to, our next generation. In an ideal world, families, schools, and communities would be united and mutually supportive in their investment in children, and recognize and value the unique role that families and schools serve in the development of young children. We hope this book will help you to fulfill your commitment to your children and to make their school years rewarding in every good way.

CHAPTER 1

WHY SCHOOL IS

SO DIFFERENT TODAY

The many changes in education, schools, and school systems.
The great impact you can have on your child's success in school.

GOING TO SCHOOL IS THE FIRST COMMON CULTURAL EXPERIENCE AMONG CHILDREN AND FAMILIES IN OUR COUNTRY. HOW PARENTS AND CHILDREN PREPARE FOR THAT FIRST DAY OF "BIG SCHOOL" AND BEYOND — THE YEARS OF LEARNING IN THE COMPLEX AND EVOLVING INSTITUTION OF SCHOOL — CAN MAKE A LIFETIME OF DIFFERENCE. IT IS NO SURPRISE THAT EDUCATION CONSISTENTLY RANKS NEAR THE TOP OF EVERY NATIONAL POLL OF VOTERS' CONCERNS.

Success in school — academically and socially — is closely tied to success in nearly every facet of adult life. Research shows that children who start off poorly in school and stay in that poor "track" have the least favorable outcomes throughout school and the rest of their lives. A good beginning matters.

Unfortunately, conditions in some schools are alarming. Media attention has focused on the weaknesses and failures — crumbling buildings, inadequate funding, poor teachers, falling test scores, violence, controversy over curricula, and high school graduates who are functionally illiterate. These problems clearly undermine children's chances for succeeding.

These issues raise the question: Are academically gifted children receiving the attention they deserve? When funding cutbacks occur, programs for our most talented youth often are considered expendable. What does this bode for the future of our country?

Beyond general concern, what can you do to assure that your child succeeds in school? That's what this book will tell you.

Scientists and educators have learned a great deal about how children learn, what makes schools effective, and how families can best support their children's education. This book provides this information so you can be up-to-date about new discoveries and well-versed in the basics — findings from years ago that continue to be upheld in recent studies.

We also think parents need information to help them distinguish fads from fact. Education is as prone to fad and fashion as any other area of life, and sometimes children are the ones who suffer. Consider two recent trends that didn't work:

- **"New math" that tried to teach very young children abstract concepts before they were ready.**
- **The "whole language" approach that failed to incorporate important aspects of phonics and prevented some children from grasping the early essentials of reading.**

Some new technologies and innovative approaches look promising. But what matters most is that every child receives a healthy dose of the right educational ingredients outlined in this book. Parents also will learn how they can determine if their child is getting enough of these ingredients on time in the proper way.

WORKING IN YOUR FAVOR

There are many challenges to a successful school experience, and we'll discuss them throughout this book. From the outset, you and your child have two powerful things going for you:

Children come to school eager to learn. This is true for children from all walks of life regardless of their intelligence, their knowledge about the world, or their parents' schooling experiences. Even children with learning disabilities are eager to learn. Our research shows that children are eager to get "facts" and find out more about life and the world in which they live. This is as important to them as social and emotional supports. This information will help them to interpret the world around them, do new things they previously relied on others to do, and enable them to have more interesting exchanges with others, from conversations to playing games and sports to making things.

Parents have a huge impact on how their children fare in school. This is one of the most robust findings in all the research literature, and one that should reassure every parent. There are many ways you can ensure that your child succeeds in school. You don't need to devote full time to the job, but you do need to be informed, attentive, and active.

A comprehensive review of children's learning shows us that student achievement is affected about *equally* by three external factors:

- **the family**
- **effective teaching practices in the classroom**
- **school and community supports for education.**

Clearly, families have much greater impact than many parents realize. Over and over we see children, even in poor schools, getting a good education and a good start in life because their parents were active, supportive partners throughout their child's schooling.

HOW CHILDREN SPEND THEIR WEEKDAY TIME DURING THE SCHOOL YEAR

For most of their growing years, children divide their waking hours about equally between school and home. Most young children need at least 10 hours of good sleep to be "at their best." A typical school day breaks down as follows:

	Hours
Sleeping	10
School day	6.5 – 7.5
Eating, dressing, bathing, going to and from school	3.5
"Free time"	2 – 3

The influence of what happens in school is clearly going to be profound and lasting. But parents can and do balance the impact of school, even though they are with their children for much less time each day.

WHAT'S DIFFERENT IN TODAY'S SCHOOLS

There have been dramatic changes in schools and the American educational system since you were a student. Issues in your own school district or private school may be much different than they were even five years ago. Moreover, schools vary widely within and among areas of the country.

In short, there is a lot of new terrain on the educational landscape. For your impact on your child's success to be as great as possible, you need to understand this new terrain.

Some features are welcome additions that offer new opportunities. Sadly, other features are troublesome. You need to fully understand both situations if you are to help your child navigate them successfully.

The issues that are transforming education today include:

Changing teacher workforce: The type of people who go into teaching has shifted over the generations. Uncertainty of funding, inadequate teacher pay, and the burgeoning array of career options open to women have changed the teacher profile dramatically. Many of our nation's talented youth will not consider a career in teaching children.

Wider cultural diversity: The ethnic and cultural diversity of children within a school and school district has increased dramatically. This presents wonderful learning opportunities to children who are exposed to many different cultures, traditions, and lifestyles. However, these differences also call for awareness, understanding, and respect by parents, children, and school professionals.

Increasing demands on schools: Schools are now expected to do a great deal more than focus on academics and teach the three "Rs" (reading, 'riting, and 'rithmetic). They are now expected to help children with a wide array of problems, including social and emotional ones. They also are challenged to fulfill the national mandate of special education for all children — in regular classrooms whenever possible.

Growing expectations for students: Students also face changing expectations. Teachers now look to even very young students to be independent and responsible. For example, most schools don't let parents bring "left at home" homework or lunches to school anymore.

New legal issues: Schools today must be increasingly sensitive to legal issues, such as equal opportunity for quality education, students' right to privacy, and prevention of sexual harassment. Moreover, conflict resolution in the educational arena is increasingly litigious. Gone are the days when parties could always resolve their differences quietly at a meeting in the principal's office.

Safety concerns: National attention on tragic incidents of school violence has raised concerns about the overall security of our schools. New safety issues have emerged as well, including those related to bitter or unresolved custody battles. How do we protect our young ones?

Changing accountability: The ways teachers, schools, and school districts are held accountable and how the performance of schools is judged differs markedly throughout the country. Many of these ways are controversial.

Communication: How and how often schools keep parents informed about everything is changing. Parents receive more information now than ever before. Nonetheless, it may not always be the *right* information. And it may be one-way, with more information from the school than from the parent.

Politicization of education: Educational quality and safety in schools are only two of the political issues at every level of government. The result is continually changing — often conflicting — goals and mandates. Accountability is also rapidly becoming a major political football. Other hot topics: parental choice, privatization of schools, prayer in schools, and adequacy and equity of funding.

Funding uncertainties: Who foots the bill for new programs? If there isn't enough money, what existing programs should be cut to free up the funding? Is the tax or private base for a school's funding stable? These uncertainties affect the school climate and the school's ability to attract talented teachers.

Debate over how to "reform" education: Falling test scores, high drop-out rates in some areas, and unacceptable levels of academic achievement are just some of the issues that have spawned a host of ideas about reform — what is needed and how it can be accomplished. Many ideas are being adopted with little proof that they work.

Inadequate preschool care: With more children in non-parental child-care for a significant period of time prior to school entry, the quality of that care is under intense scrutiny. The results are not encouraging. Too many children are in mediocre or poor-quality non-parental care *prior* to kinder-garten. As a result, they start out behind their better-cared-for peers from day one.

These are a few of the changes affecting today's schools. Not all of them are bad, nor are all schools in a crisis. But you can see why it's important that you be informed on these issues to a much greater degree than your parents had to be.

WHAT MATTERS, WHAT COUNTS

Research clearly shows that the most advantaged children are those whose par-ents are "there" for them in the right ways, at the right time, not doing too much or too little, recognizing and supporting their child's individuality and right to learn more.

Well-informed parents often are the most discerning and demanding about the quality of their children's education. They invest early, substantially, and selectively in their children's education. For these parents, education is synonymous with their children's future prospects. But well-informed parents also know that school is not the only factor that determines whether their child receives an excellent education for life.

Well-prepared parents are in the best position to assure that their chil-dren receive the best education. They know how to support their child's adjustment to the school setting, and they have effective ways to solve the inevitable problems that will arise.

Well-prepared parents also are likely to be less stressed, tired, uncertain, worried, or critical. They discover how much fun they can have while helping their children succeed in school and life. Such parents consistently find that their child's elementary school opens new opportunities for *them* as well as their children, including new friends, new activities, new ways to contribute to their community, and a chance to learn (or learn *again*) new and interesting things. This manual is designed to make you a well-prepared parent.

A BIT OF TRANSITION TO SCHOOL HISTORY

In the original "Dr. Spock" book of 1945, advice on children ages three to eight occupied a very small section. The topic of "fitting into the outside world" was under the section titled "from six to eleven" — far later than parents and society now expect children to fit into the outside world. The chapter on schools was only 14 pages long (in a book over 500 pages long!), and covered only two topics: "what a school is for" and "trouble with lessons." Clearly, this was an era when educators were in charge of schools and parents were in charge of family life. Close collaboration and frequent communication between schools and families didn't exist. When parents went to their child's school, it was for a special event or because there was trouble and the principal had called. Parents often had little idea of what was being taught in the classroom, much less what educational theories guided the teacher's organization of the classroom, methods of teaching, and criteria for measuring individual student progress. How much the world has changed in 50 years!

However, one third of the 13-page chapter "From Six to Eleven" was on "comics, radio, and movies." Some things stay the same.

KEEP IN MIND

Whether your child is young and you are just starting to think about schools or whether your child is already in school, there are some basic issues to keep in mind as you read this book:

Childcare is a form of education, and quality matters. The care your child has received right from birth has been shaping his readiness for school. Good preschool care — from you or a high-quality group setting — will provide a good foundation for learning and social interaction. In the period from ages three to five, your child can be guided and encouraged in important ways to set the stage for a good transition to school.

Once your child starts school, the quality of care is just as important. Parents and family life provide the balance in a child's day — a support for achievements and a critical buffer for the inevitable bumps.

New friends and new families. School offers a new world of friends and new lessons in social negotiation. School is a social conduit as well as an information conveyor. Your child will learn to build on the work of others, to collaborate, to accept challenges and criticism, to seek and win approval. Your child may question how and why other families do things the way they do. Sometimes your child will want to change.

From now on, peers will steadily assume an increasing influence over your child, especially for such things as style, likes, and dislikes. Peers will introduce new words, ideas, and actions (it's always other children who teach our own those "bad" things).

But research shows that *parents do not lose their influence.* Even as friends rise in importance, school-age children still look up to and value the special role their parents have in their lives.

BE PREPARED – AND ENCOURAGED!

We wrote this book to provide parents with up-to-date, comprehensive, and practical information on the most important things you need to know to promote your child's success in school and life. Some special topics may not seem that relevant just now. But perhaps they will next year.

Sometimes, parents are certain that they know what their child's talents and weaknesses are. Then something new emerges — a passionate new interest, a previously hidden talent, a difficulty in learning something. This is normal and part of the fascination of teaching and parenting.

We encourage you to keep thinking about school and education. Share your ideas for improving education for your child and for all children.

Above all, we hope that feeling well-prepared as parents will help you throughout one of the most wondrous experiences you have ever embarked on — that of being parents who care about their children and are preparing them for their future.

THE MULTICULTURAL WORLD OF TODAY'S CHILDREN AND FAMILIES

The word "multicultural" is not just a buzz word or a politically correct word. It describes what the world is really like today for young children and their families. Multiculturalism recognizes the cultural, linguistic, and historical diversity among our citizens. It celebrates the achievements, as well as acknowledges the struggles, of different groups of people who have made our country (and indeed, the world) what it is today as people live and work together, thrive, and learn in a way that is unprecedented in humankind.

Children in today's schools will learn words and ideas that come from a rich and ever changing heritage. Today's children will come home singing songs, telling stories, and recounting the biographies of people from all walks of life and all parts of the world. The history books are being re-written, and the literature children read comes from many cultures and countries. This is a time for celebrating and accepting, and for preparing children to live, work, and play with others from many cultures. Indeed, increasing numbers of children themselves are multicultural and have the lifetime benefits of experiencing the world from more than one perspective.

The information in *Going to School* is for all families and for the common culture of school that all parents value as a life-launching stage for their children.

CHAPTER 2

HOW CHILDREN LEARN

AND HOW PARENTS CAN HELP

The extraordinary growth of the young child's brain and mind. How a lifelong love of learning starts in early childhood. Seven Essentials proven to promote children's learning and development.

THIS CHAPTER DESCRIBES HOW RESPONSIVE CARE FOR VERY YOUNG CHILDREN SETS THE STAGE FOR LEARNING. SUCH CARE DOES NOT PRODUCE A SELF-CENTERED OR SPOILED CHILD. IT TEACHES A CHILD TO TRUST, BE CURIOUS, STRIVE TO LEARN NEW THINGS, AND BE SKILLFUL IN SOCIAL INTERACTION. ALL OF THESE CHARACTERISTICS ARE ESSENTIAL TO LEARNING AND SCHOOL SUCCESS.

One principle has been consistently supported by research findings: The adult a child will become is shaped by the *totality* of the child's experiences. It is the aggregate of everyday living that profoundly shapes how children grow and learn. There is a great deal of scientific evidence that children's home environment, the quality of parenting, and preschool experiences contribute in important ways to their emerging competencies in social, emotional, and academic development.

A PRIMER ON EARLY BRAIN DEVELOPMENT

One great contribution of scientific research in recent years has been to show the power and growth of the brain in early childhood. These findings have profoundly affected our understanding of the impact of early care on children's growth, from language and social skills to cognitive and emotional development.

Your child has been learning since before birth. A child is born with an almost full complement of brain cells — some 100 billion. However, these cells, called neurons, are not fully connected or necessarily used at birth. The main task of the brain in early childhood is for these neurons to forge connections. By age three, the brain has formed an estimated 1,000 trillion of these connections, called synapses. An individual cell may be connected to as many as 15,000 others.

This tremendous growth is fueled by the child's experiences, heredity, and maturation. The amount of positive stimulation a child receives is directly related to the child's behavioral and brain development. This positive stimulation includes responsive forms of play, affection, discovery, and language interactions. In situations where children are deprived of enough such early learning opportunities, brain and behavioral development slow or fail to progress in normal ways. Exactly *what* types and *how much* early stimulation young children need to promote "optimal" brain development is a topic of vigorous scientific inquiry.

During the first 10 to 12 years of life, it is estimated that approximately half the synapses formed in early childhood will be shed or pruned. Most likely, the synapses that are used repeatedly are strengthened and are more likely to endure. Those used less often are more likely to be pruned or re-configured. By early adolescence, the number of synapses will have declined to about half the number of those in the three-year-old's brain. A great deal of research is underway to understand these basic developmental processes and their practical significance.

What has been well-documented for more than 30 years, however, is that the way in which the adult brain functions can be profoundly affected by early experiences. A lot of this research has focused on children from extremely deprived or enriched environments. Therefore, less is known about variations within the so-called normal range of life experiences.

EARLY BRAIN WIRING

Recent research confirms that brains get "wired" in different ways to achieve positive ends. But a brain is not a living "computer" waiting for the "software" of experience. Evidence indicates that brains are as unique in their appearance and their functioning as everything else about us. There are many compensatory and probably idiosyncratic processes at work in the early years that contribute to each child's brain development.

What should parents do about brain development? Mostly, they should do what good parents have done for generations. Be sure your child is well cared for, well nourished, rested, happy, engaged, and allowed to play and learn with all the delight and energy of each stage of development.

SAFETY FIRST

Protect your child's brain by always using seatbelts correctly. Don't be deterred by an occasional protest. Always use safety helmets for sports that have the risk of head injury, such as riding bicycles or skateboards or roller blading. Be sure others who care for your child also follow these safety rules.

THE MANY WAYS OF LEARNING: HOW YOUNG CHILDREN'S BRAINS (AND MINDS) WORK

Early brain development produces a large, complex brain by the age of three. A three-year-old's brain is estimated to be 90 percent of the adult brain in terms of structure and function. Yet the brain's development is far from complete. What children learn and do continues to affect the brain's function and refinement. Such changes will continue throughout life into old age — something not fully appreciated until recently. The primary basis for this refinement appears to be experience and active use of the brain.

There are many different forms of learning. Learning includes a wide range of human behavior characterized by the *active process* of acquiring new knowledge and skills, as well as creating new connections among existing knowledge and skills. Learning occurs in informal, everyday contexts as well as in structured learning situations. It involves associations or relationships between and among elements. These elements can include objects, representations of objects, actions, feelings, and many abstract ideas and concepts. In the early years of life, most learning occurs in the frequent transactions the child has with people and objects. Here are some examples of different forms of learning that occur early in life:

Learning to ignore things. This is an important form of learning, called habituation, that occurs early in life. It allows the child to tune out "background" sights and sounds and irrelevant stimuli, such as the sound of the refrigerator making ice, or noise from a nearby playground. Habituation is important in setting the stage for the infant's ability to concentrate.

At first, habituation may be reflexive. Infants initially respond vigorously to external events, such as sound, light, or touch. However, if a baby hears a bell ring repeatedly, she will soon stop turning her eyes or head to look for the source of the sound.

This very early form of learning — making connections and adjusting one's behavior to the external situation — is part of intelligence. An infant's pattern of habituation is one of many behaviors that are correlated with later intelligence. As far as we know, this is not a form of learning that parents need to actively promote. Your young child will likely have many opportunities to tune out or ignore repeated, inconsequential forms of stimulation.

Forming concepts. This type of learning also originates in infancy, and becomes increasingly sophisticated and apparent during the school years. Concept formation is a type of abstraction. In the early years, such abstraction is closely linked to experiences with objects and events. As the child matures, the abstractions involve mental or physical manipulations of signs, symbols, or classes of events and objects.

One of the best-studied examples of concept learning involves object constancy — coming to know that an object continues to exist when it is out of sight. This discovery enables young children to enjoy playing peekaboo and "discovering" a hidden object. Object constancy includes understanding that an object can be seen, heard, or experienced in different ways. For example, an object rotated through space looks different from varying angles. Brain maturation and experience contribute to learning different aspects of object constancy.

As the child grows, more structured experiences are the basis for concept formation. Children's toys and common household objects can promote the acquisition of concepts. For example, blocks, food, or clothing can be sorted by shape, color, or size. Shape, color, and size are abstract concepts that children typically begin to learn a lot about in the second and third years of life. They learn and test increasingly sophisticated concepts about properties of the physical world.

At the same time, children are learning concepts about intangibles, such as emotional expression and self-regulation of behavior. In the second and third years of life, children have quite well-developed concepts about different emotions and what causes or ends them. Much of their learning about emotions occurs through direct experience and is assisted by parents attaching words to different feeling states and behaviors that reflect emotions.

Learning to read, spell, and write involves a great deal of concept formation. These concepts include understanding that letters and letter combinations represent sounds; letter combinations represent words that can be decoded (analyzed and sounded out); and words can be understood in context, such as getting hints from the words that come before and after, the pictures on the page, and the flow of a story.

Learning Cause-and-Effect Relationships. This form of learning also begins early and continues throughout life. It is based on children's observations and experiments with things and people. Parents can help set the stage, although this is not necessary for much of the early cause-and-effect learning. Children naturally seek to make sense of their experiences and to find order and reliable patterns in what happens around them. It also is important for children to learn which of their behaviors produce desirable effects, and to eliminate those that do not. This cause-and-effect learning is the foundation for much of what happens in the first years of school. Teachers set up many situations where children can manipulate objects, solve problems, and observe orderly patterns and variations.

As children get older, cause-and-effect relationships contribute to their understanding of probability — that some things are more or less likely to occur under certain situations. This may be why very young children prefer a clear "yes" or "no" to "maybe." By eight years of age, however, most children would prefer a "maybe" to a "no" concerning something they want.

Scientists divide learning into different categories. The table below provides a partial list of these types of learning. Your child is engaged in almost all of these forms of learning, at one level or another, every day. What matters is that you encourage your child's natural curiosity in many ways. Even before children speak, parents can promote learning through example, play, reading, talking, and reinforcing positive behavior.

TYPES OF LEARNING

- **Figuring out action–reaction and cause-and-effect relationships**
- **Learning through observation**
- **Copying others to learn new ways to do things**
- **Tuning out what's irrelevant to focus on what's important**
- **Distinguishing what's different and what's the same**
- **Classical conditioning, especially involving reflexes in early infancy (like Pavlov's dog)**
- **Trial and error (from informal to highly systematic experimentation)**
- **Conceptualizing ideas and themes**
- **Verbal learning involving words and gestures**
- **Logical or deductive reasoning.**

These types of learning can occur in and be applied to many areas, including creative arts, athletics, academics, social relationships, mechanics, imaginative or fantasy play, and other forms of adaptive behavior.

SEVEN ESSENTIALS TO PROMOTE CHILDREN'S LEARNING

Over a decade ago we began to look for a way to translate the wonderful and exciting findings about brain growth and child development into practical advice for parents. We felt the research was too valuable to be confined to the pages of academic journals, and it had to be shared with those who could benefit most — parents and children. And so our list of Seven Essentials was born — a synthesis of findings from more than a thousand research projects and scientific presentations.

SEVEN ESSENTIALS PROVEN TO HELP YOUR CHILD EVERY DAY

- **Encourage** exploration with all the senses, in familiar and new places, with others and alone, safely and with joy.
- **Mentor** in basic skills, showing the whats and whens, the ins and outs, of how things and people work.
- **Celebrate** development advances, for learning new skills, little and big, and for becoming a unique individual.
- **Rehearse** and extend new skills, showing your child how to practice again and again, in the same and different ways, with new people and new things.
- **Protect** from neglect and inappropriate disapproval, teasing, or punishment.
- **Communicate** richly and responsibly with sounds, songs, gestures, and words; bring your child into the wonderful world of language and its many uses.
- **Guide and limit** behavior to keep your child safe and to teach what's acceptable and what's not – the rules of being a cooperative, responsive, and caring person.

These Seven Essentials are based on studies about children's emerging intellectual and language competencies in the first five years of life. Based on the evidence, we recommend that every child have all Seven Essentials *every day* to be engaged in active learning, to remain positive about the challenges of learning, and to be well prepared for school. Children who receive lots of these Seven Essentials through their exchanges with parents and others show the healthiest and best development.

Think of these essentials as daily "vitamins and minerals" for your child's heart and mind. They really are worth memorizing and doing every day. Most are fun and easy to do anytime, anywhere. A single activity can easily include several at once. There are many ways to personalize them to reflect your interests, your culture, and your values.

Your child will never outgrow the need for these essentials. Just adapt them to meet your child's growing capabilities and changing interests. Over time, these Seven Essentials will help strengthen your child's development in every way.

1. ENCOURAGE EXPLORATION.

You should actively encourage your child's curiosity and investigation of the world. Help your child to seek new experiences, new information, and new forms of stimulation. It is not enough just to allow your child to explore.

For the three-year-old, parents can point out new things when it is safe and profitable to check them out.

By age five or six, your child's curiosity will be more selective and wider-ranging. You won't need to have your child explore everything all the time. But you can point out delightful or unexpected opportunities for learning. Share the many ways that your child can explore — talking to experts, going to the library, visiting museums, going on outings, paying close attention to things in your house or yard, and conducting experiments. From five to eight years of age, many children are really impressed by what they can learn from such trial-and-error discovery.

2. MENTOR IN THE BASICS.

Mentoring for young children becomes increasingly direct and systematic. Mentoring is a form of teaching with love and an appreciation for the individuality of the learner. From three to eight years of age, children are like sponges. They love to learn and share lots of facts and skills. They want to understand most things that interest them. They will question parents and others extensively. You may well need new books about topics that your child is eager to learn more about. But what, exactly, are the important "basics" to teach your child during this period of life?

For children to learn, parents do not necessarily need to create formal lesson plans or purchase expensive learning programs. Instead, you can "be yourself" and teach your child what you know and what interests you in everyday interactions. Such instruction and sharing are key components of mentoring. Also, when you teach what you enjoy, you invariably convey enthusiasm for learning and a love of knowledge — a powerful way to build your child's enthusiasm for learning later in school.

Dr. Howard Gardner of Harvard University, a leading theorist and researcher in children's learning and intelligence, strongly advocates that children be oriented to and accomplished in the familiar three "Rs" — reading, 'riting, and 'rithmetic. Another "R" that he and most early childhood educators add is "reasoning" or higher-order thinking. Some add a fifth "R"— responsibility. We concur that all are important and can readily be provided by parents in their mentoring.

Most teachers do not think that parents need to teach reading *in a formal sense* before their child goes to school. Yet parents may want to know how to mentor for reading skills. Please note that there are stages in children's reading. These stages are not exact, and your child does not need to learn these in a strict order. However, earlier skills are important for learning the later ones.

If your child is in a good school, the teacher will likely give you constructive suggestions for mentoring in school-related topics, including the three "Rs." Remember also to mentor in social skills, and include reasoning and responsibility. In all your mentoring, be loving, patient, encouraging. Provide lots of examples for your child to follow and learn from. Be sure you, too, are having fun.

Activities for mentoring children in reading, writing, and spelling

- **Sound out** the different letters of the alphabet.
- **Say the name** of a letter when you see the letter.
- **Make sounds** and guess what letter they stand for.
- **Read single-syllable words,** especially words you see often in books, on signs, or on objects at home.
- **When reading** with your child, point to words to show the direction of your reading.
- **Try to match** pictures and words.
- **Learn lots** of nursery rhymes and rhyming songs.
- **Using easy-to-pronounce** words, take turns thinking of rhymes.
- **Combine or blend letters** into sounds, especially those that create new and unexpected sounds. You'll probably enjoy thinking of the many combined letter–sound combinations, but you can also use a dictionary's "pronunciation key" and guides for sound–spelling correspondence.
- **When your child** is ready, try reading simple words in text, starting with books your child knows well and loves.
- **Progress to practicing** more difficult multi-syllable words. There are many excellent "learn to read" books that are graded according to children's ages that provide helpful hints to parents to encourage children's recognition of words in context.
- **Play word detective games.** Look for parts of words that give clues to their sound or form words inside of other words.
- **Talk about words** and what they are made of – letters, letter combinations, syllables, vowels, and consonants. Discuss prefixes and suffixes that give clues to the meaning of a word. (But remember that some of these are advanced concepts.)

- **Identify words** (with the same or different spellings) that sound the same but have different meanings, such as weather and whether; they're, there, and their; be and bee; watch (as in watching a movie) and watch (that tells time).
- **Identify words** that have the same spelling but can be pronounced differently and then mean different things, such as wind (that can howl), and wind (as in winding a clock); read (in the present and past tenses); and lead (as a horse) and lead (as in pipe).
- **Think of a letter** that sounds like a word, such as b and bee, t and tee, l and elle.
- **At all stages** of your child's development, expand your child's vocabulary.
- **Talk about** how language can serve different purposes – providing information and instruction, conveying feelings, and being fun and interesting in its own right.
- **Help your child** to follow increasingly complex directions.
- **Combine words** into sentences aloud, or with printed words once your child recognizes them.
- **Test your child's** memory for details from a story, for arrangement of events, and for clues that help predict the ending. (You are likely to be impressed.)
- **Think of words** that start with different letters. As your child's vocabulary grows, try thinking of words that go from a to z, especially in a category, such as foods, animals, actions, or silly words.
- **Read** increasingly longer, more complex stories. Be sure your child continues to enjoy and follow them.
- **Identify** the main ideas or messages from conversation, stories, and books.

3. CELEBRATE YOUR CHILD'S ACCOMPLISHMENTS.

From age three on, there will be many opportunities to celebrate your child's remarkable advances. Every day your child will learn or do things that warrant your attention and praise. This will not make your child conceited or self-centered. Instead, there is ample evidence that children learn more and faster in positive circumstances. Research on brain chemistry shows that children are unlikely to direct their attention fully to the learning at hand when they are stressed, fearful, or confused. But pleasurable sensations help children want more of the events that produce these positive sensations. Acknowledging children's achievements helps them know that you notice their success in learning, and increases their enjoyment.

This does not call for unlimited or non-specific praise. Let your child know that you notice and value efforts to try new skills and learn new things. Sometimes your child may respond by saying, "It's not all that good," when you praise a drawing or a story. Or he may tell you, "It's really easy," after you have shown how impressed you are by some achievement. This does not mean that your positive words are not appreciated. Rather, your child is letting you know that he understands that some achievements require more or less effort. He may have his own standards of accomplishment and be striving to do better.

Not every advance means your child will show the same maturity and intelligence at all times. She may show remarkable sensitivity to others one day, but not the next. Your child may be eager to read a challenging book aloud to you every day for a week and then refuse to read a book of comparable difficulty the next week, announcing, "This is too hard."

This pattern of "a step forward and then a pause, or step back" is normal. For example, children who learn to add "ed" to verbs to create the past tense often overuse their new skill, making mistakes in speech that were formerly correct. This is temporary and does not require vigorous intervention. Children's self-correcting, coupled with consistent (but not insistent) encouragement will do wonders.

4. REHEARSE AND EXTEND NEW SKILLS.

The early years in school are filled with the need to practice. Yet some of the best ways to practice aren't repetitive, forced, or dull. Children love to see how a new skill can be used in different ways. Young children often love repetition of favorite stories or songs. Once again, brain chemistry is at work. Certain pathways linking positive emotional states and increasing comfort with a repeated task or experience are being activated and strengthened. It also is likely that new connections are being forged and that your child may be thinking in new ways about something familiar or already mastered. This happens often with numbers. Children who can answer correctly to simple addition or subtraction queries may suddenly want to experiment on their own with new ways to get the answer. They may be testing out new mental strategies or ways in which physical props can be helpful to solve more complicated problems.

Here are some suggestions for what parents can do with their children to practice academic and social skills:

- **Ask them to show how they did something in class.**
- **Encourage them to keep journals to write and draw in at home, just like at school.**
- **Have them find new words in a book that you can read and practice together. Try remembering these new words and using them in an invented sentence or story.**
- **Teach children to call a friend or relative on the phone and use appropriate greetings, self-identification, and polite goodbyes.**
- **Have them practice manners and thoughtful acts at home and elsewhere.**
- **When your child begins to show empathy or generosity, find ways to follow through and do this again.**
- **Help your child write thank-you notes, create original artwork, and find other ways to let others know your child appreciates them.**
- **Try out new social lessons, such as "smiles are catching" or the Golden Rule ("Do unto others as you would have them do unto you").**

Help your child learn that some rules can be applied at the wrong times or in the wrong situations. Even if your five-year-old would love to have someone squirt him with a water gun, he should *not* apply the Golden Rule and do it to you without advance permission. Or your four-year-old may really want you to sleep with all her favorite stuffed animals, and you may need to explain that not everyone likes to fall asleep in exactly the same surroundings.

5. PROTECT FROM NEGLECT AND INAPPROPRIATE DISAPPROVAL, TEASING, OR PUNISHMENT.

During the three- to eight-year-old age period, children will encounter more teasing and many more reprimands than in their earlier years. This is because they are more self-directed, and can understand and benefit from appropriate guidance and constructive criticism (as detailed in Essential number 7 about guiding and limiting behavior). But your child still should not receive overly harsh punishment for things that are not intentionally bad or harmful. Also, it is unreasonable to expect perfection in everything your child does. Here are examples of normal child behavior and appropriate responses:

- **Behavior:** Your four-year-old is playing catch with you and runs through a patch of flowers in her eagerness to catch the ball. Several new buds are broken.
  - *Appropriate response:* "Great catch, but oops, you went into the flowers. Be careful and let's move away so this does not happen again. When flowers are broken, they can't be fixed."
  - *Inappropriate response:* "You killed those flowers. Don't you ever look where you are going? What's wrong with you? That's the end of our game of catch."
- **Behavior:** Your six-year-old lost his first tooth. He is very embarrassed to go to school because he thinks he looks "terrible" and other children will laugh at him. That night, he begs to stay home the next day.
  - *Appropriate response:* You sympathize and say that you felt just the same way (or that someone else in the family did). You ask what ideas he might have to look extra good even with his tooth missing. You also say that he looks like some other children in his class who lost teeth. Although you do not agree to let him stay home, you may plan a trip for an ice-cream cone the next day or tell him that he may invite a friend over for a favorite game. And the Tooth Fairy can pay a visit and leave a note to mark the occasion.

- *Inappropriate response:* You get angry that your child is being so immature. You say, "Well, if you think the other children will laugh and make fun of you, I'll do it now so you'll get used to it!" You tell him the Tooth Fairy will not come at all because of his ridiculous feelings and behavior.

Behavior: Your second-grader is practicing spelling words. For two nights in a row, she got all the words right and was very cooperative. Tonight, she said, "I know them all and I don't want to practice." You insist it is good to practice and then she misspells the first word on the list when she recites the letters.

- *Appropriate response:* You continue through the spelling list and then ask her if she thinks she may have misspelled any of the words. You then can correct the errors or say, "Boy, it's lucky we are practicing. Even when you already know a word, sometimes when you are in a hurry or upset, you may not think and remember to be careful." Or you may ask her to write down the words so she can compare her written list to a master list. Thank her for practicing even when she didn't feel like doing it.
- *Inappropriate response:* You immediately shout, "See, you aren't so smart, and that serves you right for acting like a know-it-all. You don't even know that easy word. We are going to practice twice as long, and if you keep on making mistakes, you may not get to play tomorrow."

Behavior: Your family is at the dinner table ready to celebrate your child's birthday. Just as you start to eat, the phone rings. Your child jumps up and runs to answer it, shouting, "Maybe it's Grandma calling to wish me a happy birthday." In your house, you have a rule that everyone asks to be excused and waits for permission before leaving the table. Also, you usually let the phone be answered automatically when you are eating, so that your dinner together is not constantly interrupted.

- *Appropriate response:* Because it is a special occasion, you simply ignore the behavior, since your child usually follows family rules. OR perhaps when your child returns to the table, disappointed that it was not Grandma, you say, "Why don't we follow our usual rules and not answer the phone until after dinner? If Grandma leaves a message, we'll return her call right away."
- *Inappropriate response:* The minute your child returns, you say, "You disobeyed the rules about asking to be excused. I want you to apologize. You will be punished and you won't be allowed to talk to Grandma when she calls."

These examples have two things in common. First, all the transgressions were relatively minor. Second, these behaviors are typical for children of the three- to-eight-year-old age period, especially when enthusiasm or fatigue can influence their judgment. None reflects willful, disruptive, or thoughtless behavior. Therefore, you should teach with this in mind. When parents respond inappropriately to such normal types of behavior, the toll on children can be great.

Some parents who treat their children harshly mistakenly believe they are doing their child a service. We cannot imagine that this could ever be true. Rather, they are actively teaching their child to disregard the feelings of others, to ignore the big picture, and that if children are not perfect, adults will get mad at them.

Sadly, parents who ignore this Essential are often unaware that they are hurting their child or responding excessively to age-typical behavior. For example, all children make some messes in helping prepare food, and when at the table. Adults make the same mistakes, but usually less often or on a smaller scale because we are bigger, more coordinated, and more practiced. Some children are highly sensitive. Others seem not to care when they are teased or treated harshly for minor transgressions. Do not be fooled by appearances. Many children learn to hide their feelings in the face of such treatment, sometimes to avoid a double dose of teasing and punishment.

This Essential extends to protecting your child from bullying and rude or insensitive behavior from others, including other children, friends, or relatives. Children typically tease each other, but innocently and at a level that they can handle. But when it gets out of hand or is the dominant form of interaction between your child and someone else, you should intervene. Whoever the consistent offender may be, you should be sure that contact between your child and this person is reduced or eliminated, at least for a while.

This Essential does not imply that children can never be reprimanded or gently teased in supportive ways, or that punishment can never be used. But harsher parental behavior should match the child's behavior. Intentionally harmful, rude, or defiant behavior warrants a response — one that can teach your child the importance of positive behavior and the need to avoid the negative. Save parental guidance and limit-setting for what really counts at each age. Be consistent, clear, strong, and in control when you respond to inappropriate behavior.

Do not laugh about your child in front of him or others in ways that you know will be hurtful. Do not embarrass your child or tell stories about him that make him feel incompetent, or self-conscious, or that belittle his feelings. Show your child the same respect and thoughtfulness that you show to your friends, and that you expect from your child.

6. PROVIDE A RICH LANGUAGE ENVIRONMENT EVERY DAY FOR YOUR CHILD.

From age three on, and particularly during the first years of elementary school, this is the most important Essential for your child's school success. Your coaching and your use of language are important in helping your child become more adept.

Right from birth, children start learning their native language or languages. Infants discern the key features and many uses of language long before they speak. In the second year of life, when language growth is typically rapid, children show many signs of recognizing that language is both powerful and delightful.

Language reflects thoughts and thoughts help language. Language involves formal features, like vocabulary and grammar, but there are lots of implicit rules about body language and the ways that tone, volume, inflection, and gestures can alter the meaning of the words. Language is also the primary mode for teaching in our culture. Teachers in elementary school spend more time on the language arts and on enhancing your child's language than on other areas of development.

Converse with your child. Use everyday exchanges as a natural way to teach new words for feelings, objects, events, places, time, and abstract ideas. Use books to help with language. Talk about the books after you read them. Let your child tell stories or "read" books, even before formal reading skills appear.

Do the same for writing. Even three-year-olds can "write," and they can interpret the squiggly lines or pictures they draw to "write" down their story.

Remember that some topics and words are not appropriate for your child's age and comprehension. Many topics covered on the front page of newspapers and on the evening news may be unsuitable for your child's ears and mind. Be cautious. Be aware of how highly impressionable young children are. Children will be introduced naturally, and hopefully gradually, to the full range of human experiences and use of language, but this should not all occur in the three- to eight-year-old period.

Beware that your child is likely to pick up some words that you do not approve of. Remember that most young children have no idea what those four-letter words mean. They just know they are "bad words." Also, children typically go through stages of telling "bathroom jokes" and being interested in their bodies and other children's, too. Deal with this appropriately — not excessively. Yes, you can shape your child's language and indicate that certain words are off limits and forbidden in your household. Should *you* use these forbidden words, expect your child to notice and comment!

For more information about the language arts, see Chapter 10.

7. GUIDE AND LIMIT YOUR CHILD'S BEHAVIOR TO PROMOTE POSITIVE BEHAVIOR AND TO AVOID HARM.

This Essential is about socialization and behavior modification, which are so important during the transition-to-school years. This is the time that your child will probably learn more rules about social conduct than at any other time in life. Children catch on quickly to many of these rules, but there typically are a few stubborn areas that they don't grasp as readily.

What areas need the most vigorous guidance? First, anything involving your child's health and safety. These issues must be addressed consistently and with appropriate explanations so that your child learns about such things as crossing streets, not running into traffic, not ingesting foreign substances, etc.

Basic civility is another vital area. Children typically need many prompts and reminders. They may go through periods of shyness. Help your child to know why thoughtful behavior matters. It will be very important for your child's acceptance and ease in school.

It is extremely important that you teach your child about physical play and aggression. There are documented differences in play and aggression among children from different cultures and social classes. But your child must understand the basics of acceptable play in preparation for school. Remember that three-year-olds handle frustration much differently from, and with less self-control than, a six-year-old. But even a three-year-old's behavior can be shaped in lots of socially acceptable ways.

Do not try to teach that physical aggression, such as hitting, kicking, and biting, is unacceptable by doing these things *to* your child. This old-fashioned technique is not the best. It just teaches that parents are bigger and stronger.

Instead, use immediate and harsh verbal reprimands. If need be, physical restraint or removing your child from the situation may be in order. For some behaviors, it may be effective to place your child in a "time-out" or other limited situation for a specified time, and be sure that you have explained clearly why the behavior is unacceptable and will not be allowed again. If such behavior continues, you may choose to end or deny enjoyable events, such as an outing, or playtime with a friend. Privileges also can be taken away from older children when they are mature enough to understand the connection between their behavior and the punishment.

Many important forms of socializing actively encourage mature and thoughtful behavior. Your socialization should not focus only on preventing or eliminating unacceptable behavior. You can set a powerful example for your child by the way you behave. Also, as your child matures, you can read and discuss books about good behavior and the consequences of bad behavior. Relate what you read to your own life and to your child's actions and thoughts about these matters.

For more information, see Chapter 11 about the social side of school, which includes a section on how parents can guide their children's behavior.

PLAYING AND LEARNING

Play is an extremely important way that children learn. Play provides natural, fun ways to explore and to have trial-and-error experiences in a safe, enjoyable setting.

In fact, research shows that children learn best when they are having fun. When an emotion is engaged, events and ideas are committed to memory more strongly. Even as adults, we recall more easily events in the past that are associated with strong emotions, including those that delighted (as well as frightened) us. We also remember more from the classes we enjoyed than from those that didn't interest us. This is why young children learn more from interesting and creative play than from rote memory routines that are the staple of many accelerated learning programs.

Learning and memory are inextricably linked to emotions. Brain chemicals, called neurotransmitters, that affect and are affected by emotion can help the brain to be more receptive to new information, and better able to store and retrieve it. While negative emotions, such as fear and anger, can reinforce learning, the most beneficial learning occurs from lessons or experiences linked to enjoyment and pleasure.

ACTIVE AND PASSIVE LEARNING

There is a great deal of scientific evidence about the importance of children's own actions in learning. When children initiate activity or are actively engaged, they typically learn more. A key form of such activity is called response-contingent learning, in which a child learns that certain actions or words produce predictable results. Another highly effective form of learning is when parents teach about something that has already captured their child's attention.

Parents should be aware that television, in addition to its negative effects on children's behavior, is generally ineffective in teaching. This holds true even for so-called "educational" television. Such programs may not be truly harmful. Others may teach children some things, particularly when parents reinforce what is taught in active ways that engage the child.

WHY CHILDREN ASK "WHY" SO OFTEN

Children's curiosity, inquisitiveness, and asking "Why?" are universal. What is the role of these behaviors in development and learning?

Without doubt, children's queries are a genuine expression of what is interesting or perplexing to them. Parents who answer their children's questions attentively and appropriately teach much more than just the answer. They are teaching their child that (1) asking questions is a good way to get information, (2) adults can be counted on to provide information, and (3) even trusted grownups don't know everything, because they often say, "I don't know," or "Let's go find out more about that." These are worthwhile lessons. And, of course, children often get the real answers they are hoping for.

It is easy to overlook that children come into the world with little or perhaps no specific knowledge about how the world works. While children can seem remarkably intelligent and insightful, their reservoir of knowledge is limited. Children often use words correctly long before they know what they mean.

Your answers are a way to apply the Seven Essentials and a great way to proceed on the path of lifelong learning. You will undoubtedly enjoy how your child's comprehension of "why" questions and answers changes with age.

As a caring parent, you will get tired. You cannot be expected to answer *all* of your child's "why" questions. Sometimes you won't know the answer, don't have the time to answer, or may not want to answer. This is fine every now and then. Each parent must find the right balance between being a responsive "parent–teacher" and meeting the demands of everyday life.

Use your friends, your family, and your social support network. If your child is very curious, enlist others who know about subjects that interest him. Arrange get-togethers and outings so they can explore and learn together. Also, get some good dictionaries, reference books, and encyclopedias that are ideal for young children. Expect to learn a lot yourself.

HOW ACTIVELY SHOULD YOU PROMOTE LEARNING?

This is the question we are asked most often by parents. The answer is that parental teaching does, without question, make a difference in what young children know and what their skills are. Whether such teaching needs to be planned, however, is a different matter. Many parents teach naturally and without awareness in their everyday exchanges with their children. Others are less comfortable or skilled in this role, especially with very young children who do not have well-developed verbal skills. Overly forceful and ambitious parental teaching seldom, if ever, works well. This can be frustrating to parents and children alike. It can also create negative emotions connected to later formal learning.

Each child is an individual. Pay attention to your child's interests, talents, curiosity. Capitalize on them. Do not waste time comparing your child to others at this stage. Instead, appreciate your child's uniqueness and remarkable development.

Children with few opportunities to learn, whose parents are not highly responsive, and whose families do not provide a rich language environment are at a decided disadvantage when they go to school. It is difficult for these children to make up for the years of inadequate encouragement, mentoring, celebration, practice, and language experiences. Even when these children learn a lot from what schools have to offer, they trail significantly behind their classmates who came from more enriched families.

The learning opportunities that preschool children in our country have are profound. Children from families, preschools, and communities that are rich in the Seven Essentials — the natural forms of everyday teaching and encouragement that work best — are at a clear advantage when they go to school. These children are prepared for what schools do best — building and expanding children's competencies in academic and social areas.

In the long run, active parental teaching makes a huge difference. But effective parents balance the teaching of life skills and school skills. Good parent-teachers recognize the many ways that children learn from experience, observations, and reflection.

Some children have learning difficulties and disabilities. All children have learning differences, only partly understood at this time. But all children can and do learn under the right conditions. And this learning is vital to their quality of life, their health and well-being, and the ways they will become contributing citizens as they grow up. Being close to a young child is the most precious reminder we have of how vital learning is to our society, how basic it is to want to know more, and how joyful it is to gain new skills and understanding.

Cherish your own sense of wonder at your child's remarkable growth and learning. Notice, too, how much you are learning and what a skillful teacher you are becoming!

CHAPTER 3

TEN HALLMARKS

OF CHILDREN WHO SUCCEED IN SCHOOL

What research shows about children who succeed.
How you can foster each hallmark and prepare your child for early and lasting success.

THE PAST DECADE HAS SEEN REAL RESEARCH BREAKTHROUGHS IN UNDERSTANDING HOW CHILDREN ADJUST DURING THE EARLY YEARS OF SCHOOL. RESEARCHERS NOW TAKE INTO ACCOUNT HOW COMPLICATED CHILDREN'S LIVES ARE AND HOW MANY FORCES SHAPE SUCCESS IN SCHOOL, INCLUDING INTERGENERATIONAL EDUCATION, FAMILY VALUES, PEER CULTURE, THE MEDIA, EXPECTATIONS FOR CHILDREN'S SUCCESS, TEACHER EFFECTIVENESS, PARENTAL INVOLVEMENT IN CHILDREN'S LEARNING, AND CHILDREN'S OWN NATURAL COMPETENCIES AND MOTIVATION TO DO WELL.

The results of these new studies are more accurate. They also are far more useful to parents, showing concrete ways in which they can promote their children's well-being.

Current research indicates that *no one factor accounts for children's success in school and learning — not even a high level of intelligence.* On the contrary, *many factors foster success, including a child's cumulative supports and experiences, and the influence of parents, family, and school.* Further, even children who succeed in school go through ups and downs, including how much they like school, how hard they try, and how well they perform. The new findings can help every parent, whether their child needs major assistance or a helping hand to weather a bump in the road.

Research also shows the profound and lasting impact of the family on a child's success in school. *Families affect success as much as schools or teachers.* Nearly every hallmark of children who do well in school is completely under parental control or heavily affected by what parents do.

THE HALLMARKS OF CHILDREN WHO DO WELL IN SCHOOL

During the past 25 years, our research and that of others consistently show some characteristics common to children who succeed. Recent studies have given these findings more weight and a clearer focus. Each hallmark shows up repeatedly in studies on different types of children in different parts of the country. They are not limited to cut-and-dried differences in children's intelligence or temperament when they start school. Rather, they are *dynamic processes that can be positively influenced by parents.*

TEN HALLMARKS OF CHILDREN WHO SUCCEED IN SCHOOL

1. They are eager to learn.
2. They ask lots of questions, and they ask for help.
3. They work hard and know that their effort matters.
4. They have well-developed social and emotional skills.
5. They are good at assessing their skills.
6. Their parents are role models for learning.
7. Their parents promote learning by "natural" teaching at home.
8. Their family routines support doing well in school.
9. Their parents are effective at setting and maintaining limits.
10. Their schools have high expectations for student achievement, support teacher development, and communicate frequently with parents about their children.

Parents should be encouraged by these hallmarks and the findings that *there are many different paths to success.*

- **Many children, especially boys, have been "late bloomers."**
- **Other children, often girls, have shied away from some difficult subjects, such as math and science, because the teachers and children underestimated their capabilities and/or the importance of learning these subjects.**
- **Some other children seem to lack real passion for school, neither failing nor soaring during the early years. Yet later in life, something or someone brings out their skills, builds their motivation, and enables them to flourish.**

The following explains why and how each hallmark works, and how each can be shaped in a strong and lasting way by parents.

1. THEY ARE EAGER TO LEARN.

These children are curious. They love to explore and typically have been encouraged to learn *right from birth.* By the time they enter school, they usually know a lot because learning has been so much fun. For them, learning is associated with many positive emotional and social experiences — neither boring accelerated learning programs nor repetition with materials that are not challenging.

Such children typically have many interests, and some can become passionately (or stubbornly) interested in one or a few things that they really "get into" for some period. Rarely have these children been criticized in their efforts to learn. Neither have their parents structured all their learning experiences for them.

Parents seldom need to stimulate a very young child's interest in learning new facts, new words, new ideas, and new ways to do things. The challenge is to keep from dampening this remarkable and vital quality. Some parents inadvertently become overly protective or cautious. They may worry that their child's curiosity will lead to harm or may be interpreted by others as impolite — "too nosy" or "too forward." Other parents may routinely ignore or discount their child's interest in the world. They may even provide harsh treatment in response to a child's desire to do something new or spend more time learning or exploring.

Clearly, parents can't promote their children's curiosity and interests full-time. It would be too demanding and unfair to others in the family. But parents should ask themselves, "Do I let my child know that I value exploration and learning? Do I encourage and allow (in a safe and responsible way) my child to discover how things work, look, sound, smell, feel, and taste? When I restrict my child's natural curiosity, do I provide clear reasons that are readily understood, such as 'That is very dirty,' 'That is poisonous and will make you sick,' or 'That is sharp and can hurt you'? Do I give my child the freedom to make mistakes and to figure some things out on his own?"

To encourage your child to love learning:

- **Encourage your child to explore** in a new setting. "Let's go find out about..." "I wonder what would happen if we..." "Let's look over here, too." "Maybe someone can show us how to..." "Let's see what this feels like..."

  Guide your child's behavior if the setting is one where certain types of exploration are not appropriate (touching things at a museum or picking up delicate objects in someone's home; reaching out to animals at a zoo or even on the street; going up to a stranger to ask a question that is too personal). Rarely does this guidance require that exploration stop. Rather, it is a matter of redirecting curiosity in appropriate ways.

  Exploring is fun, and has great lifelong survival value. Many fields of human endeavor are advanced by adults' curiosity, desire to explore, and eagerness to learn. Scientists and explorers, adventurers and inventors, great political leaders, teachers, and the best parents all love to learn and keep on exploring.

- **Don't overlook familiar settings.** The everyday world contains surprises, too. At home or outside, be sure to point out things that can be looked at, used, or thought about differently. Notice something that previously was unnoticed (a shadow on a wall, the shape or color of something, how two things that seem different are really alike in some way). Ask your child to point out something to you, so you can learn from your child. Such reciprocity – that we can learn from each other – is a great lesson for your child. You, too, will benefit.

As parents ourselves, we know that cherishing and protecting this hallmark can at times be burdensome, especially when we are tired or rushed. Vigilance over an eager child can be demanding. Curiosity takes time to follow, and children rarely like being rushed, interrupted, or thwarted repeatedly. But these years will fly by, and seldom will you regret allowing yourself to just "go with the flow" a bit more often. Curiosity can sometimes lead to trouble, but mostly it leads to lots of learning and fun.

2. THEY ASK LOTS OF QUESTIONS, AND THEY ASK FOR HELP.

They ask questions to help them learn more, move ahead, and avoid confusion or mistakes. They are not afraid to ask for help or seek more information in order to do something that is important or interesting, although sometimes they want to do something or solve a problem "all by myself."

Asking good questions is one of the most efficient ways for a child to gain information. Knowing the when, how, what, why, and who of questioning is a skill that children should increasingly master during the early childhood years.

Asking the right question at the right time can spare a child lengthy or boring trial-and-error efforts in solving a problem or learning something new. Good question-asking can also save a child needless embarrassment. Moreover, teachers view children who ask good questions as interested, motivated to learn, and eager to be cooperative and socially skilled. Asking the right questions is a sign of intelligence.

Research shows that some parents encourage "compliance without questioning" (old-fashioned "blind obedience") when it comes to teachers or other figures of authority. Very young children who are taught never to question authority often interpret this to mean that they should not question the teacher at all. Unfortunately, teachers and children's peers often judge these children as passive, disinterested, or not very bright. Usually, more highly educated parents promote questioning in their children, especially encouraging them to ask for help and explanations.

To encourage your child to ask questions and ask for help:

- **Respond positively** at home to questioning and provide help when it's needed. Children who receive answers, directions, and help at home – offered with warmth, encouragement, and useful specificity – naturally expect that their eachers also will be good providers of information. In school, however, children will need to make some adjustments in asking questions, conforming to the rules about how and when to ask questions, such as raising their hands, waiting their turn, and listening to questions other children ask.

  Balance is needed here, too. Your answers and help should encourage your child's learning, not replace it. Don't be over-helpful. But don't let frustration get out of hand.

QUESTIONING TO AID READING COMPREHENSION

The organizing and learning potential of questioning are further shown by Dr. Ann Brown of the University of California at Berkeley, a scientist who works with children who have difficulty with reading comprehension. Although these children often can read the words correctly, they may have difficulty extracting the meaning, the sequence of events, or the larger theme from a story or essay. Studies show that these children can be taught to use questions to aid their understanding. For example, when they read, they ask themselves questions every few paragraphs, such as, "What is the most important thing happening? Who did it? What came before and after? Are there any words I do not understand?" Such strategic questioning helps the child monitor understanding of new material. Children then selectively seek information or guidance as needed from adults.

We know that asking lots of questions improves a child's memory, probably because the child is actively engaged. When children want to know something, and then receive an answer, they are far more likely to remember the answer than if they hear the information passively. Good teachers usually let children ask lots of questions because they understand the importance of the child's initiative in the learning process. Older children can even learn to ask themselves questions silently when a teacher is presenting new materials. Very often, the flow of the teacher's presentation will quickly answer the child's question. This process enhances the child's learning.

Although asking lots of questions is a hallmark of children who do well in school, there are exceptions. Sometimes a child will be shy in a new situation, such as at the beginning of a year with a new teacher, or when a stranger comes into the classroom. At other times, a child may feel like trying to get an answer without help. There is no reason to be concerned about these situations as long as the child is generally willing to seek help when needed.

3. THEY WORK HARD AND KNOW THAT THEIR EFFORT MATTERS.

Children who succeed in school believe success depends on their own work and skill — not on luck or someone else's actions.

At first, almost all children try to do their best. If they are adequately stimulated and challenged, this will mean some hard work on their part. Unfortunately, some children come to believe that doing well in school is not under their control. These children ascribe problems in the classroom to others or to bad luck. Researchers call this the "locus of control," and their findings can help you and your child.

Locus of control represents a continuum along which individuals perceive that they have a greater or lesser effect on what happens in their lives. Research shows that children who have been encouraged to work hard and have been helped by adults to succeed in the task at hand know their efforts count because they have seen the results time and again. Children who don't get this encouragement don't learn the importance of hard work and sustained attention.

Research also shows that children who have had lots of cause-and-effect learning experiences in their preschool years are more likely to believe that their own efforts make a big difference. Cause-and-effect learning teaches children that their actions produce predictable results, from the toddler's experience of a jack-in-the-box that pops up when the handle is cranked, to stacking a tower of blocks so they do not fall down, to turning a page in a book to see new pictures and continue the story.

In contrast, children who have had far fewer of these learning opportunities are more likely to think that doing well in the classroom is influenced by how much the teacher likes them, how lucky they are, or whether they are having a good day. These children do not link their own behavior and concentrated effort to how much they learn and how well they do. In turn, these children don't do as well in school.

To encourage your child to work hard and know that effort matters:

- **Notice and praise** your child for extra effort. Reinforce good behavior when your child takes extra time to do a task well or really concentrates. The ability to sustain interest and activity on a focused task is one of the most important general skills that teachers want children to have.

  There are many opportunities at home for parents to allow children to practice this. Cake batters need to be stirred a lot (maybe a few hundred strokes or three minutes with an electric mixer) in order to rise properly. Children's ability to draw something (a house, a person, an animal, an airplane) often gets better after practicing more than once. Learning patience for some things that cannot be rushed (waiting for a painting to dry, listening to the middle of a story before you can know the end) is part of this as well.

  Following two-, three-, and four-step instructions is another great "at home" activity that will help your child at school. It builds a child's power to follow a sequence which requires paying attention and remembering. Such practice can be done with building structures, gathering things for an activity, or just as a game unto itself. (Get the object, put it above/below, inside/outside, or in front of/behind. Then say or do something, such as clap your hands, turn around, or repeat a word.)

  A note of caution: your child does not have to work hard at everything. Some things will come more naturally, and sometimes children will be tired or less motivated to work hard. So encourage your child, but don't overdo it. Also, sometimes children will say that something is easy when it isn't. There's no reason to worry as long as there are no adverse consequences.

Sometimes children refrain from doing their best for fear that they will not succeed. Be gentle in encouraging your child. Use humor to teach that everyone fails at times, and that the point is to keep trying. We know that "The Little Engine that Could" story is told to children in many cultures and in many languages for a reason. The little engine was able to do the nearly impossible because it was convinced that sustained effort would win the day.

As your child gets older, you will want to start to teach that simply trying the same thing over and over again is rarely an effective strategy in itself. You will also help your child judge which tasks are possible and which aren't. This is closely related to Hallmark No. 5 that children have good appraisal of their own skills, including their strengths and weaknesses.

- **Provide many types** of cause-and-effect learning experiences. This need not involve expensive toys. Play simple card games that require the use of strategy (like "Go Fish"). Put together puzzles. Household chores and simple activities are great, too. Conduct simple science experiments at home (there are lots of books and kits to help with this). Remember that learning social cause-and-effect relationships counts, too. Be generally consistent in your parenting. The most powerful cause-and-effect learning occurs within the context of social relationships as your child learns which behaviors cause what type of reaction from you and others.

4. THEY HAVE WELL-DEVELOPED SOCIAL AND EMOTIONAL SKILLS.

These are essential to learning and to getting along well with people, especially teachers and classmates. Children who do well in school also get along well with others. They usually like their teachers and many of their classmates, and these feelings are reciprocated. Qualities such as consideration, sharing, being cooperative, waiting one's turn, following classroom rules (most of the time, anyway), and being able to have fun all count a lot in the early school years.

When children have severe school adjustment problems, there is almost always difficulty in both the academic and social arenas. Of course, even well-

BASIC SOCIAL AND EMOTIONAL SKILLS

For first graders:

- Showing helpfulness toward peers when they ask for help.
- Agreeing to take turns with another child.
- Listening quietly to the teacher when instructions are given or a story is read.
- Being able to work alone on a task (assigned or self-initiated) without distracting others.
- Waiting to be called on to ask or answer questions in a group situation.
- Being able to control one's emotions (most of the time) when frustrated or when treated unfairly by others.
- By age six or seven, being adept in finding constructive ways to show negative emotions, even though it is unlikely that children can or should entirely hide them.
- Expecting clear and timely consequences, both positive and negative, that are linked to their social behavior.

For third graders:

- Knowing a lot about the value of "being a good person" and "doing what is right," for more than just immediate, tangible rewards or avoidance of punishment.
- Offering help to a peer or teacher, even when it is not requested.
- Suggesting ways to solve a social conflict or to settle a disagreement, even when not instructed to do so.
- Expressing spontaneous empathy and concern when someone else is hurt, rejected, disappointed, or confused.
- Being able to show joy when someone else wins or succeeds.
- Expressing a desire to do something thoughtful, and sometimes doing this independently or at considerable expense to themselves (giving up money saved from their allowance, staying home to make or do something for someone rather than going out to play).
- Being interested in reading biographies about the lives of other people, which often convey important lessons about the social-emotional side of life.

developed social skills in a five- or six-year-old are far from the adult version of "ideal." Good teachers and parents definitely know this!

Many teachers have a well-defined set of consequences for certain transgressions — ones that children can describe and usually seek to avoid. These can include time-outs and procedures, such as receiving a yellow or red light, losing special privileges in the classroom, or not getting stickers or a colorful stamp on a card. These techniques are more useful with younger children, who require external and tangible evidence of consequences, than they are with older children, who have a more developed internal sense of right and wrong.

The harsher, old-fashioned ways of disciplining students for transgressions, such as placing a child in a corner with a dunce hat, verbally berating a child, or physically striking a child, are now recognized as highly ineffective and even counterproductive. These techniques may have scared other children, perhaps preventing further transgressions, but they also served to disengage some children, and to lead all too many students to see teachers as mean-spirited and unforgiving, rather than as caring adults committed to children's true learning.

To encourage your child's social and emotional development:

- **Provide positive, responsive, and consistent parenting.** This is the best way for parents to promote good social and emotional skills. Start early. Model good social behavior and positive emotional coping. It's hard to teach your child anger management and self-control when you lose your temper and let your emotions dominate over reasonable actions. For encouragement and advice as you fine-tune your parenting skills, keep seeking expert advice and talk with other parents (including your own).

- **Explain good behavior.** It's important to talk with your child about school rules, what pleases (as well as irritates) teachers, and how to get along with other children. As your child grows, there will be obvious advances in the ability to understand social rules, the feelings of others, and the consequences of social transgressions. You can guide this process wonderfully.

However, be prepared for the inevitable. Almost all children will have their share of spats, outbursts, disappointments, frustrations, and fears related to things happening at school. There will be notes from your child's teacher (or other school personnel) telling you about these at one time or another. As one world-class first-grade teacher once told us, "You wouldn't want to have a child who *never* gets a red light. Such a child would not be normal or very much fun!" View these ups and downs in the social realm of school for what they are — first-rate teaching and learning opportunities.

5. THEY ARE GOOD AT ASSESSING THEIR SKILLS.

Children who succeed in school generally do not vastly over- or underestimate their academic abilities. This ability to accurately appraise one own's skills and level of understanding is essential to the learning process.

The ability to evaluate one's own skills and level of understanding *with reasonable accuracy* will be valuable in many situations beyond the classroom. This serves as the basis for strong, positive self-esteem, the type that is grounded in a child's actual accomplishments, rather than the type based on wishful thinking, or derived from empty compliments that imply "you're great" no matter how well you really do.

The area of self-appraisal has typically been studied by measuring children's self-esteem. The results show that children who do poorly in school do not necessarily have low self-esteem. To the contrary, many children who perform below grade level actually think they are just as capable as others. Conversely, children with proven high academic achievement may rate themselves as only moderate or moderately high. Perhaps these children have set very high standards for themselves.

This research indicates that the young children who overestimate their skills and successes usually do so for three reasons. First, the child may be unable to correctly assess his or her own performance. Second, the child may be trying to deny, disguise, or compensate for a sense of failure. Third, the child's self-esteem may not be closely connected to actual behavior in the school setting. Research has not yet adequately resolved which explanation or combination of factors is at work here.

Parents and educators don't always agree on the role of competition in school and in life. Some people believe that individuals thrive under competitive conditions, and this can bring out the best in a person. Others view competition as unduly stressful or distracting, taking away some of the intrinsic motivation to achieve. Yet others value cooperation and a selflessness that may seem at odds with individual competitiveness.

Unfortunately, researchers have not yet looked at children's competitiveness and cooperation over a long period of time, and they have not related childhood competition and cooperation to adult levels of achievement and personal life satisfaction. Perhaps a balance of competitive and cooperative skills, as well as individual goal-setting, will best prepare your child for the future. Without question, there are ample opportunities to use cooperative and competitive skills in constructive ways in the classroom, just as there are times when an excess of one or the other will be inappropriate or ineffective.

To encourage your child's self-assessment abilities:

- **Have an ongoing dialogue** about your child's self-appraisal. This is one of the most effective strategies for helping children know how much they know or whether they are realistic judges of their own classroom behavior and achievements. This technique of self-monitoring allows a child to stop at the right times to try to find out more, or to clear up things that are confusing. For example, a child who is taught how to think about what is happening while he is learning new things will be able to:
  - ask himself questions, in the same way a teacher or parent might, to see if he understands
  - rehearse or practice new things he has learned, even without prompting from an adult
  - give himself a "grade" on his mastery of a new skill or his grasp of a new idea to see whether he needs to work on it and improve

- ask the teacher (or you) questions that make it clear what is confusing to him or what he wants to check so that the adult will become a more effective and responsive participant in the learning process.

- **Praise your child** for specific behavior and specific achievements. This is an invaluable way to help your child acquire a realistic and positive sense of self. For the most part, base your praise on your child's progress compared to an earlier period, rather than making comparisons with other children.

- **Explain that differences** among children are normal. Sometimes comparisons with other children may be appropriate and constructive. In the classroom, children see proof of such differences every day in the work placed on the wall, in who can answer what types of questions, and in the teacher's praise and guidance. They also see differences in non-academic settings, including during gym and recess times. Talking about differences, and how great it is that the world is filled with people who are good at doing different kinds of things, is reassuring to a child.

  Talk with your child about the fact that there are differences among children in how well they do things. Tell your child, "Most children are really good at some things and not as good at other things. This is true for grownups, too." This allows your child to begin to see his own behavior in relation to that of others without feeling superior or inferior.

  Such comparisons need not contribute to unhealthy competition, but can help children assess their own skills. Differences are not limited, of course, to academic achievement, since children differ just as much in their physical growth and appearance, musical and artistic talents, athletic skills, leadership abilities, and friendship skills. Talk about your own feelings, especially when you were the same age, about being good in some areas and not so good in others.

6. THEIR PARENTS ARE ROLE MODELS FOR LEARNING.

Success is said to breed success. When it comes to parents and children, this often is true. Why? Is it just a case of good genes? We think this is only part of the answer. To a great extent, children do learn from what they experience directly. Learning to learn begins at home.

THOMAS ALVA EDISON: A ROLE MODEL FOR LIFELONG LEARNING

Thomas A. Edison's life was a tribute to a passionate love of learning, exploration, and discovery. His insights into his own success are refreshing and informative. When asked about the secret of his remarkable successes, he often offered these two observations: "Genius is one percent inspiration and ninety-nine percent perspiration" and "There is no substitute for hard work."

Even as a boy he is reputed to have loved to experiment and learn things on his own. He was persistent in both discovery and invention, fortunately for all of us who rely on the electric light bulb, recording devices, and a host of other discoveries he made. As he doggedly pursued one quest, he received admonishment not to feel like a failure. His widely quoted response was: "Why, I have not failed. I've just found 10,000 ways that won't work" — a great approach for children and adults alike.

Children who succeed in school have parents who are actively engaged in reading, acquiring new skills, and taking on new challenges. If children see their parents eagerly and actively learning, reading daily, talking about wanting to learn more about some topics, and even making mistakes and benefitting from these, then children are more likely to feel comfortable in taking on new challenges themselves. Learning is a way of life — not just something that happens in a classroom.

Interestingly, many well-informed parents are the *least* reluctant to say, "I don't know," or "I was wrong" and *then go find the correct answer* to a child's question. They also are willing to admit that they, too, make mistakes. How could it be otherwise in the process of learning (and parenting)?

Remember, that for children under the age of eight, two of the most important ways of learning are through observation and imitation. Your child is likely to learn a lot about learning if you set an example.

How to set a good learning example:

- **Learn together.** Interestingly, parents often are stimulated to learn more about some things because of the questions their children ask, the interests and talents their children show, and what their children are learning at school. This leads to a type of "family learning," in which parents and children are engaged in discovery together.
- **When parents get interested** in a new subject, start a new hobby, or discover a new fact, they can share this with their child. Children can become mini-experts in a remarkable range of topics – some useful, some just fun. This can lead to amusing examples of very young children who can discuss details of a sport, the real estate or stock markets, cooking and dining, clothing, politics, or the history of a particular place in the world long before they really understand what they are saying.

7. THEIR PARENTS PROMOTE LEARNING BY "NATURAL" TEACHING AT HOME.

These parents communicate often with the school, and they arrange extra learning opportunities when their children have special interests or need extra help. This is the best kind of parent involvement in a child's learning, and such involvement is central to a child's success in school.

Such involvement begins at home. Parents are, after all, their children's first teachers. The best teaching by parents often occurs in the course of everyday activities. For an infant, this includes talking during caretaking activities, naming foods when eating, pointing to something interesting to look at or touch, and listening to sounds in unexpected places. For a toddler, learning extends to interactive sessions with books and storytelling, singing songs, and playing simple turn-taking games. By the time your child is preparing to go to school, more school-like learning often has begun, including counting, naming the letters of the alphabet, recognizing shapes and colors, and being able to tell ways things are similar or different.

Research literature strongly endorses the value of children having early successes in learning. As a child acquires new skills and knowledge, she is more prepared to go on to the next stage of learning in that same area. This leads a child to become more expert. This has many inherent rewards for a child who already is eager to learn. Further, the more early success a child has, the more likely she will be to tackle increasingly difficult tasks.

In contrast, children who have many early failures are likely to be wary of new learning situations and may seem less interested in trying to learn something challenging. This is true for all children, even those who are capable and highly intelligent. As a parent-teacher, you can help to ensure that your child's learning experiences have a high ratio of successes to failures by your support and participation.

Just as important, parents need to make sure that their children are exposed to more and more challenging and complex activities, so that they neither lose interest and grow bored nor are stunted in their development. J. McVicker Hunt of the University of Illinois, a prominent theorist in human intelligence, wrote eloquently about this as "the problem of the match." That is, the match must be right between the child's level of understanding or thinking about the world and the learning opportunities presented to the child.

How to promote natural teaching at home:

- **Bring school subjects** into home life. When your child is in school, you can reinforce and expand school-based learning by bringing it into your home life. Help your child to recognize different coins and know their value. Pin up word labels or practice new songs or poems. Write something together, like a story about what your child is studying in class. Talk about the seasons, holidays, nature, and feelings.

  Parents often will be asked by teachers to help at home in specific ways. Even when you aren't, make it a regular routine to incorporate school topics into everyday life. Just be sure that your role as "parent-teacher" does not undermine spontaneity, flexibility, and just having fun "hanging out" together. Not every moment has to be a learning moment!

- **Spend time with other families** with children the same age as yours. You will see how other parents teach, and you may get new ideas for your own family. Parents who incorporate teaching in the natural flow of events seem to do things like categorize, label, define words, offer synonyms and antonyms, tell stories that make points come alive, ask children questions that are fun to answer, and ask questions themselves ("I wonder how far away the moon is?" "What really makes leaves fall in autumn?" "Why do dogs wag their tails so much?" "Why does sodium bicarbonate fizz?").

  Parent-teachers often seem like magicians to their children, because they can demonstrate things that seem phenomenal. Pour a cup of water into two different size glasses and see how different it looks! Take water and transform it into ice (and vice versa). Take a cup of water and boil it away (almost)!

  For parents who are not skilled in home science experiments, crafts projects, or in writing books, there are dozens of books and kits that make it easy to do some pretty impressive things. Any parent can quickly learn to create a mini-volcano that overflows or make ink that becomes invisible. Building with blocks, assembling a rocket, putting together puzzles (from easy ones to the more complex jigsaw and three-dimensional ones), also are natural teaching opportunities. Assemble your own book by hand or on the computer. Do some origami. Each activity will lead to great learning.

- **Communicate with your child's school.** The best way to do this is to stay in touch with your child's teachers. This can include in-person conversations, written notes, attending parent events, and reading the newsletters sent home by teachers. In the coming years, we anticipate that technology will continue to revolutionize our daily forms of communication. Teachers and principals in some schools already are using e-mail messages, bulletin boards, and web pages as a means of communicating with parents. This is just the beginning.

- **Encourage extracurricular activities.** These can be valuable assets in your child's overall education. The hours after school and the long summer weeks for those in a traditional school-year program also are vitally important to children's overall rate of learning and development. Research shows that children who do not participate in organized programs or activities during these hours do not continue to extend their school-based learning as much as those children whose parents help to arrange for the extra learning experiences.

PLAYGROUPS FOR LEARNING AND FRIENDSHIPS

We know a group of parents whose children attended the same preschool who decided to create their own Saturday Morning Playgroup. The parents have continued this for five years, and plan to keep on going as long as they can. Children and parents alike have benefitted immensely. Parents take turns planning an activity (about once every seven weeks) and are responsible for getting the details to everyone else. Although the children are now in first and second grade, scattered across different elementary schools, the special friendships among children and parents have been sustained. They go to lots of different places, have tried a remarkable number of new activities, have learned an enormous amount over the years, and enjoyed every minute of it.

Your child might take lessons (music, dance, science, drama), participate in sports, attend community school programs (such as tumbling, foreign languages, and art classes for children), and enroll in religious education. Playgroups can provide a wonderful way to enrich a child's early school program. Look into creative ways that you and other parents can rotate responsibility in planning what the group does.

At summer camp (day camps are increasingly available for very young children) your child may learn to swim, take arts and crafts classes, learn the words and tunes to lots of new songs, and go on field trips. In the process, there is a lot of teaching and learning, all in a very enjoyable setting. Children who attend show the clear benefits of participating in high-quality summer programs, even when there isn't an explicit educational curriculum or focus.

Once again, however, don't overdo. Avoid over-programming your child or yourself. You both need "down" time and relaxation. You also need time when creative ideas and free-flowing thoughts can occur. (See Chapter 5 on family life for more information about priorities, family values, and getting to do what matters the most.)

8. THEIR FAMILY ROUTINES SUPPORT DOING WELL IN SCHOOL.

Families with good, workable routines also have children whose school performance is better. Family routines do not refer just to daily happenings, but extend to patterns of visiting with the extended family, socializing with friends, and recreation. Fortunately, many cultural and personal preferences can come into play in setting up good family routines.

Family routines matter a lot to young children. They provide children with order and a certain amount of predictability. Good routines also are grounded in children's developmental needs and balanced with those of the entire family. Remember that routines are general patterns of behavior and need not be rigid. For example, when establishing and maintaining family routines, think of the seasons of the year — how nice it is to take advantage of an unpredictably early spring or perfect snowfall or long autumn — as well as the hours of each day.

Young children clearly benefit from sufficient regular sleep — usually at least 10 hours each night. Bedtime routines and a regular time for getting ready for sleep are particularly helpful for young children. These can be coordinated with the daily necessities of tooth-brushing, bathing, and reading a book together, along with time for hugging, reflecting on the day, and having special thoughts or prayers before closing one's eyes. As in all other areas of development, there are individual differences. Some children do quite well with less sleep, and a few may need more.

Eating at regular times — often with family members taking the time to visit and enjoy one another — contributes to everyone's physical and psychological well-being. This is most important during the weekday routines as weekends afford more variety. Remarkably, our research on families reveals that many important family functions occur during mealtimes, and that this is a great time for information exchange. Great dinners can be the stuff of great lifelong memories. Unfortunately, our research shows far too many adults have unpleasant memories because their parents missed the opportunity to make mealtimes special and enjoyable events.

In some ways, it seems ironic that routines can be, in fact, freedom-granting. Certainty that important things will be taken care of frees family members to do other things. The routine minimizes having to negotiate or figure out what's what every single day. It also can create ease, harmony, and pleasure in the daily activities of family life. Routines need not be followed strictly to be effective. Rather, they represent the typical backbone of managing family life.

Organizing the house to help with your child's schoolwork and keeping information readily at hand also are important. To our knowledge, however, no one has studied this aspect of family life over time or in adequate detail. However, in Chapter 5 on family life, we pass on some creative and effective tips that families have shared with us over the course of conducting our research.

To set and maintain good routines:

- **Maintain home life schedules** and routines as much as possible. These routines should include sleeping, meals, errands, housework, television, and recreation. Don't forget socializing with other relatives and friends, as well.
- **Support your child's learning.** If your child has homework, set up a special place (or two) where he can work with as little distraction as possible. Make sure the space is equipped with needed supplies.

9. THEIR PARENTS ARE EFFECTIVE AT SETTING AND MAINTAINING APPROPRIATE LIMITS.

There are many books on how to discipline your child, and with good reason. When children are not well-behaved, they create problems for everyone — parents, teachers, and other children. There are, however, some very important principles — not just opinions — about what comprises effective parental discipline for young children.

This is not a book about discipline, and we will only touch on the subject to give you an overview of what the best research and observation on the subject show.

Starting in the second year of life, you can set consistent limits and offer clear guidelines to your child about what is acceptable and desirable behavior. With each passing year, the demands for appropriate behavior increase, but so does your child's maturity. Although all children misbehave sometimes, and seem to "test the limits" at other times, children actually prefer to be well-behaved.

Parents who are skilled in setting and maintaining limits usually have spent time thinking, planning, and agreeing on what matters the most to them and what is appropriate to teach their child at each age. They are neither overly restrictive nor too permissive. They are not harsh in their techniques. Neither are they lax or highly variable. The most effective parents (that is, the ones with the best-adjusted children) are comfortable and confident in setting limits, but are not dictatorial or overly strict.

Three disciplinary styles have been identified by Dr. Diana Baumrind of the University of California at Berkeley: authoritative, authoritarian, and permissive. Authoritative parents have repeatedly been shown to be the most effective with their children. Children whose parents use authoritative disciplinary approaches are shown to be inquisitive and exploratory, self-reliant and self-controlled, and happy and content.

Authoritative parents exert control in a supportive and encouraging manner. They are firm in their discipline, but rational, telling children the reasons why something must be done or not done. Authoritative parents are warm and receptive, but they follow through and understand the value of guiding their children's behavior in ways that are appropriate for the child's age.

Less effective are parenting styles that are authoritarian — too rigid and cold — and permissive — too lax and indifferent.

The word "authoritarian" means favoring complete obedience or subjection to authority, exercising complete or almost complete control over the will of another. When parents exert authoritarian discipline, they discount their child's needs and individuality, and in the process show little or no concern for their child. Authoritarian parents typically exert control over their children in a detached and cold manner. They also tend to be less responsive, less encouraging, and less likely to explain why they are exerting control. Very often, these parents treat all children in the family alike, even when the children's ages, temperaments, and activities might better be handled with different rules.

The authoritarian approach is *not* highly effective, because short-term control of the child is gained through fear and force, and the child often feels rejected, discounted, or abused in ways that weaken, rather than strengthen, the child–parent relationship. Children subjected to authoritarian discipline are more likely to become distrustful, withdrawn or aggressive, and discontent. The child's behavior is likely to extend to the school situation, especially because very young children see teachers as parent substitutes, and expect their teachers to behave like their parents.

At the other end of the spectrum, permissive discipline fails to provide adequate guidelines and rules for a child. Although permissive parents may be warm, their children are much less likely to learn self-control or self-reliance, and they tend to explore less. Having little or no experience with a positive authority figure, these children are not well-prepared for the expectations that are present in most good schools.

10. THEIR SCHOOLS HAVE HIGH EXPECTATIONS FOR STUDENT ACHIEVEMENT, SUPPORT TEACHER DEVELOPMENT, AND COMMUNICATE FREQUENTLY WITH PARENTS ABOUT THEIR CHILDREN.

The literature on effective schools continues to grow. Many schools are being re-structured. They are also providing continuing professional development for teachers and staff. And they are adopting improvements in the early elementary-school curriculum based on good scientific evidence.

However, several principles have emerged about what really matters in producing high levels of student achievement. Three of the most important are that the school have high expectations for student achievement, invest in teacher development, and communicate with parents.

High expectations: What do high expectations mean, and how are these shown? In effective schools, expectations are not just an externally imposed set of goals, nor are they unrealistic. Rather, teachers and the principal embrace and endorse these expectations. Most of all, they show their expectations clearly through their behavior. They treat the students with respect, encourage students to strive for higher levels of accomplishment, and have plans to ensure that all children succeed in learning.

For schools with established reputations for excellence, parents might assume that educators have high expectations for students. Do check this out. Schools, like all other social institutions and businesses, can have their ups and downs.

For example, the principal can exert a tremendous influence, for good or ill, on what happens. In good schools, new teachers may think that the students are just "smart," and may not actively convey high expectations to those in the classroom. Teachers in poorer schools may begin to believe that nothing can be done to change the situation. They may tend to blame the children's poor performance on external factors, especially if there are many children who come from homes with multiple challenges and few resources.

The good news is that there are numerous, recent examples of how principals and teachers can make a big difference and turn a school around. Check out the schools you are considering (or the school your child already attends) and see where things stand on expectations.

How to encourage high expectations for your child:

- **Make sure your child** knows that *you* have high expectations. By praising your child's successes at home – in play, exploration, puzzle-solving, learning an instrument, whatever – you convey the important message that progress and achievement are important and that your child is capable of both. You also open up her world and her expectations of herself.

Teacher development: Another important factor is that your child's schools invest in teacher development and training. Strategic investment in the ongoing education of teachers, principals, and superintendents is an investment with a proven high yield. New teaching techniques, new teaching materials and technology, and new research findings need to be conveyed in a timely manner to those on the front line. Teachers need the time to keep up-to-date and to continue to refine their own professional skills. Professional development activities often have an added benefit of giving teachers an opportunity to be with other teachers and to share information about what works or doesn't in their classrooms. We note that principal and superintendent professional development also is highly beneficial, and much more of this is needed.

How to encourage teacher development:

- **Tell the "powers that be"** in your school that you support teacher development. Find out who the decision-makers are that affect your school's policies regarding teacher training. If professional development is inadequate in amount, quality, or content, write, call, fax, or e-mail those who can change things. Teachers should not be expected to do this all on their own time or at their own cost.

Communication with parents: An occasional progress report is not nearly enough communication in today's schools to keep you up on what's happening at school and with your child. This is especially true if your child is having difficulty in any area of school, academic or social. Your child's teacher can be a great help and ally in getting your child's school experience off to a great start and keeping it that way.

How to ensure good communication with your child's school and teachers:

- **Take the initiative.** If your school doesn't have regular communications – meetings and telephone conversations with your child's teacher, written reports, parent–teacher conferences that are open to all parents – take charge. Make the calls to your teacher, schedule the meetings yourself.

DO ALL "SUCCESSFUL" CHILDREN SHOW ALL OF THE HALLMARKS?

No one study has focused on all 10 "hallmarks" simultaneously or sought to evaluate how to increase all 10 to maximize children's positive outcomes. However, numerous studies over the years lend important support to these hallmarks as truly making a difference in the lives of young children.

Can children succeed in the absence of some of these hallmarks? Yes, to some extent. But each hallmark provides obvious advantages. The more advantages a child has, the greater the likelihood of success in school.

The major point is that nearly all of the hallmarks are determined, or profoundly affected, by families. It is parents (and the child's other caregivers) who shape children's eagerness to learn, encourage their questions and curiosity, teach the value of work and effort, guide social and emotional development, teach self-assessment, practice and promote learning, and maintain supportive routines and limits. This is why families have such a huge impact on a child's success in school. When you actively provide these foundations in your child's life, you also are promoting success when your child goes to school.

CHAPTER 4

PARENT INVOLVEMENT

IN CHILDREN'S EDUCATION

Why parents must be active partners in their children's education.
How to monitor the quality of your child's education.
How to participate in your child's school and learning.

"PARENT INVOLVEMENT" IS A HOT TOPIC IN EDUCATION, PARTLY BECAUSE MANY PARENTS ARE NOT INVOLVED ENOUGH. RESEARCH SHOWS THAT WHEN PARENTS ARE MORE INVOLVED, THEIR CHILDREN GENERALLY DO BETTER IN SCHOOL. INVOLVED PARENTS ENHANCE WHAT THEIR CHILDREN LEARN IN THE CLASSROOM. INVOLVED PARENTS ALSO TEND TO BE BETTER ORGANIZED IN DAILY LIFE.

Parent involvement also is beneficial for parents. Parents who do something extra for their child, their child's classroom, or their child's school or school district have the satisfaction of seeing benefits and the thanks of smiling faces. Involved parents invariably hear about problems early and are in the best position to take action and to enact good solutions. Involved parents are also frequently in touch with other parents, sharing useful information and working to ensure that their children get a world-class education and a lifetime of good school memories.

CAN CHILDREN DO WELL IN SCHOOL IF THEIR PARENTS ARE NOT VERY INVOLVED?

Yes and no. Yes, because highly effective teachers will engage your child's mind, promote new skills, reward learning, and encourage continued intellectual growth. No, because school is only part of your child's educational life. If you are not generally well-informed about what is happening in the classroom and school, and if you do not actively expand your child's learning opportunities, your child will miss out on some valuable extracurricular experiences.

Happily, most parents have a great deal to offer their children that counts as parent involvement.

HOW ARE WE DOING?

Falling test scores among students, and the low academic standing of American students compared to those of other countries (as measured by children's performance on standardized achievement tests) are complex matters that warrant attention and resolution. Media coverage has raised parental awareness of these problems. However, these national trends provide little information to parents about how their own children are doing and how well their schools are contributing to their child's lifelong education.

In fact, survey after survey of middle-class families across the country shows an interesting finding: Parents think *other* schools (or schools in *general*) are having problems, but they believe their *own* schools are pretty good.

Further, most children are doing quite well in school and learning a great deal. This reflects the fact that parents and teachers are helping children, often in a cooperative and coordinated fashion. Whether this represents the best it can be for children and families, however, is not known. Almost all educators and parents have worthwhile ideas for how things can be improved.

The relationship between parents and teachers is another subject of debate and concern. This relationship is often characterized in the media as ambivalent or accusatory. Teachers may blame parents when children's behavior, learning habits, or preparation for school are poor. And parents may be concerned that teachers are not doing as good a job as they should be. Whenever teacher competencies are measured in a systematic way, too many teachers fall short of the mark.

At times, parents and teachers can pose problems for each other. But it is wrong to interpret occasional blame to mean that parents and schools are not working effectively to benefit children. In our research, we find parents and teachers overwhelmingly report that they like, respect, and value each other.

In short, the alarms raised about education in this country can be misleading. Yes, problems arise, but there are many ways parents can intervene on their children's behalf. Just as important, parents can work to make things better by contributing ideas to the teacher, the principal, the parent teacher organization, and the school board. Most schools offer ample opportunity for parents to get involved to support teachers and schools.

In this chapter, we offer guidelines about different ways of becoming involved and how to be sure that your child and your child's teacher know you are involved. Remember, parent involvement in education begins long before elementary school starts, and continues through the end of high school and into the college years.

WHAT IS "PARENT INVOLVEMENT"?

Parents can be involved in their child's education in many ways. Dr. James Comer of Yale University describes three levels of parent involvement with schools:

1. ***General participation,*** **the most common form, in which parents respond to teacher requests and participate in school-sponsored activities, including open houses, parent–teacher conferences, school fairs, and performances.**
2. ***Sponsoring school programs and helping in the classroom*** **is a more active form in which parents contribute time and other resources directly to benefit the classroom and school.**
3. ***Participating in school governance*** **in elective or appointed roles. This typically involves a large time commitment. Along the way, parents learn a great deal about how schools function and the problems they face.**

In addition to making their views known, involved parents also bring a fresh perspective to education and often contribute needed expertise in areas such as business, health, the arts, sports, the law, and diverse cultures and languages. Obviously, not all parents can or need to assume more active roles, although schools and children benefit immensely when they do.

When parents pay attention and show genuine interest in their child's well-being in school, they are well-positioned to know what's going on, to anticipate problems, and to resolve issues early. They also can better judge what kinds of activities at home will support and enhance what is happening at school. Such parents naturally reinforce the value and fun of learning and working to succeed.

Parent involvement does not require — or ensure — perfection. Not every school day will be reported as wonderful, exciting, and trouble-free, although most should be. The inevitable problems can be valuable opportunities for your child to acquire problem-solving skills — a big part of what school is supposed to teach.

Parent involvement of the right kind allows children to know that their parents are aware of, and care about, what is happening at school. Appropriately involved parents also know that children need some independence and privacy, and that school is primarily the *child's* experience.

As you make choices about your type and level of involvement, realize that the world of school may have changed a lot since you were in elementary school. Teachers' expectations for parent involvement will be greater and more specific; the diverse parent-sponsored activities at school are likely to have increased; and almost all educators have come into alignment with the national educational goal that, "All schools will increase parent involvement."

THE RIGHT BALANCE OF "PARENT INVOLVEMENT"

In considering your involvement, know that it is likely to be a daily endeavor. You will have many choices about the responsibilities you assume. Be realistic about what is possible. For some parents, being a classroom "parent" or planning the school fund-raiser is feasible. Others who would like to do this but don't have the time can consider sharing the role. What no parent should abdicate, however, is daily involvement in their children's school experience.

Schools expect that parents will regularly stay in touch with teachers and offer support for learning and schooling. This means reading the notes and newsletters that come home, talking with your child about each day, reading with your child every day, and helping with special projects and/or skill development, such as practicing spelling, or writing stories. Parents who travel or are not always available need to be creative in fulfilling their obligations. Having friends, other relatives, or talented babysitters pitch in occasionally is just fine.

Can a parent be too involved? When parents make their child's schooling the center of their universe, and have a disproportionate amount of family life revolve around the child's school progress, then parental involvement may be getting out of hand. This helps no one. Similarly, daily visits or calls, or extensive notes to the teacher are overdoing it (unless a special issue is being worked out). Balance is essential.

You may also be overdoing it if you feel overwhelmed, exhausted, or frustrated with your level of involvement. Check with other parents whose children are in the same classroom. If a teacher's expectations are unrealistic, parents should work with the teacher to resolve the problem. Alternatively, perhaps you are taking a teacher's suggestions too literally or too far. You don't need to carefully study every piece of work your child brings home.

Finally, if your child shows frequent signs of distress at your school-related activities, take stock. Are you remembering to spend time with your child doing other activities and just having fun? Without meaning to, are you placing undue pressure on your child to achieve at the highest level at all times? Are you mis-timing your activities, maybe when your child is tired, hungry, or in need of a hug or vigorous play?

What is too little involvement? When parents do not create time to read notes from the teacher, review what a child brings home, or attend parent activities at school, the child is likely to suffer. Very young children cannot remember that this is the week to bring in something for "the letter D," the topic of autumn, or something with the color red to help with a class activity. They also cannot be expected to reliably remember which days school ends early, or when parents need to return a signed permission slip so they they may go on a field trip. When parents do not meet these obligations, their children are embarrassed and often become detached and sometimes are prevented from participating. This can happen in families from all walks of life. Being a parent who is constructively involved in your child's education takes commitment, forethought, and time. All parents can do this well, if they are open to suggestions (especially from their child, the teacher, and other parents).

Some parents are understandably frustrated if they think the school has become excessively demanding. Your child, however, cannot be the mediator or asked to join sides. Please keep your criticisms away from very young children's ears and seek effective ways to resolve the situation.

Finally, some parents may think that the schools are "babying" their child by requesting parents to spend so much time on school-related activities at home. This is particularly true for parents who have no recollection of their own parents (your child's grandparents) spending so much time helping with schoolwork in the early years. There is little research on how much and what types of parent involvement are best for children at different levels. Good parent involvement always fosters a child's self-initiative and responsibility in learning and performance. Parent involvement does not mean that parents do the children's work. Rather, it is a way for parents to complement and extend the learning that occurs at school.

WHY HAS PARENT INVOLVEMENT BECOME SO IMPORTANT?

Twenty-five years ago, most teachers did not make suggestions to parents about what to do at home, nor did most parents interfere with (or even know about) what went on in the classroom. While this may have been easier, it also was true that too many children had unpleasant early school experiences and no help from parents to improve things.

Teachers and parents today are expected to communicate openly, frequently, and effectively. Today's teachers now take college courses about families and how to invite and accept parent involvement. Why the change? We think there are at least three reasons:

- **Everyone wants all children to do well and fit in. Keeping parents informed is one way to ensure that everyone is working to achieve these results. Also, classrooms now serve a much greater mix of children, including children with disabilities and special health-care needs. Information for parents of a child with special needs can be vital in optimizing the child's school adjustment.**
- **The education world has become more legalistic. Schools want to be sure that children are safe, that they will report "accurate" information about what is going on in the classroom, and that they experience continuity between home and school. Schools also want to prevent acrimony and avoid lawsuits. Frequent communication is one way to prevent misunderstandings.**
- **There is a great deal of evidence that children whose parents spend time at home helping to strengthen, review, and extend what is taught in the classroom do better on measures of academic achievement. Teacher–parent communication is essential if parents are to provide the right types of support at home. Also, as teachers change what they do in the classroom, parent–teacher communication keeps parents up to date.**

The extra communication can be time-consuming, but the benefits are substantial. Let your child's teachers and school administrators know what you like or don't like about the communication you have. Are you getting too much or not enough information? Do you have suggestions for improving communication? Perhaps you have ideas based on your experience in the workplace or your child's preschool. If so, share these. Your input is likely to be welcomed.

HOW TO MONITOR THE QUALITY OF YOUR CHILD'S EDUCATION AND SCHOOL EXPERIENCE

Monitoring your child's education is the cornerstone of parent involvement. Every aspect of parent involvement is geared to providing the best schooling possible for your child, and you can't do this if you don't know what's going on. Yet we know of no topic more difficult to cover than this one, for two reasons. *First,* parents cannot be everywhere, and you will not know everything that happens to your child. *Second,* there is no clear consensus about what constitutes a "quality" education. There are many strongly held, divergent opinions about the most important aspects of a child's educational experience. This is why school choice has become such an important topic. That said, there are several useful ways that parents can gauge whether their young children are receiving a high- quality education.

1. EVALUATE WHAT YOU SEE IN YOUR CHILD AND THE SCHOOL.

- **Is my child showing evidence of learning a lot about many topics?**
- **Does my child appear to be interested in and eager to share what is happening at school? (Beware: Don't just rely on your child's response to "How was school today?")**
- **Are books and other educational materials and activities challenging for my child?**
- **Does my child have many opportunities to succeed in ways that are meaningful and represent advances in skills and knowledge?**
- **Does the classroom provide different ways for students to be actively engaged in the learning process?**
- **When I go to school, are there visible signs of children's work that reflect learning? Artwork is fine, but there should be other products as well.**

- **Does the school seek to engage parents in promoting learning at home? If so, are the instructions to parents clear and useful? And do the recommended activities seem worthwhile, rather than rote exercises that are not fun or interesting?**
- **Do all or almost all of the children seem engaged and happy when I visit the classroom? (Note: This refers to typical classroom times, not to special events like parties, performances, or field trips.)**

2. TALK TO YOUR CHILD.

Children are remarkably apt reporters of their own classroom experiences. They also can provide a fairly trustworthy account of whether they are learning new things and whether school is interesting to them. Be sure to talk with your child about school. This goes far beyond the daily probe of "What happened in school today?" which yields a highly variable response from many children, ranging from the stereotypical "Nothing" and "I don't remember" to lengthy discourses about what really happened.

Research studies indicate that children are far better about revealing information that is true and reflects important dimensions of their experience when they are not quizzed directly with questions that call for expected answers. The style that works the best with young children involves a dialogue in which topics are introduced in a general, sometimes indirect, manner, followed by clear probes and specific comments to anchor and guide the discussion.

Because it is a dialogue, parents will join in, sharing their own ideas, describing relevant experiences, and asking for clarification or elaboration of what their child has shared. There are no right or wrong answers. And it's important to avoid strong judgments, since these are likely to shorten or end the dialogue. Also, try not to redirect your child's conversation so that only certain things are shared while others are hidden or denied. Don't try to control the dialogue (even if you do initiate it). But also don't be a passive listener.

Beyond the dialogue, you can have constructive conversations that will tell you a lot. Ask open-ended questions that encourage your child to tell you how things could get even better at school:

"What would you do if *you* were in charge of things at school?" (Followed closely with "And would this help you do better in school?")

"Can you think of something really good that could make school even better for *you*?"

"What is the best way to help children *like you* learn?"

"What do other children in the class think about the way [teacher's name] teaches?"

3. COMMUNICATE WITH TEACHERS AND OTHER SCHOOL PERSONNEL.

You need more than your child's view about school to effectively monitor what's happening. You need the perspective of teachers and school personnel. In getting their views, four things are vitally important in how you communicate — clarity, brevity, timeliness, and sensitivity.

Clarity: Convey your message clearly. There are many ways messages can get garbled and misread. One is poor handwriting. Teachers tell us that they get a lot of notes that are hard to decipher. Write neatly (just as your child is being told to!) or type your message. Avoid using jargon, slang, and extreme statements.

Make sure your meaning is clear. Some parents are so busy being polite, clever, or accomplished in their written notes that they don't make their point. Ask someone else to read or listen to what you've written. Likewise, if you are going to meet with your child's teacher or principal, jot down your thoughts and, if necessary, practice what you intend to say. Make sure your practice partner understands your message.

Brevity: Teachers have many parents, students, and issues to deal with. Be brief and to the point.

Timeliness: Good communication is a two-way street. When teachers and school personnel ask or need something from you, give them the response they need *when* they need it.

Being on time reflects your consideration for the teacher and the school, as well as your organizational skills. There will be many times when parents need to respond to a query, sign a note or progress report, turn in a reading list, or return a signed permission slip *by a specified date*. Mark it on a calendar (or two!). Leave yourself reminders. Be on time. Better yet, be early.

If you won't be able to respond on time, send a note or contact the person ahead of time to explain why. Remember, the teacher or school is responsible for bringing together information from many parents, not just from you. Even if a request concerns only your child, there probably is a reason why the teacher or school wants a timely answer. Show that you care by not being late. This also sets a good example for your child about completing schoolwork on time.

Much as we encourage parents to deal with issues promptly and early, we also encourage you to think about whether some matters can wait and might resolve themselves in a day or two. Selecting the right time, as well as being clear and brief, can make a big difference in how effective your communication is.

Remember that every communication need not be about your child, you, or your child's classroom. If you see an interesting article about education, want to offer to do something extra for the school (plant a garden, freshen up a mural in the hallway, create a new parent mentoring program for kindergarten next year), speak up! Share! What better way to be seen as a supporter and a contributor, one who is responsive, responsible, and ready to help?

Sensitivity: Be considerate. Think about what would be the best way to convey your message — informally in person? in a written note? in a planned meeting? Don't waste a big meeting on a small item. And don't try to deal with an important subject on the fly. The setting and timing of your message matters. Running into the classroom just before class to discuss an important topic with your child's teacher is inconsiderate and generally counterproductive.

Manners count. Be diplomatic. Avoid accusations or laments. Be open to other people's points of view and additional information. If you are in the wrong, acknowledge the fact promptly and openly. And remember to thank the teacher and others for their time and thoughtfulness, even if the problem is not immediately resolved or if uncertainties remain.

Include upbeat and encouraging words in your communication as well as the problems. Express appreciation appropriately (not through excessive gifts or words that might easily be misinterpreted). But also don't be afraid to let the teacher or principal know when things aren't going right.

Some teachers now routinely share their home phone numbers with parents; others still choose not to (and may have unlisted phone numbers). Those who give their home number often tell parents under what conditions to call. Please respect these wishes. Also, teachers usually tell parents when they have free time for consultations. Record this information early in the school year.

4. TALK TO YOUR CHILD'S FRIENDS AND THEIR PARENTS.

Ask your child's class friends what they think about what's happening in the classroom and at school. Ditto for talking with other parents, including those with children in this year's class and those whose children previously had the same teacher. In a good educational setting, almost all of the children will have positive experiences — not just your child or a few children, and certainly not just children at the "top" or the "bottom" of the learning curve.

As you get to know other parents, an effective way of eliciting their honest opinions is to avoid leading questions such as "Isn't [teacher's name] a great teacher?" or "Are you upset [worried, concerned, angry, frustrated, confused, irritated] about what is happening at [name of school or name of classroom]?" Instead, begin the conversation with queries like "How do you think things are going this year for [the name of the parent's child]?" or "What do you especially notice about the way [teacher's name] handles the class?" If you discover that other parents are seeing things differently, investigate further.

Finally, be sure to reflect on your goals for your child. What do you want for your child in life? How do you see the role of the school in achieving these goals? This should help you to evaluate whether the school is engaged in a collaborative partnership with you and your child. Look beyond rhetoric. Go beyond what the school brochures and the principal say. Pay attention to the everyday things that happen, little and big, because these represent the true substance of your child's school experience.

THE MANY WAYS PARENTS CAN (AND SHOULD) SUPPORT SCHOOLS

Schools are vital to our communities and our society. While parent involvement directly helps your child, it also strengthens the school. Ideally, at the end of each school year, parents should be able to look back and identify specific things they have done to leave their child's school a better place.

Help the school personnel feel appreciated. Every parent can provide thank-you notes, cards for holidays, and individual or class presents (modest, but thoughtful ones are best). Do not limit your show of appreciation to just the classroom teacher. If there are regular classroom assistants or special resource teachers, thank them as well. What about someone who went the extra mile for your child in the lunchroom or playground? Thank him and tell the principal, too. Nominate a great teacher for a Teacher of the Year Award. The time it takes to keep school personnel feeling good for their hard work is small compared to the benefits it reaps.

Are there tangible contributions you can make during the year? Some schools have fund-raisers in which you can participate. This counts! Just as important, you may can help to repair something, to decorate something, or to donate something to the class or school.

Contribute your time. Some of the busiest parents make time to volunteer in their child's classroom or school. You can accompany children on a field trip, make phone calls to share important information, come to the classroom and read to children, or help with a special project.

Teachers usually make requests to parents about their needs, or you can ask the teacher how to make something happen. What about doing a special show-and-tell session for the children? This is especially helpful if the topic is connected to other learning activities occurring at school. Even routine work, such as addressing envelopes, filing papers, or helping the librarian or media center director put new labels or cards in books is valuable. Chances are, you will enjoy this volunteer time and your child will be proud of you for doing it.

Talk constructively with other parents about the school and its direction. This is another form of supporting your child's school. Sharing information is valuable, and it means that more parents are able to cooperate to strengthen their child's school. Don't think that your child's "good school" can't get better. Parents at some of our country's premiere schools are the most active in seeking improvement.

Take a leadership role or complete a major project. Only a small percentage of parents can do this each year, but if you do so at least once every four years, you will be a true agent of change. It is such sharing of leadership responsibility for schools (and in other areas — the workplace, organized religion, political organizations, community activities), that makes a democracy strong and successful. Even if you have limited time and energy, attending a public hearing or a parents' planning meeting may allow you to offer a valuable perspective or creative idea that others may act on.

FORMAL PARENT ORGANIZATIONS: WHAT YOU NEED TO KNOW AND DO

The traditional PTA (Parent Teacher Association) has been transformed in many places. New names include Parent Teacher Organization or Parent Teacher Student Organization. Some groups have their own names. Some are affiliated with regional and national groups. You will definitely be invited to join. Read the invitation and ask other parents about it. Many schools pride themselves in having 100 percent parent participation.

These groups organize and energize parent talent for schools. They also fulfill an important role of challenging schools, seeking information about what's happening and why, expressing concern about changes that are not optimal (at least on the surface), and lobbying with the school board or state government about important matters. These organizations can be inspirational, bringing in new ideas through a speaker series, a newsletter, or creating a parent resource room at the school.

These associations often respond to parents' schedules and preferences. Some meet in the evening, others during the day. Some raise money, while others concentrate on a wide range of activities. Most change over the years as school needs and family needs change.

HOW PARENT INVOLVEMENT MAY SHIFT WITH YOUR CHILD'S GRADE AND TEACHER

Some parents just get parent involvement down pat for the kindergarten class when they encounter a first-grade teacher with very different rules and expectations. Then along comes a second-grade teacher who ups the ante or changes the parameters again. You, like your child, will need to be flexible and open to benefitting from change. Below are a few guidelines about the increasing expectations that come with your child's promotion through the elementary school grades:

- **Homework:** Earlier grades expect less time per day to be spent on traditional homework activities. However, the requests for daily reading plus regular sleep habits may make the early grades not seem much easier for parents than the later grades. In a recent national survey, parents reported that children's time spent doing homework more than doubled between the first few years in school and fifth or sixth grade.

  Schools vary a lot about their homework policies over the weekends and over school holidays. Fortunately, whatever your child has to do, so do the other children. This helps parents in supervising their child's use of study time. As children get older, they can study with other classmates, but this is not likely to be effective in the first three years of elementary school. There may be some exceptions, such as rehearsing for a play or concert, or having a pretend spelling bee.

- **Independence:** By the second grade, teachers expect greater child independence in completing assigned tasks. Your role will be more supervisory compared to kindergarten and first grade when almost all homework requires your direct participation.
- **Tests:** Formal tests and projects will increase. It is important for your child's well-being that you pay attention to the dates of tests and when projects are due. Children this young do not need calendars and electronic organizers, but you may!
- **Study space:** The need for a child's own study space will increase tremendously from kindergarten through the end of second grade. If at all possible, have both family spaces and a private space where your child can study.
- **Supplies:** The variety of supplies you will need for homework and learning activities will increase with the years. Have your child help select them. Personalize them in ways that help your child to be responsible for them. This is excellent preparation for the continuing academic demands your child will encounter.

THOUGHTS ON WHAT PARENT INVOLVEMENT MEANS FOR YOUR FAMILY

Beyond all you are already doing for your child, going to school will present a new set of demands. To some extent, you must forge a partnership with your child's school and the key players if your child is to benefit fully from the school experience. As with any good partnership, attempts to gain total control on one side or the other are likely to be useless and counterproductive.

Schools are reaching out to parents more than ever — inviting participation in new and exciting ways, as well as in traditional ways. Participate fully and with good cheer. Make your wishes known, give your creativity free reign, and expect occasional imperfections and inconsistencies on your part and the school's. But most of all, be a player. If you do, you will be able to look back on wonderful experiences that enriched your child, the school, and your community.

CHAPTER 5

FAMILY LIFE AND ACADEMIC SUCCESS

How home life affects the transition to school and success in school. Building a family life that's enjoyable for everyone and that helps your child succeed.

NOTHING IS MORE IMPORTANT TO YOUR CHILD THAN YOUR FAMILY LIFE. THE QUALITY OF YOUR FAMILY LIFE INFLUENCES ALMOST EVERY ASPECT OF YOUR CHILD'S LIFE IN THE EARLY YEARS. CHILDREN FORM THEIR FUNDAMENTAL BELIEF SYSTEMS LARGELY ON WHAT HAPPENS OR DOESN'T HAPPEN IN THE FAMILY.

What happens in your family, including how your family relates to the world outside, will create powerful memories that shape choices, habits, values, and achievements for the rest of your child's life. These memories also will be passed on to the next generation. What happens in your family in the coming years — your activities and traditions, your ways of doing things and solving problems, your zest for life and your family's values — will be your family's legacy in the stories your children will tell their children.

In our many research studies of families, especially the studies where we get to know the families over many years, we know of no single lesson more worthwhile to share than this: *Your family life is tremendously important and worthy of your most thoughtful and loving attention.*

In this chapter we discuss the strategies, attitudes, and behaviors that have been shown to work for different kinds of families. We also describe many ideas that families with school-age children have adopted or abandoned in their journey toward what they define as "the good life."

HOW THE FAMILY MIRRORS SOCIETY

A family is not defined adequately by legal, biological, or geographical circumstances. Rather, the family is a wonderful mix of social, psychological, and practical endeavors. Ideally it lasts a lifetime, despite transitions in external circumstances and internal features.

There are many analogies of what a family is like, from a corporation or a beehive to a never-finished work of art or a real-life rehearsal for a long-running play. But none adequately captures the complexities and richness of the family or its unique role in our lives.

Every family is a microcosm of the world at large. Within each are individuals who:

- **Assume clear and distinctive roles, but also have some overlapping functions**
- **Endorse shared goals for the family, while maintaining individual agendas**
- **Do many things cooperatively, but sometimes compete or conflict.**

The natural ups and downs that occur in societies, corporations, and governments also occur in families. What happens in the lives of individual family members creates opportunities and challenges. They, in turn, teach children valuable lessons about relationships and managing emotions, as well as how to do many worthwhile things, from the practical and necessary to the ethereal, aesthetic, and fun.

Family life at its best protects, encourages, teaches, and supports family members, renewing and preparing them for success in life. Such families also are where people acquire the desire and learn the skills to make the world a better place.

WHAT THE CHANGING AMERICAN FAMILY MEANS FOR YOU

Family circumstances and individual choices directly impact family life: who gets married to whom (or not), who has children at what ages and stages in their lives, who spends time with young children (day and night, weekdays and weekends, school year and summertime), and who lives at home. These circumstances and choices also contribute to shifts in decision-making, responsibility, and everyday life in the family.

Family lifestyles today are more varied than at any other time in our nation's history. Think of how some of the nation's demographic and lifestyle trends may already be expressed in your family:

- **More parents are delaying the ages when they first become parents.**
- **More parents are having "two" sets of children (that is, children who do not all share the same original family unit).**
- **More single parents are heading households.**
- **More parents aren't living in the place they were born.**
- **More people are marrying someone of a different religion, country, culture, ethnicity, or educational attainment (rather than someone who is "just like them").**
- **More families are adopting children, including older children, from around the world, and of ethnic backgrounds different from the parents.**
- **More families are difficult to put into any conventional category.**
- **More people with all kinds of disabilities are now becoming parents and having successful families.**

These lifestyle changes are not inherently good or bad for children. Each situation requires adaptation and awareness to ensure that children receive the consistent, responsive, positive parenting they need. Each situation also provides opportunities to learn about and appreciate the diversity that exists within and among families.

No matter how families start off, most change over time. This is true even for those that continue to be strong, happy, and successful. Being prepared for and able to adapt well to changes is a great family strength.

All types of families can provide supportive homes for children despite the different challenges they encounter. Hopefully, the challenges from outside the family that are based on fear, prejudice, negative stereotyping, and insensitivity will decrease as people strive for fairness and civility and overcome their own beliefs that reflect lack of experience and knowledge.

well as that of many others, confirms that children remarkably well when:

- economic resources
- have positive and active relationships with both their rents do not fight!)
- ve strong social support to assist with parenting and

rted for families where single parents who have l ild, for blended families with two or more sets c r families where the parent has a chronic illness o vith gay or lesbian parents. These positive find- ir these families have more challenges in provid- in their children. But parental dedication, good pl ing, a strong spiritual belief system or philoso- ph sense of humor all factor into the equation of suc

K OF YOUR FAMILY: ND GOOD PROGRESS

Take time to reflect on your family's life: how you spend time; what your dreams were and are today; the wonderful and not-so-wonderful aspects of your family's life; the sources of help and inspiration you draw upon; your family's remarkable achievements, talents, and strengths; the problems you face, worry about, or ignore; and your family's health, wealth, and happiness.

People have high hopes for their families. Children dream about having their own wonderful family when they grow up. Young adults actively explore different ways of living and building a strong family of their own. Most try to learn from the successes, mistakes, and missed opportunities in their own family and others. Powerful thoughts and emotions surround the formation of families and contribute to what results.

Most people know of families with a young child that have experienced tragic conditions. Such events often cause us to realize how precious and important life is. None of us knows how long we will live, how far our resources will go, what life-shattering or life-changing events might occur. It is neither maudlin nor superstitious to live your life, and to be part of your family's life, as though each day really matters.

Many forces can compromise your dreams for your family. Sometimes these reflect differences in what the parents want. But *more often the erosion of a family's quality of life results from an accumulation of small things.* Sometimes while attending to the immediate needs, parents forget to place "family life" itself on the short list of things that warrant serious thought. The constant demands of parenting young children can push such reflection to the "back burner." Don't let this happen. Periodically reassess your situation. Don't let minor problems go unchecked. Keep adjusting your activities to match your priorities. Make sure your values in life are reflected in your activities, your words, and your plans.

Above all, cherish your own family's sense of optimism, striving, and hope. Preserve your dreams openly and with foresight. Successful, strong, loving families do not happen by themselves or overnight. Families continue to evolve. Take time to be grateful as you continually take stock of your family.

WHAT FAMILIES CAN LEARN FROM SCIENTIFIC STUDIES OF FAMILY LIFE

Scientific study of family life is relatively new. Gathering the right information to get a clear picture of what happens and why, and assessing the consequences is a complex and challenging endeavor. Scientists who study families readily acknowledge that much about family life is likely to remain beyond the realm of systematic inquiry. Nonetheless, a great deal of practical and interesting information has been learned from tens of thousands of families.

The methods used to study what happens in the changing American family include interviews, questionnaires, and direct observation. Some new technologies even allow scientists to document biological changes that occur when family members interact with one another. Other experiments monitor what happens when families agree to change specific aspects of their family life, often with outside assistance or guidance.

Here are some of the most useful and fun things we have learned from our own research on families with children in the "going-to-school" age range of three to eight years old. These findings apply to a wide range of families, and they are not based on families with major mental health, substance abuse, or legal problems.

About priorities for the family and children: More than 90% of families studied cite two "big concerns" in their lives:

- **Helping their children to do well in school**
- **Figuring out how to get all the household chores done in a fair and easy way.**

  As for qualities parents most want for their children, "highly intelligent" and "physically attractive" are not high on the list. Instead, parents want their children to be eager to learn, helpful, sensitive to others, responsible, honest, loving, good-natured, creative, happy, and independent.

  Families place a lot of importance on the family goal of having "good relationships with other family members," and "developing character" in their children and in themselves.

About dinner time: The old-fashioned family dinner time has not disappeared, but it has changed. Here are some recent findings:

- **Duration:** Middle-class families report spending less than half an hour together at dinner and do so about four or five nights a week.
- **Food:** Tops on the menu for families with school-age children (at least on nights that they invite researchers into their homes with video cameras): Hot dogs were the number-one choice, followed by spaghetti with red sauce.

- **TV or not TV:** Some families eat with the television on. Not surprisingly, these family talk a lot less and show fewer signs of enjoyment of and interest in one another.
- **Conversation:** When families are observed during dinner, much of what they discuss relates to family management and logistics. This appears to be a great time to plan, evaluate, and share information. Laughing and good-natured teasing also are part of family dinner, although parents spend quite a bit of energy telling their children to use good table manners.

  When parents start to lead a family discussion about what everyone did during the day, they start by asking, "What happened in school?" or "What did you learn in school today?" Children's first responses often are "Not much" or "Nothing special." But parents who pursue the conversation through other leads learn the most about what really did happen.

  One good strategy for encouraging conversation about this topic is for parents to begin with a lead, such as "I know today was the day your class was going to do [something]. Did you like that, or was there anything fun or surprising about what happened?" Or "Aren't you studying about the season of [autumn, winter, spring] now? Well, I noticed [something interesting in the yard or park nearby]. Let's take a look at that later on." These types of specific lead-ins often work well.

  Parents with talkative young children need to manage the conversation so that everyone can talk, and the discourse is not entirely taken up by either the parents or the children.

  In general, parents are remarkably skilled in dividing their attention equally among the children at the table, although babies, of course, take extra time. In single-parent households, the single parent appears to do double duty, interacting about as much as parents do in a two-parent family. Thus, children are receiving good responsive parenting in many different kinds of families.

  As with dinner, many family routines in and out of the home are part of the daily and weekly lives of families with school-age children. Families find most of these routines satisfying and valuable – an important way of putting their family values into action. Many wish they had more time for some of the special family routines and traditions.

About school involvement: Studies have produced interesting findings for schools and families alike:

- **School supports:** When schools provide extra supports to parents related to their child's schooling, such as parent resource rooms at schools, parenting classes, a parent-teacher liaison, and monthly newsletters for parents, many families tell us that these are very useful. These parents feel more knowledgeable about what is occurring in their children's classrooms and school. As a result, they are more confident in their ability to help their children at home.

- **Parent involvement:** There are many ways for parents to be positively involved in their children's learning. In general, parents who had positive school experiences as children are more active in their own children's education. For parents who did not, including parents who did not complete high school, personalized assistance from the schools has led to measurable benefits. In one study, parents who received this help spent about 15 extra minutes each day helping their young children with school-related work.

  Other studies show that coaching parents in how to help their children has resulted in greater learning by the children, improved study habits at home, and greater enjoyment by parents and children. Some coaching hints include:

  - Focus on praising specific efforts or behavior while working on a problem, even if the answer is not complete.

  - Give suggestions and guidance, but not too early and not while your child is actively trying to figure things out, such as trying to sound out a new word while reading aloud.

  - Do not make general negative accusations about your child's ability or attitude.

  - Avoid saying things like "Try harder" or "Think some more," because they do not provide useful help. Instead, offer suggestions for specific behaviors your child can use to make progress in the work at hand.

  - Take your child's age into account. Sometimes parents unknowingly try to stop their child from using problem-solving methods that are normal and helpful to younger children, such as moving lips while reading "silently" or using one's fingers to add and subtract. These behaviors will cease later when they are no longer needed.

Home-based strategies: Parents use many strategies to help their child in school. These include the obvious direct forms of help, such as with homework. But many families also report that parents try to be good role models by reading books, talking about current events, and showing enthusiasm for learning new things. Young children clearly recognize and value these qualities in their parents!

- **Incentive plans:** Children and parents admit that some of their "how to help" techniques at home are not very successful. Among the least successful over the long haul are offering money, gifts, and special treats for doing well, or threatening specific punishments for not doing well, such as the loss of allowances or privileges. We suspect this is because such incentives are not closely linked to the learning process and because children already care a lot about doing well in school. These same families also admitted that it was nearly impossible to fully carry out the reward or punishment systems they tried.

- **Judging academic progress:** Parents use various ways to measure their child's academic progress. Most defer to the teacher's evaluations. However, some seemed satisfied if their child simply attended school regularly and did not complain. Others had almost impossibly high standards, such as expecting an elementary-age child to engage successfully in a serious intellectual debate with the parent or to be "at the head of the class" all the time. Fortunately, there were remarkably few parents who put such high-pressure demands on their young children.

About children's perspectives on teachers and school: In the first few years of school, children tend to see teachers as surrogate parents. This means that young children expect teachers to care about their feelings, to help them feel good about who they are, and to be happy (or sad) when things go well (or not). Only later, between third and fifth grade, do they shift to viewing teachers as more specialized in their role as educational or information specialists. In elementary school, children give their teachers very high ratings — almost as high as parents — in how helpful they are.

- **Liking the teacher:** For young children, liking school is practically synonymous with liking their teacher. Further, children often like school a great deal, even when they tell us that their school achievement is just "all right" or "average," rather than "at the top."

- **Self-assessment:** Many academically competent children were either modest or somewhat tough when they rated their own levels of school performance. In general, this does not appear to be harmful, since these children also share many other positive impressions about school, their family, and themselves.

About children's views on parents and their families: Young children really like their parents and give them fabulous marks when it comes to how helpful, supportive, and informative parents are. Of course, the children's words for these views are different, but they are a testimonial to the effective parenting that predominates today in middle-class homes that are relatively stable (in terms of residence and family structure) and free from major problems associated with substance abuse, domestic violence, and serious mental illness.

CHILDREN'S OWN WORDS ABOUT PARENTS

Young children's opinions of themselves are, to a considerable extent, a reflection of what they think of their parents. When children rate their own qualities, such as how honest, responsible, helpful, loving, creative, and happy they are, the profile they generate is a lot like the profile they report for their parents. For example, children who think their parents are especially helpful, responsible, and eager to learn also tell us that they themselves have lots of these same qualities. Children who see their parents as creative, happy, or sensitive to the feelings of others also think these are among their own strengths. The finding extends to those qualities that are not considered strong — that is, young children tend to say that they share (or show) their parents' weakest points as well.

Children decidedly agree that their parents care a lot about school and that doing well in school is an important family goal. Children say that they themselves concur: young children truly want to do their best in school.

Families that had the greatest number of stress factors or disruptions recently tended to be those where the children had slightly more negative impressions of their families and their school life. The children's ratings of their family and their social support also showed more fluctuations or changes in a short period of time (three to six weeks) — while children in more stable family situations tended to have more consistency in their reports about their feelings and impressions of their families and themselves.

IS THERE AN IDEAL FOR YOUR FAMILY?

For every family, there are images of what is ideal in the minds and hearts of the people who are most invested in the family — you, the parents and creators of your family. Professionals, educators, therapists, policy-makers, and religious leaders, on the other hand, have never reached a consensus on what the ideal family should look or act like. Experienced and wise individuals seem to know that there is no one definition that will work for everyone — not even for a majority.

In fact, restrictive societies that have sought to deny individual differences, preferences, or choices have suffered severe consequences. Our country is historically, philosophically, and pragmatically rooted in diversity. Serious shifts in this long and great tradition are unlikely. The final judgment about whether your family is successful depends on your own values and feelings.

There are, however, some widely held ideals that almost everyone endorses. These are:

- **Feeling warmth and love**
- **Spending time together in enjoyable activities**
- **Supporting the development and well-being of each individual in the family**
- **Practicing principles of effective parenting.**

Below is a list of some important areas that are likely to affect the quality of your family's life and how satisfied you are:

- **Taking time to reflect on and share your dreams, how you see the ideal family, and what you value the most.**

- **Being active in problem-solving and decision-making, often by planning, anticipating, gathering information, adopting new strategies or behaviors, and then appraising things intermittently in ways that allow your family to adjust accordingly.**
- **Being sure that any major threats to your family are addressed, especially serious problems related to health (including mental health), money, substance abuse, extramarital affairs, work, and unresolved conflicts that can include extended family members or friends.**

There is no prescription for how to deal with these areas. Just as there is no single definition of a successful family, there is no single approach to achieving one.

Another powerful factor in the quality of a family's life comes with changes over time as children develop. Caregiving for a one-month-old differs markedly from caring for a five-year-old or 15-year-old child. What is less apparent is that you also continue to develop in many ways across this 15-year period. When you take stock of the resources in your family — including the strengths of individuals and the collective strengths — and work to minimize the consequences of weaknesses, your family is likely to come out ahead.

There are many strategies to promote warmth and love, positive engagement, and effective parenting. By reading this book, you are actively seeking information and ideas, and hopefully gaining support for these efforts. Some families seek out professional help. Some schedule time for conversations or family meetings. Some gain continuous supports and inspiration through organized religion or other ways of expressing their spirituality. Many draw strength and accept help from extended families and friends. To meet the needs of all family members, given their individual personalities and different ages, you need a combination of talking and listening, doing and celebrating, planning and spontaneity, giving and receiving. Within families there is dual tension to create security and certainty as well as to sustain excitement and bring in new things. You need both.

WARNING SIGNS

Research shows that there are two important danger signals in families with school-age children:

- **Closed and rigid:** Families that operate as a closed unit with impermeable boundaries and a rigid set of habits and beliefs have more trouble than those that are flexible and better connected. Closed, rigid families are among the least prepared for life transitions, including the transition to school, which often is seen as a threat or an intrusion, because their children will come into contact with much new diversity, and the school will want to be in contact with the family.
- **Unprepared and lax:** Families that refuse to prepare for anything, assuming they can handle everything spontaneously, also have problems. Their children are likely to be left floating with no anchors, and their home life usually is fairly disorganized. Young children need a sense of order and predictability. Regardless of how much love parents have for their children, children need some tangible and daily experiences that they can count on. The school will expect such families to be involved, not just sporadically, but in a timely, responsive manner consistent with school rules and customs.

These two extremes of family style are not the norm. But many families unknowingly begin to drift toward one or the other. This may happen when a family that previously functioned well begins to act in desperation or has failed to deal early and decisively with a serious issue, such as substance abuse, verbal or physical abuse, a financial crisis, or mental health problems.

Take stock of your family's style. Be honest in your appraisal of such tendencies within your family.

As your child enters school, you may encounter families that are affected by serious problems or extreme patterns of family behavior. Be sympathetic and supportive to their children. Also, if you ever suspect abuse or neglect, talk with someone at the school about your observations. Be informed about your local laws and agencies that protect vulnerable children. Even in families where there is never a reportable level of neglect or abuse, children often suffer the consequences of parents who are unwilling to change their minds or ways. Indeed, one goal of a good education in a democratic society is to foster active thinking of life's important issues, and adapting as needed.

LIFE TRANSITIONS

The transition to school will be a major event for your family, and preparation will pay off in many ways. It is like getting ready for a long road trip and making sure that your car has had a tune-up, and you have thought about directions, accommodations, snacks for the trip, etc. Well-planned trips have the fewest number of unwelcome surprises and the greatest opportunity to enjoy chance encounters. The same holds true for going to school.

The transition to school should contribute to your child learning a lot, gaining new friends, and becoming more independent. The transition to school is also a chance for you to broaden horizons and get help in successfully educating your child.

But there will be huge demands on your time related to school. Some things will be sacrificed to the patterns of daily life. Plan in advance for ways to adapt.

CREATIVITY AND INNOVATION IN FAMILY LIFE

Creativity abounds in family life. There is a constant flow of opportunities to plan, choose, solve problems, invent, change, respond, compromise, and reflect.

Through observation, reflection, conversation, and direct experience family members learn.

The creativity and innovation in the dynamics of family life extend beyond the family boundaries. During your child's transition to school, you will see remarkable examples of how your child will use what she has learned from her family in school, in new friendships, and in the community at large.

Not everything families do well needs to be original. Successful families borrow and adapt ideas and activities that have worked for other families. A creative family remains open and inquisitive, continuing to learn from others and from mistakes within the family. Mistakes are inevitable, and they can teach important lessons.

FAMILY LIFE IS NOT JUST FOR CHILDREN

Family life is important beyond its role in launching children in their own lives. Family life matters for parents as well. Success in family life involves everyone. Conscientious parents who strive to be sure that their child has the best possible start in life may forget that they, too, continue to develop. Parents have needs and wants that deserve attention. Moreover, attention to themselves will not detract from their children's well-being. In fact, it may make life better for children and parents.

Parents who achieve a balance in their family — neither "child-centered" or "child-ruled" nor neglectful of their children ("parent-centered" or "parent-dominated") — are more likely to deal effectively with stresses and challenges. Such families also are well-positioned to create and take advantage of new learning opportunities.

Make time to cultivate your own intimate relationship, your close friendships, your interests, and your talents. Perhaps you may not be able to pursue all endeavors as fully as you'd like, especially during your child's early years. But you shouldn't stop or neglect these entirely. To avoid feeling like your own life has been put on hold, take action to see that this doesn't happen! This is one area in which families can be very creative and cooperative.

A great family life need not be an all-consuming task. But neither is your family likely to be at its best without some conscious effort. The strategies that work for different people under different circumstances are not fully understood. What is known, however, is that many satisfied families have the following:

- **A healthy dose of optimism**
- **Reasonable tolerance for little problems**
- **A sense of being able to control the important things in life.**

Families which appear spontaneous and effortless often have thoughtful parents who frequently take stock of their priorities and appreciate the good things in their lives. For families with serious challenges, such as a child's disability or a major parental illness, a source of great strength appears to be religion, spirituality, or a well-developed philosophy of life.

Families reporting the highest levels of satisfaction are ones in which the parents perceive that they have strong social support related to parenting and family management. These parents are willing to talk with others about family issues, to learn from others, to ask for and accept help. Such families are not isolated units within their communities, but are connected in multiple ways to many people, families, and social and religious groups.

PRIORITIES, PRIORITIES, PRIORITIES

The single greatest issue raised by families in study after study is that they do not have enough time. Time to do what? Mostly to be together as a family and

THE FAMILY ENVIRONMENT

DOMAIN 1:
Physical Development and Health

- Meeting basic needs for survival, such as providing food, housing, and clothing.
- Promoting good health (medical and dental care, good nutrition, personal hygiene).
- Arranging for childcare (responsible adult supervision when children do not have minimal self-care skills).
- Ensuring safety (protection for potential physical or social harm, procedures for handling emergencies).

DOMAIN 2:
Emotional Development and Well-Being

- Acquiring emotional self-regulation.
- Fostering positive expression of emotional states.
- Encouraging constructive ways to deal with emotions (especially negative states).
- Developing the capacity to give and receive love (both within and outside the family context).
- Learning to assess the emotional needs of other people, and maintaining good mental health.

DOMAIN 3:
Social Development

- Developing positive interaction skills.
- Initiating and maintaining relationships.
- Acquiring the ability to avoid and/or resolve social conflict.
- Recognizing the role of the individual in group contexts, both within and outside the family unit.

DOMAIN 4:
Cognitive Development

- Fostering intelligence and academic skills.
- Fostering daily living skills, such as money management, transportation use, and future vocational competence.
- Learning to think critically and creatively.
- Understanding how to evaluate and direct one's own thought processes.

DOMAIN 5:
Moral and Spiritual Development

- Helping family members acquire beliefs and values about ethical behavior and a philosophy of life. Examples of activities that foster the acquisition of such beliefs and values are religious education and practices, discussion of basic values, and reasoning about moral dilemmas.

DOMAIN 6:
Cultural and Aesthetic Development

- Fostering an appreciation of one's own and others' cultural heritage, folklore, and traditions.
- Developing a personal sense of beauty and art.

to do things they enjoy and value, from recreation and hobbies to spiritual pursuits and keeping up their homes and gardens.

This does not mean that parents and children don't spend a lot of time together. Rather these parents indicate that they don't have enough time for a leisurely pace, having fun, dawdling, resting, or choosing something to do. They tell us they can't fit some things they most love into their schedules. They often feel rushed and always behind schedule.

If you are in this situation, we suggest that you review whether everything you now do is essential. Have you taken on so many commitments that there is no time for other things, including spontaneous ones? If so, what adjustments can you make?

At the heart of your family life are your values and priorities. There are some broad and universal functions of families that transcend cultures. Review the chart on The Family Environment. How important is each of these domains to your family, and what are your goals for each, especially in this time of the transition to school?

In clarifying your family's priorities in the important domains of family life, realize that your resources are important in fulfilling your goals. Money is not a family function. Yet having enough economic resources to meet basic needs is, of course, a concern. Allocate those resources to match your priorities. These will change over time, so periodically reassess your budget.

When you think about how you spend your time, consider the family goals or values each activity relates to. For example, many families with young children get involved in organized sports, which is a very time-consuming family commitment. What is organized sports accomplishing for you or your child at this time? Is emotional, physical, or social well-being promoted? Cognitive development? Ideals of cooperation and competition? Your answers will help you be sure that you are not spending too much time, or too little, in certain endeavors. Assess other activities in the same way. Is each achieving results that make sense in light of the time and money you invest?

The popularity of books about how to simplify one's life is not surprising. These books are great sources of ideas on ways to give up some things that you have traditionally thought of as essential. There will be trade-offs. But most families would do a lot to have time, and it takes more than money to buy time. In fact, families with much higher incomes do not think they have any more free time than those with more modest incomes.

Changing your attitudes or increasing your efficiency in household necessities may buy you precious time. Staying more connected to your extended family and friends will be one reward, along with more time for special family activities — and some rest!

If everyone is well-rested, encouraged, supported, and healthy, the family will be better off all around. Eliminate the extras that are taking a negative toll on your family life. Expand the activities that are rewarding, fun, and consistent with your values and priorities. Be patient and don't try to do everything now!

ROUTINES AND GOOD HABITS FOR EVERYONE

When young children are about to enter school, organization is no longer a matter of preference. It is a necessity. Your child's school operates with timetables that will impinge on your family. Failure to pay attention or find the information you need — from preparing for days that school is closed to getting required medical forms — will place undue stress on you and an unfair burden on your child.

Getting and staying organized is not entirely parents' responsibility. By second grade, your increasingly independent child may have many ideas about how things can be more organized at home or in his room. On the other hand, if you are naturally organized, neat, and clean, having children be the same way is often a challenge.

No matter what your personal style is, you need enough organization and good daily habits to achieve your goals. Your young child will benefit immensely. If you go overboard, you will be exhausted and frustrated a lot of the time. As in almost everything else, seek balance. Ask others what they do. Try new things until you find what works best. There is a wealth of material on the subjects of organization and simplification. Take advantage of it.

Before you add anything new to your life — such as a pet — think through the implications for your schedule. We know many families that routinely threaten to get rid of their darling (dog, cat, swimming pool, vacation home, vegetable garden, etc.) so they can be "free!" If you have not yet acquired these, consider offering to be godparents to someone else's pet, house-sitters for their vacation home, or assistants in a garden that is overflowing with bounty in the summer.

GUIDANCE AND DISCIPLINE FOR SCHOOL

The transition to school will place new demands on your child for self-control, hard work, active learning, social cooperation, and patience. Your child will have lots of new rules to learn, as well as a new daily schedule. Does this mean you should change the guidance and discipline at home — to be gentler, to give your child a break, or tougher, for a lesson in what the outside world is all about?

We think not. Good parental guidance and discipline should be adapted gradually as your child becomes older, understands more, and can accept more responsibility. A kind ear to your child's concerns is essential. But raising or lowering your home standards is not likely to help.

You might see if there are major differences between home and school expectations that could lead to problems. If so, think about whether some gradual adaptation is in order. At least explain why things are different. Some schools may have lunchroom rules that are helpful for kindergartners or first-graders, but that make no sense to enforce at home. You may have rules about manners, such as requesting to be excused or staying seated until everyone is finished, that would not work at school. Most children quickly understand the differences. But if this does not come so easily to your child, talk with her and the teacher to see how you can make things go well.

Be sure you have read your school's handbook about discipline approaches and the school's responsibility to inform parents of transgressions or problems. Decide how you will handle things at home when your child makes such transgressions. We know of no children who do not receive a least an occasional reprimand from school. Most often, it's because eager young children find it hard to keep quiet at all the right times.

In general, do not view these transgressions as requiring double punishment or double reprimand. Do not take over the teacher's responsibility. Rather, endorse the importance of good behavior at school and express disappointment when this does not occur. However, if a pattern of frequent transgressions occurs, talk with the teacher about how you can help at home. Above all, be sure your child understands the seriousness of the situation and how to correct problems.

INVESTING IN YOUR OWN WELL-BEING

Parents who are not at their best physically and mentally find it extremely difficult to do their best as parents. There is probably nothing more important for the long-term success of the family and the child's future than being sure that each parent is well taken care of. Parents have the right and the responsibility to take care of themselves as adults and individuals. There are many ways to accomplish this. Such care is not in competition with the well-being of the family or child.

Many children take pride in their parents' accomplishments at home and outside. They also can learn to appreciate their parents' friendships with other adults, and their ability to fulfill other responsibilities, such as caring for their parents (the child's grandparents) and assuming valued roles at school and in the community.

Although children may protest initially when parents spend time on others, the long-term advantages far outweigh the temporary hassles. As children grow, they also accumulate a life story, a unique set of remembered experiences. How their parents managed their own adult lives, had fun, made contributions, did things for others, and took care of themselves combine to set an example that will be helpful when children become adults.

Finding the time to "do it all" may make this admonition of "don't forget yourself" sound like one more thing you cannot fit into your life. That's why the earlier part of this chapter was so important — to get organized, develop routines and rhythms that are easy and effective, and set priorities, so that there will be enough time for the adult members of the family to be nurtured, too.

SCHOOL-FAMILY TIES

The transition-to-school period is a time of phenomenal learning for children and parents. It's also a time of expanding social connections for every member of the family.

Meeting this period with forethought, organization, and humor can make a world of difference to your family and your child's school success. Periodically adjusting to everyone's changing needs and interests can help immensely. This is an active, evolving time. You need to evolve with it. If you do, you will help ensure your child's success in school and build a lasting family legacy of love and support for generations to come.

CHAPTER 6

HOW TO PREPARE FOR "BIG SCHOOL"

The importance of early care in preparing for the transition to school. Understanding your child's learning style. How to foster the skills, attitudes, and behaviors that will help your child adjust and do well in school.

THERE ARE MANY WAYS THAT PARENTS AND CHILDREN CAN PREPARE FOR THE FIRST DAY OF "BIG SCHOOL" AND THE MONTHS AND YEARS THAT FOLLOW. MOST OF THE IMPORTANT PREPARATION ACTIVITIES ARE THE SAME ONES THAT BUILD YOUR CHILD'S FOUNDATION FOR LIFE, INCLUDING PLAYING, EXPLORING, SHARING, LEARNING, LISTENING, AND TALKING.

There has been a great deal of emphasis in the media on accelerated learning programs for very young children. It is important for parents to know that *no short-term early learning program has been shown to have lasting benefits.* Instead, your child's readiness will be influenced by the aggregate of the experiences and opportunities during the preschool years.

Some preparation activities are linked to success in the early years of school. These activities promote a child's comfort, well-being, and ability to participate in school. Among the most important are those that enhance language abilities, social skills, and emotional control.

What can you do to ensure that your child will make a successful transition to school? This chapter provides lots of ideas for this preparation period, one that really begins long before children go to school.

What works best? A mix of daily activities and special events, talking about and visiting your child's school, and encouraging your child's curiosity and active participation in the learning process. This chapter focuses on assessing your child's strengths and needs, and then adjusting your preparation activities accordingly. We also discuss what to *avoid.*

PREPARING *YOUR* CHILD: TAKING STOCK

Children differ in how they adapt to new people, places, and ways of doing things. It's important to take stock of your child's special interests, talents, quirks, and disposition. Which of your child's propensities and behaviors will create positive learning opportunities in the early school years? Which are likely to present challenges? Which school settings or teaching styles might be more conducive to your child's learning, comfort, and happiness? Which might be a *mis-match*?

Children differ widely in temperament and personality. But neither is static or unchangeable.

- **Many once-shy children become talented, *outgoing* adults.**
- **Children who may not have been early readers often become highly skilled readers and writers later in life.**
- **A young child's attention span and concentration with structured activities is not a good predictor of later ability to concentrate and complete important tasks.**

Parents can have a huge impact on their child's school success by how they guide and shape their child's temperament and personality as well as how they encourage specific learning skills.

In all aspects of preparing for school, keep your child's individuality in mind. Respecting who *your* child is and is becoming is key to responsive and effective teaching and parenting.

WHAT *NOT* TO DO

From a vast body of research on school preparation, one key finding emerges:

The best preparation for school does not *require directly learning what will be taught in school.*

Many adults spend countless hours teaching the academic subjects that they think will be taught in kindergarten. They assume that such teaching will give their child a head start and a long-term advantage. They may also have their child practice "compliance" behaviors, such as sitting still for long periods. These preparation activities are not highly effective. Here's why:

- **The activities for a three- or four-year-old child that best promote skills for the next several years are different from those that good teachers provide in first and second grade.**
- **Inappropriate demands on a three-, four-, or five-year-old to learn academic skills and to display mature forms of behavior typically leave adults and children frustrated, stressed, and disappointed. In turn, these reactions may lead to a new set of problems.**
- **Too much time in practice-and-drill sessions takes away time from much-needed play with toys and other children. Constructive play, which children help guide and control, enhances intellectual and social skills that are invaluable in the classroom.**

What children need for school are the following skills:

- **Comprehension and love of language**
- **Ability to play well with others**
- **Manipulation skills**
- **Knowledge about the physical and social world**
- **Ability to trust adults who help them when they can't do something by themselves, to comfort them when they are hurt or confused, to show them new and interesting things, and to make them feel good about their many daily accomplishments.**

YOUR CHILD'S INDIVIDUALITY

There are many well-tested, proven ways you can build your child's foundation for early learning. Understanding and responding to your child's learning style and abilities are the starting points. By age three, many aspects of your child's temperament, personality, interests, and preferences are in evidence. Take these into consideration as you plan activities and participation in early childhood education. Which of the following activities does your child especially enjoy?

DOES YOUR CHILD LIKE...

- Being read to?
- Learning songs or nursery rhymes?
- Putting together puzzles?
- Playing actively with other children?
- Creating make-believe situations?
- Drawing, painting, or "writing" activities?
- Practicing new motor skills, like running, jumping, climbing, throwing, and catching balls?
- Finding out what new words mean?
- Making rhymes and silly sounds?
- Copying what you and older children do around the house or yard?
- Taking care of younger children or pets? Or showing caretaking behavior toward stuffed animals or play people?
- Building with blocks or other objects?
- Playing board games that have rules (like Candyland, tic-tac-toe)?
- Playing vigorous games like tag, hide-and-seek, and tug of war?
- Watching plays, movies, videotapes, or children's educational programs on TV?
- Talking about the characters or themes in what they have watched on the stage or screen?
- Attending concerts and performances?
- Visiting museums with hands-on activities? With look-at-but-don't-touch exhibits?
- Helping make choices in stores, like grocery, toy, hardware, office supply, or garden shops?
- Visiting relatives and joining in special family or holiday celebrations?

Your answers provide useful information about your child's talents, interests, and learning styles at this age and stage of development. Use this information to expand your child's natural learning opportunities. If you can't answer some questions because your child has not yet been exposed to certain places or things, incorporate these into your future plans.

Be flexible. Your child's enjoyment of various activities can be influenced by the subject matter or by who else joins in. Involve friends and favorite people. Build on favorite themes. Experiment. Try things more than once. It's okay to leave a concert at intermission. Crafts projects or putting on a play don't have to be elaborate or lengthy.

Open up your child's world. Don't inadvertently close off options based on gender stereotyping. Does your daughter have a baseball glove and ball? Blocks to build with? Toys that go fast? Does your son have stuffed animals or dolls? Drawing materials? Cooking tools or toys? Put worries about being a tomboy or

A LESSON IN ACCELERATED LEARNING

In a famous experiment conducted many years ago, preschool children were taught advanced motor skills. Initially, these children were more advanced in their playground skills. Yet within one or two years, they had lost their early advantage. Children without the advanced training quickly caught up and learned these skills, and performed at comparably high levels.

Today, there is an explosion of competitive sports for children as young as three and four years of age. Many of the team sports involve a level of motor coordination, thinking, and strategizing that are far beyond the capabilities of most children this age. Later, when parents see their children "catching on," they may think that the early practice really helped. But research indicates that for most children and most sports, this is not the case.

This lesson also applies to academic areas. Bright children are not always early readers. Promoting early reading for a child who is not interested or ready is unlikely to yield long-term benefits. However, if your child spontaneously shows interest in sports, reading, or puzzles, by all means encourage these skills to flourish.

sissy aside. Children have many sides to their interests and talents. Teachers will encourage boys and girls to try a lot of different things when they come to school.

WHAT SKILLS ARE NEEDED?

There is a good deal of confusion among parents as to what skills and attributes really help a child in school. Study after study shows that early memory of numbers and letters or other academic "facts" have little impact on school success. Instead, the major attributes that help a child adjust well to school are:

- **Showing an interest in learning about new things**
- **Being willing to join in new activities and new situations**
- **Having good language comprehension skills**
- **Being able to adjust well even when things don't go just right or as planned**
- **Expressing ideas and feelings clearly most of the time**
- **Asking for help appropriately**
- **Showing consideration for the feelings of others**
- **Taking initiative in planning and doing things**
- **Being proud of progress and achievements**
- **Thinking of ways to solve problems**
- **Learning from adult guidance**
- **Observing others to learn what to do**
- **Remembering and reflecting on things in the past.**

Children with such abilities are well-prepared for going to school. These skills and attributes count *more* than knowing the alphabet or numerical skills. For children with the abilities listed above, learning in kindergarten will be certain, easy, and fun most of the time. Alternatively, memorizing letters, words, numbers, or facts *without* the above skills and positive attitudes will be of little help.

Two broad categories of experiences best enhance the behavioral attributes your child needs for going to school:

- **Many and diverse types of learning regardless of the content**
- **Positive, sustained relationships with children and adults.**

For three- to five-year-old children, three excellent types of activities that provide these learning and relationships are:

- **adventures outside the home**
- **literacy activities**
- **social interactions with children and adults (in addition to parents).**

ADVENTURES OUTSIDE HOME

Wherever you live and whatever your circumstances, you are surrounded by wonderful learning opportunities for your child. If you live in a large city with many museums, parks, and other cultural institutions, wonderful. Take advantage of these often. But small towns and rural communities have an endless variety of opportunities, too. Remember that things and events that seem ordinary to adults may be new and wondrous to a young child.

Excursions are invaluable in teaching and preparing your child for school. Going places to do things introduces your child to the larger world in a way that cannot be duplicated by books, videotapes, or TV. Lessons from these excursions are complex, multi-purpose, and support social and emotional growth as well as intellectual and academic achievement.

Your local newspaper is a great place for ideas about what to do and where to go. Most newspapers have weekly sections devoted to family activities. Many communities have a free monthly publication focused on children and families, which includes coupons and discounts for events. Look for the local version of the *Child Times* in cities you visit.

Everyday errands offer learning opportunities, especially when you can plan extra time to explore some corner of the mall or shopping district where you don't normally stop. Look at a display of fresh flowers or exotic fruit in the grocery store. Talk about the construction of a building or road en route to your destination.

Learning about and negotiating new situations. Learning opportunities abound on excursions, both special trips and everyday errands. The sheer sensory delights are lessons in themselves — the sounds, smells, and appearances of animals at the zoo or the plants, birds, and people in a park. Even if some information is beyond your child's grasp, you can discuss the topic at a level your child can understand — such as how animals are like and unlike one another, what's funny about them, and what they eat.

In preparing to go to a concert (or during intermission), talk about different kinds of music, sounds, instruments, and roles people play (conductor, solo performer, member of the symphony). At the state fair, watch people doing things with and for animals, from shearing sheep (maybe there will be someone spinning yarn from the wool) to milking cows to grooming horses.

Remember, the biggest, best, and most expensive event is not necessarily more impressive to a young child. A small local fair can be as interesting and fun as the huge state fair that may be more distant, more expensive, and more crowded. Ditto for the performance by a world-renowned orchestra compared to the free concert at your local high school or community college.

Interest in learning. The more excursions your child experiences as interesting, the more the learning benefits accrue. Just as important, taking trips, big or small, is a form of practice for trying new things; being open to new sensations, words, and ideas; and getting comfortable with people and practices that differ from those at home.

Use your imagination. What can you do on a trip that is different from the last time? Even in ordinary settings, such as the grocery, your child has a chance to see other parents with their children, and people from many different walks of life. If and when appropriate, use these as opportunities to talk about families, people, and the world.

Remember that children like repetition. Your child may want to visit the same place at the zoo, museum, or botanical garden time and again. Not everything has to be brand new. Besides, there will undoubtedly be nuances to notice. More than learning can occur from these repeated outings. Hopefully, you also will enjoy creating some of your own family "traditions" related to your community outings. Celebrate with a treat of some kind, take photos, write a story when you come home, or call a friend or relative and tell them what you did.

There will be unexpected sights and sounds on many excursions — sirens from an ambulance, an interesting sign along the road, a building under construction or one being torn down, and changing weather. Talk about these. In the process, new words, expanded understanding, and opportunities to reason, make choices, or solve problems are likely to appear.

Throughout your trips, one of the most important things your child will learn is how you behave in the outside world. Are you friendly? Interested? Cautious about some things before you proceed? Patient or impatient when you have to wait? Considerate of the feelings of others? Pushy or cooperative? All of these behaviors contribute to your child's sense of what works and what doesn't in public.

A few words about how to treat your child in public. Avoid embarrassment. Don't talk *about* your child in public in ways that make him uncomfortable or self-conscious. Do not make fun of him or criticize him for normal mistakes or misunderstandings. Remember the awful things you have seen other parents do in public? *Don't* do them yourself, especially in matters of discipline and guidance. Instead, encourage your child's best behavior. It is desirable to limit and prevent undesirable behavior. But avoid a big public display if things do not go as you would like. Don't humiliate yourself or your child. If necessary, leave a situation to find a private place to deal with a concern. This is an important lesson for your child about being out in the world — *there is a time and place for everything, and sometimes you handle things differently when you are in different places.*

One of the first and best places where children learn about variation in behavior is at the homes of relatives and friends where the rules will likely be different from those at home. In these settings your child learns new rules about climbing or jumping on furniture, whether it's OK to open or close certain doors, using extra-polite behavior, showing affection, and from whom to seek permission or gain information.

Cooperation and flexibility. Excursions require more coordination of people and their desires than being at home. Parents make the vast majority of decisions about where to go, what to eat, when to leave, etc. But children should be able to contribute opinions on some of these matters. In the flow of the outing, there are natural opportunities to talk about what will occur and to make adjustments or change your minds as things progress.

Some limits may be set in advance, and reminders shared throughout. ("No, you may not go on the very big slide." "We will get to have one treat only." "After we see the paintings and statues, we will go home for a nap.") Others may simply not be anticipated. To promote sharing and the give-and-take of decision-making — things that will occur frequently in school — parents need to allow their child to offer ideas and then be part of a joint decision. This does not need to be a 50/50 deal, nor should all choices be open to negotiation. But many joint decisions help your child to think ahead about what to do, to gather useful information, to listen to other ideas, and to think about what is most important. Your child will have many opportunities to practice coping with the fact that people change their minds sometimes and that no one gets his way all the time.

Think about the length of your outing. For younger children, shorter outings usually work best. If the trip will be long, plan rest times and a change of pace. Even when you pay admission to an event, don't feel you must stay longer to get your money's worth. The goal should be to have a good time, one that you can reflect on and perhaps do again. Don't let an otherwise great visit become an ordeal because you mistimed the event, rushed to accomplish too much, or stayed too long. For families with older children or guests, plan for someone to take your child on a break or home early or while the others continue.

On trips, children can learn about different rules of conduct for different settings or kinds of activities. Explain why we must be quiet in the library or theater, in contrast to amusement parks where it's OK to scream and yell on rides. Discuss how we dress depending on where we are going, how we introduce ourselves, and why we clap to show appreciation for a fine performance.

Besides showing your young child how to behave through your example, find time to talk about rules and norms, and to compare and contrast what you can do in some places but not in others. There are many wonderful books that teach about these rules and norms, often through amusing stories. The Berenstain Bears series, all available in inexpensive paperbacks, is a well-known modern classic in this area, and almost every topic you can imagine is addressed in one or more of these delightful, instructive books. Look for other books that contain messages about these societal expectations written at a level for your child's understanding. Reading old-time children's literature allows for a natural discussion of how times have changed.

Remember that a big part of going to school will be learning that classroom behavior is different from just being at home, and that ways in which children can and do behave differently depends on where they are: classroom, hallway, playground, gym, cafeteria, media center, computer room, etc.

Expanding language skills. On trips, children are exposed to many new words and the ideas they represent. You can introduce some before your outing, and continue to discuss them afterwards. A larger vocabulary will help your child better enjoy books, conversations, songs, and activities.

It's not just the number of words your child knows that matters. What also counts is how they are used, their varied forms, their subtle and not-so-subtle meanings, and their effectiveness in adding specificity to communication.

The more children grasp language, its components and structure, its versatility and necessity, its richness, and its playfulness, the better prepared they are for going to school. They can ask questions better. They can better communicate their likes and dislikes. They can better follow a teacher's instructions. They can benefit more from a teacher's or classmate's comments, suggestions, and praise. They can excel at show-and-tell, making up and writing down stories, reading for ideas and themes, and learning from lectures or videos.

A good grasp of language allows even very young children to teach others about new things they have seen, heard, tasted, touched, and done. Help your child grow in this important skill. In conversation, take into account your child's comprehension. Anticipate possible confusion in words and their meanings. Play games with synonyms and antonyms. Practice pronouncing words that are difficult to say or that just feel good when you say them. Recall a new word several times throughout the day or the week. Depending on your child's age, you can even write a word down or draw pictures about new words. And by all means, use those dictionaries, encyclopedias, or computer-age methods of learning more about a new word.

A lot of what happens in the first few years of school involves language learning — from vocabulary expansion to learning about letters, phonemes, words, and sentences; from improving grammar to developing descriptive complexity and specificity; from using words to make interesting sound patterns in poems and songs to inventing increasingly creative and long stories. Besides learning new words, outings often lead to lengthier conversations about a topic or theme. The absence of the usual household distractions also encourages conversation.

Conversations with your child are a good reason to use cell phones and beepers judiciously. One of the saddest changes we have observed in recent times is the number of parents who accompany their children to a playground, zoo, or restaurant, but spend their time on a portable phone. This compromises the outing for the parent and the child. Outings are special times. Keep them as free from intrusion as possible so you can fully enjoy the moment.

Problem-solving. Trips offer unexpected problems — getting lost, getting caught in a traffic jam, encountering bad weather, or being disappointed in an event you had looked forward to. When these situations arise, your child will see how you handle things and hopefully will learn new ways to behave in the face of disappointment. These are invaluable lessons that prepare your child for school.

Sometimes parents don't tell their children what's going on when the unexpected or unpleasant happens. At some times and in some situations, this shielding can be appropriate. Let your child in on what's happening whenever possible, especially if you need to pay attention to something or if your mood has changed.

Not all surprises are bad. You may meet a friend while out and then modify or expand your plans. You may intend to do one thing and then discover an opportunity to do something else as well. Perhaps the book you hoped to check out at your library isn't there, but there are even better ones available. Since libraries have rules that limit how many items can be checked out, this is a perfect opportunity for a lesson in making choices. Thus, the *positive* unexpecteds are just as likely as the negative ones to require action. By engaging your child's participation whenever possible, you are teaching valuable problem-solving skills as well as fostering adaptability and positive emotional self-regulation.

"NEW" IS IN THE EYE OF THE BEHOLDER

We took our son, then two years old, on a trip to Paris. In a city bustling with art and culture, Sam was truly fascinated — by sticks. He discovered big ones, little ones, smooth ones, rough ones, musty-smelling ones, ones that snapped, ones that bent, straight ones, crooked ones, curved ones. It was a learning delight that engaged him fully at every level. We didn't need to buy any souvenirs, and we brought a smile to the face of the customs officer as we traveled home with Sam's new stick collection.

For many families, frequent and varied outings are part of their daily mode of operating. They often are a necessity. Whenever possible, allow extra time to enjoy your child's company and natural curiosity. Talk about where

PLACES FOR LEARNING

Cultural institutions and events:

- libraries
- parks
- botanical gardens
- zoos
- art museums
- special children's events, such as plays and musical performances
- museums of history and specialty museums (maritime, cartoon, neon, doll, automobile)
- science centers
- planetariums and observatories

Everyday destinations:

- grocery stores
- stores and shopping malls or districts
- restaurants
- movies (targeted for preschoolers)
- playgrounds
- homes of relatives and friends
- walks or bike rides or drives around your neighborhood or new areas

Activity destinations:

With forethought, these can provide a wealth of positive experiences for a young child:

- parents' workplaces
- offices of health care practitioners
- banks and businesses where transactions occur
- post offices
- city hall or public buildings with displays

you are going, why, and what will happen. In these ways, the practical business of living can become more enjoyable and highly educational. Not surprisingly, parents who do a good job of negotiating everyday living tend to have children who are well-prepared for school. A few suggestions from successful parents:

Make the most of your excursions. Trips increase your child's sense of competence in multiple settings, encourage exploration, increase the desire to seek information outside the home, and build social and academic skills. Outings also give you a lot to talk about. The conversations you and your child have are natural ways to teach and to promote the use of memory skills.

Collect souvenirs. Souvenirs can be fun, too, if you can keep their number, size, delicateness, and safety under control. Consider collecting smaller and more original things. We know of families that have collected grass seed, sand, pebbles, colorful pins, patches, or decals. How about stamps or coins?

Build your family's archives. Most people document special family events and vacations. But don't limit your family archival history to these events. Consider gathering books or pamphlets about what you do. Commercial maps may be too complicated for a preschooler to understand, but you can make simpler ones. Postcards are wonderful and affordable for children to collect. They make great props for sharing with others and often contain useful information. Collect postcards about your own home town. You could even have an outing to find a new postcard.

Building a library or archive of family outings is a wonderful prelude to the years of show-and-tell, and will be a lifelong source of stories about what your child and family did. Make family "scrapbooks" with photos, videotapes, computer images, diaries, stories, tape recordings, and mementos. Scrapbooks make for great storytelling and reading. They help children reconnect with the good feelings of family events. Albums help teach language skills and reasoning. They also strengthen memories for specific places and activities. Many lifelong skills and memories have their origins in these experiences and their preservation in the recorded family history.

LITERACY ACTIVITIES

Reading and storytelling are among the most powerful ways to build your child's skills, interests, memory, and language. But reading to your child has benefits far beyond promoting language, because reading — done well — involves queries, responses, and turn-taking, as well as review and exposure to new ideas, people, places, and consequences.

Reading promotes all of the attributes that help children succeed in school:

- **The stories in books are excellent for teaching ways to *learn about and negotiate new settings, be cooperative, and solve problems.* The central characters are frequently in wonderful, memorable, often funny circumstances that they have to learn about and cope with.**
- **Books are outstanding for encouraging a child's *interest in learning.* You can select books on new topics and explore new subjects.**
- **Reading to and with your child contributes immensely to building *effective communication skills,* through the give-and-take between parent and child as well as in the stories.**
- **Books and interactive reading are powerful ways to build your child's *capacity to think,* such as *reflecting on past events and anticipating future ones,* as well as to remember, imagine, plan, and figure out things.**

Why is reading so engaging and so beneficial for young children? First, in the hands of a skilled teacher, a book becomes a prop. The reader can bring the words on the page to life by pointing, asking questions, modifying words to bring the child and others into the story, and relating the story to familiar things in the child's life.

A skillful reader allows a young child to interrupt, knowing that this reflects curiosity and a desire to learn, not rude behavior. The child may ask a question or make an observation about something said or shown. Besides conveying new information, reading is a natural opportunity for extended interaction which builds your child's social and emotional skills.

The stories often contain valuable lessons, from having fun to showing care and respect for others to understanding how people build or fix things. You can extend these lessons by relating what happens in the story to other situations. Many classic stories, such as "The Boy Who Cried Wolf," "Chicken Little," and "The Little Engine that Could" are wonderful for this purpose.

For good reading choices, use parents' guides to children's literacy at your local libraries and bookstores. Many preschools and elementary schools also have lists of recommended books. These guides usually are arranged by children's age level and by topics or themes. Your local librarians and experienced bookstore staff can help. Tell them what books your child likes. They will likely know many new books to suggest!

A special thought for families in which one or both parents come from other countries. Be sure to blend your own childhood stories and books with those of traditional American culture. This gives your child the best of each culture. Elementary school teachers are likely to assume that all children know about classic stories, such as "The Little Engine that Could," and may simply say, "I think I can, I think I can, I think I can," as a shorthand to encourage the child to put forth extra effort. By introducing these traditional stories and rhymes, your child will become that much more a citizen of the world.

Similarly, parents who share the same background should read books from other parts of the world and from other traditions. This helps prepare children for school, and it's fun for parents, too. Some of the most beautifully illustrated books and fascinating tales come from faraway places.

How, what, when, and where to read to your child. Reading to a young child is a skill. Almost everyone can get better at it. Most parents enjoy reading because children are such a great audience. They often listen in rapt attention and beg for an encore. And there is a delightful array of books to choose from.

By the time your child is three, reading should be a part of everyday family life. Have lots of reading choices available. Take advantage of libraries and book swaps. No matter what your book budget is, be sure your child owns at least some books — ones that are durable and easy to use. Keep repair tape and glue handy, especially for the books with tabs that make things move. If you get a book that does not interest your child now, save it. Interests change. Remember that books make great gifts.

Have several places in your home for your child's reading materials — places that are easily and safely accessible. Some may be shared places with books for you and your child. It helps to keep a separate place for borrowed books so you can find them when it is time to return them. Allow room for expanding.

Parents are usually amazed that very young children learn the titles of the books based on their appearance, and sometimes appear to "read" the words (memorized, most of the time) on the page. Celebrate these signs of your child's emerging literacy skills, and build on them. Look for words that look alike or start with the same letter or sound. Think of different words that mean the same thing. Add a new twist or ending to a story. Beware: sometimes children love this; other times they rebel when you deviate from the "real" story!

Encourage friends and relatives to read to your child, too. They often love this special role, and your child gets a variation of something familiar. Children also can show others how much they know and how much they like books. In all our years of working with parents and children, we have *never* heard a parent say that their child did not like to be read to. In fact, parents consistently tell us how much their children enjoy this, and how much children want to hear their current favorite story over and over.

We suspect children learn a great deal from repetition and gain much from the social dynamics of reading and rereading. Encourage your child to tell part of the story. Guess what is going to happen next. Think about reading some of the pages in a new order or playfully skipping a page. You even can try to act out part of a book, especially one with great dialogue or action. Then reverse roles or bring somebody new into the story. Play "what if" games. These are easy ways to have one book provide more than one story.

Enjoy the illustrations. Invent your own story to go with the pictures. Think about what else you could draw pictures of and add your extra pages to the book. Read a favorite book when another child visits. Don't limit reading to bedtime or quiet time. Parents can share reading a book, taking turns with each page or reading different voices. The opportunities are many, and the rewards are huge.

Most literacy experts think 15 minutes of reading is a daily minimum, and 30 to 60 minutes a day is even better. (Note: For very young children, this may mean five to 15 books per day!) Even if your child has books read by other adults during the day, don't forsake this special opportunity to promote learning at home with you. Individualized and interactive reading is the best kind of all, and a parent's way is very special, indeed.

If you are pressed for time, reading can be combined with other activities. You can read or discuss a story while you sit outside, or while your child splashes in a wading pool, or while you prepare dinner.

After dinner is a universally favored reading time. Some reading may hold the interest of several family members. Add special rituals, like an extra hug, a healthy drink at the end of the story, or a song. But the real joy for children is the reading itself. Other rewards are not needed.

When parents love to read, reading becomes a natural part of life for the whole family. When your child sees you read, she observes that reading is important to you, that you get new ideas from it, that you talk about what you read, and that you enjoy reading. Allow your preschooler to see that you read mail, read signs on the road, read messages on the computer or television screen, and read notes left to you by others. Write notes to your child and read them together. Ask friends and family to mail your child a letter or card. You do the same. This personalizes the excitement of reading.

Improving your own "read aloud" and interactive reading skills is mostly a matter of being adventurous, unself-conscious, and "getting inside your child's head." Pay attention to what your child likes and knows. Notice a quizzical look or a big smile — a signal for you to elaborate on something or repeat what you've read. When you discover a book that is especially enjoyed, consider finding more books on that topic or with the same characters. Ask your child what type of books he wants. Include him on trips to the library or bookstore to make selections. If possible, help your child to establish a friendly relationship with the librarian or the bookstore manager. They will make helpful suggestions and confirm for your child that many people love books and reading.

LEARNING IN A SOCIAL CONTEXT

By three years of age, most children are ready for greater challenges and opportunities for vigorous play, interaction with other children, and learning about the physical and social world. There are many ways to meet these needs for learning, play, and companionship, including planned playgroups, preschools, and child development centers.

In the past two generations, preschool experience has become the norm for all families, including those where both parents do *not* work outside the home. Research findings confirm that high-quality preschool experiences can be beneficial to children, and that poor-quality ones can be harmful. In this section we provide guidelines for parents in selecting a place to give their child these learning opportunities in a beneficial way. Parents whose children already have been in such a setting should be sure that their child's needs are being met as well now as they were when their child was first enrolled.

Good preschools and playgroups broaden a child's range of experiences, especially social experiences and opportunities to learn about friendships, cooperating, planning, resolving difficulties, following directions, and how others talk, think, and behave. The finest preschools have talented and dedicated teachers, exciting and interesting play and teaching materials, an organized, age-appropriate curriculum, and a philosophy of educating young children.

Good preschools also have the indoor and outdoor space to provide certain types of activities that are not possible or welcomed in most homes. Even the families who create their own playgrounds and large preschool-like rooms at home discover that for a child there often is something "extra" or magical about the play and learning areas at a great preschool or public playground.

A child does not need to be in a preschool every day or all day long to benefit. Many parents create weekly schedules for their children that involve more than one setting or primary caregiver. Most children thrive under these conditions. Parents also can add playgroups, special lessons, or group activities, including sports-related ones. These can be fun and rewarding for children and parents. However, it is worthwhile to experiment to find out what works best for everyone.

What to look for (and why) in quality early childhood education. There has been much debate about the impact of non-parental childcare on children's development. In the largest study to date, the National Institute for Child Health and Human Development has tracked more than 1,300 children in 10 cities for the past seven years. The results show that there are some lasting benefits from high-quality care regarding children's intellectual and linguistic development. These important findings do not negate the importance of parental care, but rather confirm that children who have expanded learning opportunities in high-quality educational environments do tend to achieve at higher levels.

Many children are in the care of someone other than parents for much of the first five years of life. Other children do not enter a social learning setting until around three — the age when the majority of children begin to participate regularly in an out-of-home program. Selecting the right learning environment for your child, and becoming actively involved, are important ways to help your child prepare for elementary school.

A good preschool program fosters the hallmarks of good learners described in Chapter 3. The more hours a child spends in a center, the more important the quality of care, and of early childhood education, becomes. For children who spend 30 hours or more per week in a childcare center, the teachers' ability to foster these hallmarks, especially a love of learning, social and emotional development, and good play skills, is critical.

Based on our years of helping to create, direct, and evaluate early childhood education programs for children from birth through age eight, we encourage parents to seek out a preschool program that offers more than just safe, responsible care and nurturance. Find one that represents the best practices and endorses fundamental principles about how young children learn.

Look for teachers who are:

- **Highly responsive to children**
- **Filled with ideas about things to do and make and places to go**
- **Love being with children and are fascinated by them**
- **Value play and help set up opportunities for lots of natural child-initiated play**
- **Encourage a child's development *in all areas***
- **Celebrate a child's achievements**
- **Are patient, kind, and warm**
- **Provide limits and guidelines to promote positive behavior**
- **Know how to handle difficult situations**
- **Are eager to learn more about young children and what is beneficial for them**
- **Are interested in you and your family and want a good deal of contact with you.**

This last point is especially important. Don't assume that your child's preschool teachers are too busy to spend time with you or that you don't need to know what's happening in your child's program. All of the great childcare programs we know *want* frequent, informal contacts with parents and the extended family. If a center or person seems too rushed or not interested in you, beware.

Of utmost importance, the adult-to-child ratios should be high. Guidelines from the National Association for the Education of Young Children are:

- ***Birth to 12 months:* one adult to three children in a group no larger than six (or one to four in a group no larger than eight)**
- ***12 to 24 months:* one adult to three children (group size of six), up to one adult per five children (group size of 10)**
- ***24 to 30 months:* one adult to four children is ideal (group size of eight), up to one adult per six children (group size of 12)**
- ***30 to 36 months:* one adult to five children (group size of 10), up to one adult per seven children (group size of 14)**
- ***Three- to five-year-olds:* the generally recommended ratio is one to seven (group size of 14), up to one to 10 (group size of 20).**

The adult-to-child ratios are important for an adult to provide sufficient one-on-one attention. Although the number of adults alone doesn't guarantee high-quality or responsive care, poor ratios are a major deterrent. Imagine yourself trying to nurture this many children, often of varying ages and abilities, from different types of homes, and with different needs and strengths.

Good preschool teachers need to know a lot about the development of very young children in general and as individual learners. They must recognize and value the individuality of each child, understanding that all children have strengths and weaknesses. Good childcare routines and teaching also are grounded in the social and cultural contexts in which children live.

Preschool teachers with formal training and continuing professional development prove to be more effective in promoting learning and positive social and emotional development. Of course, training alone can't ensure motivation or skill. And there are some excellent self-taught educators.

A nearly universal goal in this country is that children be cared for and taught by qualified personnel with certification in early childhood development. Preschool programs with favorable teacher-to-child ratios and certified, talented teachers tend to have the best programs. Not surprisingly, this comes at a cost. More teachers cost more. Better trained teachers cost more.

All preschool staff should be entitled to good work benefits. Sadly, the majority in our country today still lack these. As parents involved in your child's education already, you can help to elevate these standards for your child and others to follow.

Don't rely solely on a school's or center's reputation. Spend as much time as possible in the groups and classrooms, on the playground, and even sitting through lunch or break time before enrolling your child. This will take a minimum of two visits. It's worth taking vacation time or sick leave to be confident that your child is getting the best experiences to enhance and complement all that you do. In the process, you may learn some things that will help you at home — from new ideas about toys, games, and outdoor equipment to strategies to promote positive behavior.

WHAT TO LOOK FOR IN CHILDCARE

The quality of care your child needs can be met in a variety of settings. But in any setting you should look for:

- Energetic, well-trained, friendly, and child-oriented teachers
- Low child-to-teacher ratios: Not more than 10 children per caregiver for children aged three to five
- Timely and sensitive responses to children's needs and preferences
- A program that builds a strong and balanced foundation of emotional, social, cognitive, physical, and language skills for each child
- Encouragement of each child's natural curiosity and creativity
- Activities designed to meet the needs of each child, with a way to notate special requirements
- Developmentally appropriate materials and equipment
- Daily reports from teachers for parents about each child's activities, participation, and progress
- Flexibility of schedule to meet family's needs
- Regular quality-assurance inspections and parent surveys
- Parent visits are welcome *at all times without notice*
- A safe, clean facility with good security procedures governing on-site care and picking up the child at the end of the session
- Cheerful and bright surroundings for play inside and out
- Quiet areas for sleep and rest.

Learn about the center's or school's educational philosophy. The philosophy describes an understanding of the nature of child development and the types of experiences that matter and can be helpful. The philosophy also may be grounded in the tenets of a spiritual or religious community. Does the philosophy match or complement your own parenting style and beliefs? Is it a good "fit" with your child's interests, temperament, and needs? Look into how this philosophy connects to the activities, materials, and teaching strategies used. Are there ways to ensure that each classroom or group is being led by capable and caring individuals and that the school's philosophy and policies are practiced?

JUST BEFORE GOING TO SCHOOL

In the year before your child goes to elementary school, begin to talk about school. Visit your child's future school. Get together with other children and families who go to the school or will attend next year.

Take advantage of school orientations. Read the school's materials, and let your preschooler ask questions.

Sometimes children like to pretend or play school. Help them so their play reinforces the fun of learning and realistic demands for the kindergarten situation. You can play the role of teacher. So can your child or an older friend.

There is a wealth of reading material designed specifically for young children about going to school. There also are videotapes about going to school, many with imagination and charm. Use these materials. Talk about the messages. The themes address children's normal fears and questions and often adopt a child's perspective: Will I have a friend? Can I do the same things I do at home? Will the teacher like me? Will I be lonely or miss my parents? What if someone makes fun of me?

There are many computer programs, too. However, those we see are largely focused on academic readiness. Nonetheless, many of these programs have proven engaging and educational for children. Read the family-oriented computer magazines and parenting magazines for current recommendations on programs. Many public libraries have computers and school preparation software, allowing you and your child to try something out before you invest. Your child's school may even have a parent resource room or a recommended list of software.

Check out the playground, especially if there are times when the school will allow your child to play there before enrolling. Many schools have playgrounds open to everyone in the afternoons and weekends. Others may have limited access. Your child's comfort with the physical environment will make a real difference.

Observe how other children dress so that your child will fit in comfortably. There is a lot of variation in our country's school dress codes. Seems like parents who love to dress their children in classic fashions find that their child is headed for a t-shirts and shorts environment. Others who are casual may discover that their child will wear uniforms or dress up more than expected.

Try to learn the name of your child's teacher and other key school personnel as soon as possible. Help your child to say these names. Find out the appropriate form of address that children use with teachers at the school. This varies widely from school to school, and it may differ from your family's style of addressing grownups or from your child's preschool experience. If so, help your child learn the correct form of address.

Last but not least, be sure that the week before school begins, your child:

- **Gets into a good bedtime routine**
- **Has plenty of rest**
- **Knows that school begins the following week**
- **Has all the required documents ready to take to school**
- **Is settled with clothing and shoes and backpack**
- **Gets lots of extra comfort and encouragement from you**
- **Has answers to all the important questions about going to and from school.**

Above all, double check that starting date. Many schools have different dates for kindergartners, to give them extra attention in this important life transition.

Enjoy, and have that camera (and maybe handkerchief) handy!

Most preschools blend philosophies from several early childhood educators. However, many preschools are guided or influenced strongly by one philosophy or another. We introduce you to some of the influential early childhood educational philosophers in Chapter 8. We do not strongly advocate one philosophy over the others. Instead, we hope to inform your thinking about this topic. Our philosophy and research on parenting and early childhood education has built upon these ideas, and continues to evolve as we understand more about how children learn and develop and as new techniques and educational approaches are tried and evaluated.

A CONTINUING PROCESS

As you can see from the suggestions in this chapter, the best preparation for school does not come from a single factor, whether accelerated learning programs, or teaching a kindergarten curriculum to three- or four-year-olds. Instead, preparing your child for school occurs within the pattern of daily living and in the things parents and children have enjoyed doing together for countless generations. Research findings are strong and consistent on this point.

This news should be welcomed and encouraging to parents. Don't waste your efforts on joyless early learning programs or rote memory routines. Spend your time instead on things that you and your child take pleasure in. Make sure that others who care for your child do the same. There is no limit to the effective and fun ways you can build your child's readiness for school. Enjoy!

CHAPTER 7

CHOOSING YOUR CHILD'S SCHOOL

Knowing your options. Evaluating alternatives.
Making the right choice. Deciding at what age to enroll your child.

ALL PARENTS CHOOSE THEIR CHILD'S SCHOOL. AT THE VERY LEAST, ALL FAMILIES IN THE U.S. HAVE THE CHOICE OF A PUBLIC SCHOOL OR HOME SCHOOLING. MOST FAMILIES HAVE OTHER CHOICES AS WELL. BUT IT'S IMPORTANT TO ACKNOWLEDGE THAT *YOU* ARE THE DECIDING FORCE IN WHERE AND WHEN YOUR CHILD ATTENDS SCHOOL. IF YOU ARE LOOKING AT OPTIONS, THIS CHAPTER WILL HELP REFINE YOUR SEARCH IN TODAY'S SCHOOL ENVIRONMENT.

On the other hand, you may have had a certain school in mind even before your child was born — perhaps a private school, maybe the one you attended, or the school where your friends' children go. Or you may feel that the local public school is the right choice for you.

Whether your decision is made or you are still in a "search mode," this chapter will show you important ways to assess the school you have chosen or ones you are considering. In either case, it will be invaluable for you to know a lot about the school(s) and to evaluate the "fit" with your child. This will prepare you for some of the ups and downs that are normal in school, and enable you to deal with them. You also will know whether supplemental programs — ones that you arrange for your child or activities you provide at home — might complement or compensate for what your school does or does not offer. Rarely will parents find everything they want for their child's education in one institution.

THE IMPORTANCE OF EVALUATION

By doing your "homework" on schools, you also will avoid major surprises — such as finding that the principal left suddenly and the school staff is unsettled, or that your local school is slated to close next year, or that your private school of choice now requires interviews and tests 18 months ahead of time.

As stated earlier, parents have an enormous influence over their child's success in school. But you have to be informed to use this influence. The issues raised in this chapter will teach you a great deal about school and open doors to your involvement with your child's education at home and at school. In the process, you also may make new acquaintances who may become your allies in education.

These questions are *for every parent,* regardless of your child's gifts, interests, talents, or special needs.

These issues involve everyday practical things. As you begin this journey, you may even want to designate a file drawer, an organizer, or a special place to keep the information you gather. Just think about how much time and effort people put into planning other events (vacations, weddings, family reunions, decorating or re-modeling a home) that are of far less consequence than preparing for your child's going to school.

We have observed many families spend months and months shopping for a house, but less than two or three days to learn about the educational future of their children! When asked what matters most to them, most parents overwhelmingly indicate that their child's education is of extremely high importance. Make certain that your investment of time corresponds to your own personal values and goals.

Your thoughtful choice of a school also can help your child avoid preventable mistakes. Rest assured, school and life will offer your child plenty of unforeseen difficulties to work through!

Also, your own enjoyment of the 13 years ahead — from kindergarten through high school — will likely be immensely enhanced if you like, value, and learn from what your child's schools offer. Your family life also will be affected in major ways by the quality of your child's schooling. Whether your child comes home happy and enthusiastic or bored and anxious on a regular basis has a huge impact on the entire family.

Your family's comfort and enjoyment of your child's friends and their families matter, too. A great school expands your social and support network. Your child's school and extracurricular activities will shape the group of people you spend time with. If the school is a welcoming and friendly place, you will benefit and likely be spared the hassle of complaining and trying to correct problems.

So choosing the best school that matches your family's and your child's needs is important and worth the investigation, time, and perhaps resources, needed.

Most children and parents in our studies have very positive early school experiences. But this does not mean that these were the best of all possible options. Most parents did not have a well-organized strategy to select their child's school. Many wished they had invested more time in this critical activity.

The five to 10 percent of children in our studies who did not have positive experiences might have benefitted greatly from extra investigation. The time it takes to deal with an unhappy child, a bored child, a frustrated or overly anxious child, is far greater than the up-front time to thoroughly investigate and plan well. For example, relocating a child to a new school, if the first experience is inadequate, is disruptive and very time-consuming. Moreover, the psychological toll on parent and child can be great.

There are key questions and issues that we believe every family should ask and consider as they choose their child's school. They also will help you make good choices *within* the school you select. Most schools are flexible on a number of issues. You may have a choice of teacher, be able to request adaptation of some aspects of the curriculum, and choose the age when your child should enroll. Some educational systems are in such flux or rapid evolution that they change virtually every year as to how and what choices they offer.

The questions are based on our experiences and research, including the results of a detailed study of more than 10,000 children throughout the

United States, starting when they first enrolled in kindergarten. These are issues that parents tell us they considered, as well as issues that we found were often overlooked.

The list is long. It had to be. Where your child's welfare is concerned, there is a lot to cover.

WHAT ARE YOUR OPTIONS?

The first task is to identify *all* your options. There may be more than you think.

Will you consider anything other than public (or private) school? If not, why not? For parents who already have recent firsthand experience with a school and like it, great. But consider whether your child has any special needs. If so, gather information about the school's efforts to support and accommodate those needs. Typical answers to this important question are as follows:

- **"No,"** because the school must be OK since so many families send their children there. This is not a good assumption. Even a school with a long waiting list or with the top achievement scores in your area is not necessarily the best school for your child at this time. Go through the questions that follow and look at your favored school as if you were getting to know it for the first time. At the very least, you will learn more about the educational options in your community and what the current differences are from school to school.

- **"No,"** because you can't afford a better alternative. Not necessarily true. Don't assume that the expense of the private school you really like is out of your reach, or that housing is too expensive in the school district that has the best schools.

  Over and over in surveys, when American families are asked about the most pressing concerns in their family's life, two answers are nearly universal: (1) not enough time, and (2) not enough money. No matter how much time or money people have, they rarely believe they have enough.

  Yet some families who would appear pressed for either time or money don't consider themselves to be so. We have encountered families where parents held three to five jobs, had lots of children, and judged their time problems to be only moderate!

Clearly impressions of plenty of time or a lack thereof are highly subjective. Our attitudes and interpretation of our time and money have a tremendous psychological influence on how we appraise our family's situation.

So, what does this have to do with a family's ability to consider school options for a child? You might explore alternatives afresh, from a new perspective. Set your existing convictions aside and "brainstorm."

For example, many "expensive" neighborhoods include some housing that may be within your purchase or rental budget. If such a neighborhood has the best schools, it's worth a look. The same considerations apply to having the cash for a private school. Some families choose a neighborhood with lower tax rates, or they buy a less expensive home than they could afford, in order to free funds for tuition. Also, private schools often have scholarships, offer sliding scale fees, or may allow a parent to work in the school in return for lower or free tuition. You never know until you ask.

We are not encouraging families to settle for unacceptable housing or to become martyrs on their children's behalf. Rather, we know how important a first-rate, enjoyable education is for your child's well-being and your family's. Children have survived mediocre or poor-quality education, but rarely without adverse consequences. Why should they have to undergo such an experience if there is a better alternative?

- **"No,"** because you have older children and want all of your children to go to the same school. This may not be the best option. Initially it might take more effort to ferry young children to more than one school, but you will do this anyway once the eldest moves to junior high or middle school. Everyone benefits if you find the best school for each child and make the adjustments needed.

- **"I don't know."** There's no time like the present to find out. The quickest way is to start talking with other parents, especially those whose children are in the same childcare center or playgroup as your child. Ask your neighbors. Call real estate agents. They often are great sources of information about the local schools, public and private. They frequently have recent newspaper and magazine articles about the schools that they can share, even if you are not buying a home right now. They know that many families move every three to seven years, and if they are helpful to you, you are more likely to call them when you are in the market.

Talk to your child's pediatrician. Good pediatricians typically ask children questions such as "How's school going?" "Do you like school?" "Are you learning a lot in school?" They deal frequently with schools on such matters as health and immunization requirements. They also see school-related problems such as increased headaches, stomach aches, urinary tract infections (some schools still have very restrictive policies about when children can go to the bathroom), generalized anxiety or depression, and treatment of injuries.

Pediatricians spot patterns of problems associated with certain schools, such as lack of adequate playground supervision, overly competitive or strict environments, and prevalence of learning and behavioral disorders. Be sure to discuss this on your next visit, or schedule a visit that includes a special focus on planning for your child's entry into school.

QUESTIONS TO ASK ABOUT:

SCHOOL POLICIES, MANAGEMENT, PHILOSOPHY, ORGANIZATION, CALENDAR, AND FUNDING

We have visited hundreds of schools during our ongoing studies of children's transition to school. Teams of researchers, educators, parents, and other child development experts have joined us on these visits. We find it remarkable how quickly certain aspects of a school's organization and administration are evident, even when there are efforts to "put on the best show." Extenuating circumstances aside, schools should have good management practices in place and good support for staff at all levels to ensure a smooth operation. However, the most important aspects where your child is concerned are those that affect quality in the classroom, such as teacher morale.

In the past there wasn't much difference from one school to another in these areas, especially in public schools. But today the management of many schools, including public schools, is locally controlled. Such local control is called "school-based" or "site-based" management, and it can produce wide variations in policies, educational philosophies, and funding priorities. Site-based schools typically have control over:

- **Hiring and firing**
- **Use of funds**
- **Curriculum content.**

Not every family needs to schedule a private appointment with the school principal or with central office staff to investigate school management. But in some situations, such a meeting may be needed. Often a few phone calls and a visit or two will provide satisfactory answers.

Private schools have typically adhered to a particular philosophy, such as the Montessori method or the Waldorf approach, or were grounded in the tenets of a particular religion. Today many public schools also use a particular approach or curriculum, or concentrate on either the creative or the more traditional academic elements in the curriculum.

See what's available in your community regarding school organization, management, and philosophy. Here are suggestions about how to obtain the information and how to frame your queries:

- **Handbook:** Does the school have a handbook that describes its mission and philosophy? If so, get a copy and read it.
- **Written policies:** Does the school have written policies about all important issues? Are these policies readily available to all teachers and staff? Are these shared with parents? With children? How does the school go about revising or changing policies?

  Is the school flexible in the application of standard policies and practices? For example, what happens if a family takes a child out of school for a special event or trip? Can a parent or another adult friend bring something to the school or get a message to a child under special circumstances, even if such practices are outside normal guidelines?

- **School and class size:** How large is the school? How many children are in each classroom? Remember to ask about the early grades and the older grades, since most schools have changing class sizes, with fewer children per class in the earlier grades. Is the school satisfied with its overall size and with the teacher-to-student ratios in the early elementary grades? If not, what plans are there to improve the situation? Are there any external factors likely to change the school or classroom size in the near future, such as school closures due to decreased enrollment, smaller class size because the school wants it or the district or the state requires it, the use of extra teachers or teaching assistants in the classroom, or plans to offer more enrichment options to students? Note: The effect of classroom size is mostly at the extremes. What counts more is the teacher's teaching ability and classroom management skills.
- **Location and transportation:** Where is the school located? What will be the transportation needs for your family? For very young children, will the distance affect wake-up times or bedtimes, perhaps depriving your child of needed sleep? Will your child ride a bus to and from school? If so, does this seem likely to be a positive experience? Can you car-pool? Is the neighborhood surrounding the school safe and pleasant?
- **Who is in charge?** How is the school managed? Is there site-based control over policies? Is there a close relationship with a community and/or state Board of Education? Is the management more distant, perhaps from a larger entity, such as a national program of schools or a church-guided program? Is the school pleased with the management practices? What is the reputation of the principal, director, or headmaster? What is the principal's style of leadership and management? Note: There is fairly high turnover in principals nationwide, for many reasons. Is there an assistant or associate principal or director? Is the staffing adequate to handle the day-to-day business? Do the children know the principal? Has the principal helped to inspire teachers and parents?

The school or district secretary usually can answer the factual questions. For judgments about style and quality of leadership, talk to other parents you know whose children attend the school, and to teachers.

- **Turnover:** What is the stability of the leadership and the teaching staff at the school? What credentials or skills do teachers need to teach there? Does the school acknowledge difficulties with turnover or in recruiting experienced, well-trained, and dedicated teachers? Note: Although stability often is associated with many positive features, occasionally it reflects a lack of options for teachers, or stagnation. Thus, as with most things you learn about schools, you need to have an "investigative eye" so that you don't jump to the wrong conclusions.
- **Appearance:** Do you like the way the school looks, especially in hallways, classrooms, the cafeteria, gymnasium, auditorium, central office, and library or media center? It should feel welcoming, be interesting, and convey a sense of dynamic activity and productivity. This can be seen through a variety of features (colors, architecture, decorations, messages on bulletin boards, landscaping, playground design, and equipment). Think about whether the school would be equally appealing to a child, not just grownups and visitors. It also should be clean and well-maintained. The physical side of school helps to convey:
  - what its values are
  - how it celebrates the achievements and individuality of children
  - evidence of active participation by parents and the community.
- **Reception:** Visit the classrooms during the day. Listen to the hum in the hallways. Judge how you are welcomed as a prospective parent just dropping in, even without an appointment. If needed, schedule a time to meet with school personnel to get answers you need. If you come with your preschooler, do the school staff greet your child with a welcoming tone? How are students spoken to by the central office staff? Does the central office staff seem to know individual children? Do they handle incoming phone calls as a nuisance or as an important, valued part of running a good school? In general, how easy is it to get answers to your questions?
- **School calendar:** Check out the school calendar. With some exceptions, more days at school are better. What are the hours of operation from opening to closing?

  What is the school's policy about age at school entry? Schools differ widely on this issue, and many policies are not linked to scientific data that show benefits or adverse consequences. There is a clear trend today toward academic "red-shirting" – delaying entry so that a child will be older than others in the class and, therefore, supposedly more successful. In fact, there are problems associated with this tactic that many parents don't anticipate and wish that they had considered. Among others is the need to find another environment that is as enriching as the school year the child is missing. Studies show that there are minimal advantages to holding back a child who is showing typical, positive development. For more information on enrollment age, see the special section at the end of this chapter.

- **Transition for new students:** What does the school do to help children and parents prepare for the transition to school? How does the school welcome incoming kindergartners and their families? Many schools have set up creative and effective ways to help parents and children get oriented long before that exciting (and sometimes dreaded) first day. These activities can include: visits to the kindergarten classrooms, a parents' orientation meeting, providing mentors for new parents so they can have someone to call with questions, and providing written guidelines to help parents prepare their children.
- **Funding:** Is the school's funding adequate? How much is spent on educating each child (per capita expense)? If you are comparing two or more schools, be sure the per capita expense figures include the same items, especially big-ticket items, such as capital expenditures and building-related costs. Is the funding stable? How dependent is the school upon external fluctuating factors, like decisions by the state legislature? Are there any major lawsuits or pending legislation that are likely to have a big impact on what happens in the next year or two? Information about funding for public schools is available from the state Department of Education, the superintendent's office, or the local school. For private schools, funding information is available from the individual school or from local or regional associations with which a school may be affiliated, such as a diocese.

  Although these questions may seem to reflect unusual conditions, schools are increasingly subject to swings in funding. Has the school taken any steps to supplement fees or tax revenues with private donations or endowments, an option increasingly permitted even in public schools? Citizens often fail to consider whether such a fund could help create a "safety net" or an extra "community chest" to fund special programs and opportunities for students or to handle emergency repairs that otherwise would take months to get approved and fixed.

QUESTIONS TO ASK ABOUT:

THE SCHOOL'S ACADEMIC PROGRAM AND STRENGTHS

INCLUDING QUALITY OF TEACHERS AND USE OF TECHNOLOGY

For most parents, academic quality is at the top of the list of concerns. This is understandable, although we see the academic side of school in the context of the larger school ecology *and* the child's total life experiences. Indeed, as the great educational philosophers (discussed in Chapter 8) emphasized, *education for the young child is most effective when it takes place in settings that have a balance that allows some freedom, promotes good social and emotional development, and encourages the type of creativity and activity that young children need and enjoy most.* So even thinking about academics involves looking beyond the formal curriculum.

As you explore the academic strengths of your child's prospective school, remember that the answer to one (or even a few) of the following questions will not be the determining factor in your school choice. What counts is the total picture you get from your inquiries.

In evaluating the academic quality of a school, note that there are many successful approaches to teaching academic subjects to young children. However, there are some areas in which the teaching strategy is no longer a matter of debate because extensive research has shown that certain techniques work best. A good example is the teaching of reading, discussed in Chapter 10. Most schools are knowledgeable about such findings. Be sure the schools you consider are among them.

- **Academic emphasis:** How much does the school emphasize academics? This is difficult to answer precisely, although a school's reputation in this regard is usually pretty well-known in the community. Check out the school's most recent parent handbook, directory, or manual. Does the emphasis seem adequate and balanced to you, and is your child likely to thrive in a school atmosphere with this degree of emphasis on academics? In our experience, all schools value children's learning and recognize that children need to learn the traditional basics. The issue is the school's overall approach and priorities.

- **Curriculum:** What is the core curriculum? Are there plans to change it, the teacher supports, or the school resources related to children's academic achievements? Are any important programs, such as those in foreign languages or music, scheduled to be dropped or added?

- **Student evaluation:** How does the school judge the academic progress of children, especially in the first three years, when most schools do not use group-administered, standardized tests? Are the assessment strategies reasonable, well-thought-out, and worthwhile? Are parents informed about the evaluation approaches for the general classroom and for individual "special needs" situations? How well are the children doing according to the school's own standards? What are the recent trends in student achievement – rising, stable, and very good, or going down? What is the school's reputation right now, not just in the past?

  Based on the recommendations of the National Association for the Education of Young Children, the following approaches are considered especially strong for evaluating the progress for the majority of very young children:

  - the use of multiple methods for assessing children's progress (for example, taking into account the children's actual classroom performance, children's products or "portfolios," and performance on specific tests, ideally administered by the teacher individually to very young children throughout the year)

  - taking into consideration where each child started at the beginning of each school year; and

  - making referrals for more in-depth and specialized assessments whenever problems are suspected or extra talents are noted that might benefit from supplemental academic activities. Included in the latter are testing and counseling appraisals to measure academically talented children, children with possible or known learning difficulties or disabilities, children with special sensory or motor challenges, and children with behavioral or emotional needs that may require extra teacher awareness and programs to improve the child's well-being and academic progress.

- **Student achievement:** What objective evidence does the school have about the academic progress or abilities of the children during and after the early years? Scores from later grades can be useful, but average scores alone cannot tell the full story. This is especially true of schools with a diverse student population and which do not limit enrollment to students who pass "entrance exams." What do parents of children in this school say about how much their children are learning, and whether their children are appropriately challenged? Usually parents are "wowed" and in awe of their children's early academic progress when they are receiving a good education!
- **Continuing education for teachers:** What types of in-service or continuing education and training supports are offered to teachers during the school year and the summer? These are vital to keeping teachers abreast of new material, new teaching techniques, and rapidly expanding scientific knowledge. The availability of such education for teachers is a good sign of the school's commitment to teacher quality and professionalism.
- **Technology:** What is the status of technology in the school? Are computers in the classroom, and are they actively used? Are there enough? Do the teachers have the skills to take advantage of these resources? Are computer-based activities related to the core curriculum? What about needed repairs, upgrades, and technical assistance, not to mention funds for new educational software? What does the library or media center look like? Are there plenty of books and other educational materials – videos and VCRs, tape recorders and tapes, educational toys and games, etc.? Are these in the classroom? Can some be checked out to take home? If the school does not incorporate computers or other information technology materials for very young children, is there a strong rationale or policy that makes sense to you?

In our estimation, the jury is still out on how best and fully to incorporate the remarkable new technologies effectively into early childhood education. No one knows how helpful or necessary it is for children to be computer-literate in kindergarten or first and second grade to become comfortable and highly skilled later on. We have observed many successful efforts and heard teachers praise technology in the classroom when it was used properly. However, other educators have complained that some high-

A CHILD'S-EYE VIEW OF TECHNOLOGY

Last year when our son, Sam, was five years old, he went to a garage sale and was fascinated by an old-fashioned, large, Army-green typewriter with an inked ribbon — the first he had ever seen. We bought it for him. As soon as he learned to use it, he wanted to take it to his kindergarten class so other children could use it. Why? His reason: "If the children can really see what happens when they type the letters, they probably will be really excited. This is as good as a computer!" The message here: there is always excitement around something new and different, even an old version of it!

tech equipment and programs are over-rated or not well-integrated with the rest of the curriculum and school activities. In any event, don't discount the equipment and programs you find. Even though they may not alter what or how well a child is learning, such equipment and programs have value even if used primarily to help teachers and students stay in touch with other classrooms, the central office, and parents, and to improve efficiency, such as enabling students to print their own reports and teachers to spend less time on bookkeeping.

QUESTIONS TO ASK ABOUT:

THE SCHOOL'S SUPPLEMENTAL PROGRAMS

INCLUDING ART, MUSIC, PHYSICAL EDUCATION, FOREIGN LANGUAGES, ENRICHMENT, SPECIAL EVENTS, EXTRACURRICULAR ACTIVITIES, AND SUMMER PROGRAMS

What a school accomplishes for your child depends on more than just what happens in the primary classroom setting. Even the term "primary classroom setting" is inadequate to capture the diversity of what is happening in elementary schools nationwide. For example, some children attend schools that have one or more of the following:

- **combined classrooms with different grade levels**
- **divided classrooms where children receive language arts from one teacher and science and math from another**
- **non-graded or multi-age classrooms where children may stay with the same teacher or teachers for more than one year**
- **schools where only one grade is taught, such as an all-kindergarten school for the entire school district.**

But beyond the classroom where children learn the traditional "academic" subjects, all schools have some additional supports and programs that can make a big difference. They also offer teachers time to help with overall classroom management, write notes to parents, have a break here and there during the school day, and coordinate with other teachers.

Supplemental programs open up possibilities for participation and accomplishment in many areas. It's wonderful when children discover how their new and improving academic skills can help beyond the classroom, such as reading the words to a song in music class or counting those laps run around the gym or learning to read the clock in the cafeteria or understanding the principles of how primary color paints can be combined to make different colors. These opportunities all serve to reinforce the excitement of learning and the relevance of school to life. Extra programs are a wonderful complement in this regard.

- **Program availability:** Compile a list of the supplemental or enrichment programs or activities that the school offers. Think about what matters to you and your child. In case something very obvious is missing – such as school-prepared lunches, scheduled physical education, or recess times – find out why. Do you agree with the reasons? Will the lack be important to you and your child? If you would like a particular program to be available – such as foreign language training or additional art or music courses – can things be changed? Or can you arrange for lessons or learning in another setting after school or on weekends?

- **Program quality:** Ask other parents about the quality of these supplemental programs. What evidence of them do you find in the school building or in the school newsletter to parents?
- **Parent participation:** Can parents participate in these extra programs, offering special lectures or sessions to teachers or children? Can parents provide extra hands or voices or art supplies for these endeavors? Can they bring in special guests, like authors, athletes, musicians, chefs, or local storytellers?

QUESTIONS TO ASK ABOUT: THE SOCIAL MILIEU AND HOW THE SCHOOL PROMOTES SOCIAL AND EMOTIONAL WELL-BEING

Your child's social and emotional growth are just as important to success in school and life as academic achievement. Look for signs that the school supports development in these critical areas.

- **Student body:** Who attends the school (gender, language, ethnicity, socioeconomic status, geographical or neighborhood range, predetermined talent pool, religious backgrounds, children with disabilities)? There are many social advantages when children learn to value and get along with children from different cultures and walks of life. Given the dramatic demographic changes and continued immigration patterns in our country, this social diversity can be a real plus, especially when schools see this as a strength and act on it. If the school you are considering lacks diversity, consider other ways for your child to have experiences with a broader range of children through sports, arts, and community activities.
- **Social growth:** How does the school promote: Children's friendships? The development of cooperation and caring? The ability to participate in group activities? An understanding of the importance of emotions in guiding behavior? Beware: Many schools are not well-prepared to answer these questions. However, classrooms for kindergarten and first grade may have some "rules" posted about sharing, taking

turns, listening when others are speaking, and taking responsibility for cleaning up one's own things. Similarly, a mix of activities, including some group cooperative projects or group learning, along with individual activities and total classroom activities, creates natural opportunities for children to adapt to and negotiate different social situations. Are there both teacher-structured or teacher-guided times, as well as times when children can take the initiative?

- **Problem behavior:** How is problem behavior dealt with? Often teachers have their own particular style or practices, although these usually fall under the school's established policies. Ask parents and teachers about what happens. Even better, talk with children in the school about what happens if they do something they are not supposed to. We recommend talking to older children you know (those in third through sixth grade) about what happened when they were in kindergarten or first or second grade. Ask them which teachers they liked and why. They can tell you a great deal about order and behavior modification styles of teachers as well as whether they learned a lot from those teachers.
- **Socialization:** Educators and counselors strongly encourage parents to be sure that young children have play times and free times with friends. In today's world of smaller families and fewer opportunities for children to play with siblings, relatives, and neighbors, this is an important consideration. Children learn a lot socially, emotionally, and intellectually in these social situations – *plus they just have fun!* What opportunities will your child have to spend time with classmates and others at school outside of the traditional school day? There are many advantages to neighborhood schools where children can walk to and from schools and readily get together with peers. But there are other solutions if a neighborhood school is not a likely option for you. Keep in mind that a more distant school will require extra time and effort to arrange play dates with classmates.

QUESTIONS TO ASK ABOUT:

PARENT INVOLVEMENT AND INFORMATION EXCHANGE WITH FAMILIES

This is the age of parent involvement! Dramatic changes have occurred in the expectations of educators about the role of parents in their children's education.

You will find this much in evidence right from your child's early years in school. Ask the parents of young children. You will likely hear *a lot* about the many things they are expected to (or have to) do. The reasons for this, and the hoped-for benefits, are discussed in greater depth in Chapter 4 on parent involvement.

- **Amount and types of activities:** Does the school have a reputation for having active, involved, and supportive parents? What parent-initiated activities are evident? What do teachers and the school administration expect of parents? Is there a school newsletter for parents? Do teachers have their own newsletter or way of communicating frequently with parents about the individual child and the overall classroom organization and scheduled activities?
- **Quality:** What do parents whose children attend the school say about parent involvement? Do they see the benefits for their children? Or do they feel out of touch with some things they would like to know more about? Are teachers and other school personnel readily available? When and how can parents get in touch with teachers to communicate concerns?
- **Homework and home-based projects:** Is there a homework policy that involves parent participation? Do parents sign daily, weekly, or monthly activity logs related to reading or other home-based activities? In what ways do teachers encourage parents and children to engage in projects or activities that link what is happening in the classroom to the home?
- **Parent volunteers:** Are parents in the classroom or in the school? If so, in what roles? Are they well-prepared for providing assistance that is really helpful? Can or do teachers ask parents to pitch in with special projects, field trips, celebrations, or needed routine help?
- **School visitation:** What are the policies about parents visiting the classroom? The lunchroom? Eating with their child or the entire class? Does the school sponsor special shows, performances, and open houses on a regular basis? Are these genuinely family-friendly events? Are there fund-raisers or annual fairs or carnivals? Do these seem reasonable (not too many, too few, or too pressured) to you?
- **Parent organizations and networking:** Is there a formal parent organization (PTA, PTO, or other)? Do parents seem to network informally and talk about their children's school experiences? Are there any parent-sponsored or parent-led activities

for young children outside the classroom and school day? These can include boys' or girls' clubs or newer versions that may be original in your community or unique to your school. What about sports activities and parent participation? Of course, not every child or family will want to participate in everything that's available. But by asking, you will learn about the "norm" and general patterns of parent involvement.

QUESTIONS TO ASK ABOUT:

THE SCHOOL'S RELATIONSHIP TO THE COMMUNITY

A school, just like a home, exists within a surrounding neighborhood and a larger community.

- **Local ties:** How does the school relate to the community? Are there easy-to-access community resources, such as libraries, nearby fire and police stations, stores and other businesses, community or recreational centers? Does the school take advantage of these? Is there community support for the school beyond tax dollars? If so, in what ways is this visible?
- **Availability of school resources:** Is the school used for purposes other than the traditional Monday through Friday school program? Is the playground open for community use in the afternoons and on weekends? If so, is this reasonable and advantageous? Do you see pluses in the school's relationship to the community and how this will benefit your child's education? Do you see any limitations?

USING THIS INFORMATION TO MAKE YOUR CHOICE

As parents, you are your child's first teachers, and you know more about your child's individuality, adaptability, interests, talents, and weaknesses than anyone else. Review the information you have gathered. Then stand back and look at the broader picture. Here are some of the more influential factors for many parents:

- **Does the typical day in the school you are considering look like it is well-thought-out, fun, interesting, and appropriately varied?**
- **Do the children at the school seem happy, curious, and engaged in meaningful activities?**
- **Does the school seem dynamic, upbeat, and aware of areas in which it would like to improve? Some parents are surprised to learn that the "best" schools are the ones with continuous or even big plans for further improvement.**
- **Finally, does the school achieve a good balance in developing the "total" child? Are other families loyal, enthusiastic, and positive in their evaluation of the school?**

A word of caution: Some parents are terrific about including their child in family decision-making, such as in selecting a family activity for the weekend or deciding what to eat for a special meal. This is great and developmentally appropriate.

When it comes to selecting a school, however, a four- or five-year-old is not up to the task. It's fine to take your child when you visit schools. Rather than direct query, however, you may learn more by observing your child's reactions. Answer your child's questions about a school. In the final analysis, however, you don't want to select a school solely because your child loved the huge, new playground or hated the cafeteria smells wafting into the hallway.

To help you on this journey, one that many parents begin to make when their child is about three years old, we suggest you record your findings when you evaluate schools. Include special questions that may be unique to your family's circumstances, or to your child. And if your child or family does have special needs, remember that these are not your only needs. The answers to the general questions about school choice pertain to you, too.

In the best of all possible worlds, your search will produce several good alternatives. At this point, the practical and logistical issues, such as convenience, cost, and familiarity, may influence your final choice. That's just fine. Whatever your choice, you can be confident that your child will benefit from your effort, thought, and care.

AT WHAT AGE SHOULD YOU ENROLL YOUR CHILD IN SCHOOL?

Children used to start school as soon as they were old enough. Today, however, many parents give a great deal of thought to whether their child is too young or really ready for school, even if the child is chronologically the right age. This concern has been lessened because there are many high-quality preschool education programs where children can learn at a level appropriate to their capabilities. Many such schools offer stimulating learning opportunities for very curious, bright, and mature-for-their-age children.

Nonetheless, delayed enrollment is a hot topic, and even educators and child development specialists are not of one mind. Two factors parents should consider are:

- **Why some parents delay their child's school entry.** The most common reason, and the one most strongly supported by educational wisdom, is choosing to wait if a child is immature in terms of social, emotional, and language development, particularly if the child is very close to cut-off birthdate. Such children often thrive and make great progress in the coming months. Delaying school entry and enrolling the child in an excellent early childhood educational program or center can be a good option. Such programs will help nurture the child's development in a well-rounded way, and provide extra kindergarten-like activities when the child is ready for them.

  Another reason that concerns many educators and child development experts is parents' desire to give their child a competitive edge, either academically or, later on, in sports. Such children are developing normally and are age-ready, but the parents think the child will be more likely to rise to the top of the class if enrollment is delayed a year. Yes, a child who is six and one-half or almost seven when entering kindergarten will have some skills that the five and five-and-one-half-year-olds may not. But these additional skills rarely are what kindergarten teachers care about. The child may know more facts, but may be mismatched socially and emotionally to classmates.

- **What the vast amount of research shows.** Many large-scale research studies have tried to determine how important a child's age is for school success, both in the early elementary grades and later in school and life. The findings support a two-part conclusion:

  - There are, in fact, some short-term, modest gains when a child is among the oldest in the class. But this difference is not as large as parents might think, because many factors contribute to how well a child does in school and how well-prepared a child is for the challenges of formal education.

- These early and relatively modest advantages tend to disappear by about the third grade. This shows that the children's common school experiences have become an equalizer, so that children are learning, to a large degree, what they are exposed to.

There are some caveats about the research literature, and limitations on what we know. A lot of evidence comes from studies of children who show developmental delays or come from "at risk" family and community circumstances. Other studies of general populations include a wider mix of children from all types of families. But to our knowledge, there have been no long-term studies that have assessed what happens when parents voluntarily delay a child's school entry even when the child is doing well (at least performing at or above the national level for his or her age). For these children, the practice is referred to as "academic red-shirting." In most cases, we assume it is well-intentioned, but there is no strong basis that this practice will produce any lasting academic edge for your child.

We know parents who have not thought ahead about issues such as how old their child will be at high school graduation, or when their child will be entering puberty compared to other children, or whether their child will be much larger than other children. These issues, too, have consequences.

As with almost all issues related to a child's education, there is no one best way to do things. Almost all schools now adjust, at least somewhat, to a child's readiness and skill levels. So if your child is a bit younger and needs a little longer to learn something or acquire a skill, there are likely to be good supports in place in school to help with these skills. Teachers usually know which children are younger, and they adjust their expectations accordingly. In some classrooms, children's birth dates are even posted.

We urge parents to keep your child's best interests uppermost in your thinking. Don't create expectations that are too competitive or not consistent with your child's own wishes. What happens when parents hold a child back to give him an edge later in sports (such holdbacks are invariably boys), and the child doesn't like sports?

We envision going to school as a time when all children can enter eager to learn and confident that they can advance and achieve a lot. There are many ways to measure this — not all of which rank children from best to worst. If you have questions about whether your child is ready to enroll, discuss your situation with knowledgeable teachers at the school and even educators from elsewhere. Most important, think through *all* the implications for your child, now and down the road.

HOME SCHOOLING: WHAT ALL PARENTS MIGHT LEARN FROM PARENTS WHO DO

Home schooling is the original form of education for children. Before universal education became the norm, children who received education were taught by tutors or family members.

Today parents choose home schooling for a variety of reasons. Most families who home-school do so for religious or moral reasons. However, an increasing number of families home-school because they believe they can provide superior, more individualized education. Here are few of these families and their stories:

1. **Highly accomplished twin sons.** The mother of these boys, who were reading independently by age three, was very interested in children's education and chose to create a school at home. The family lives with the grandparents, who were enlisted to further the boys' education. The boys have lots of social and musical activities to complement their home schooling endeavor. The family is undecided whether they will home-school for all of the children's education or seek a school that can accommodate the children's extraordinary academic talents.

2. **Indifference to school.** These parents sensed that their daughter was indifferent to school, although there were no serious signs of difficulty. The mother decided that spending a year or two in home schooling might be fun. She did so, and the daughter flourished and discovered a greater passion for learning. The girl stayed in touch with her friends from school and eventually returned to public school in a seamless transition. During the two years of home schooling, the family traveled a lot, took many educational day trips, and read extensively. The parents grew even closer to their daughter and helped her to blossom academically.

3. **Behavioral difficulties.** Parents whose child had encountered serious behavioral difficulties looked for options when the school refused to serve the child in a mainstreamed setting. They considered residential or segregated special education settings, but felt the educational supports were dismal. So the parents and the school worked together to create a home-based schooling experience for one year. The child gained self-control, and he advanced considerably in many academic areas. He then joined a part-day program in a mainstreamed class. The family continues to provide additional support in the afternoon, and extra teaching.

4. **Around the world.** These parents of three children had always dreamed of sailing around the world. They turned to the Calvert School, famous for providing a full curriculum that has been used for years by many "sailing families." The parents, who were not teachers, were unsure how skilled they would be at teaching. But the family decided the worst that could happen would be that the children might have to repeat a grade. In fact, the whole family thrived that year, and extended their sail to three years. The children did very well, and the parents are certain that the children's progress on all fronts was greatly enhanced.

What these and many other successful home schooling stories affirm is that parents and children can enjoy and benefit from such close engagement on academic matters. However, some parents cannot sustain this effort, which is truly a full-time job. They also may find that the effort challenges the line between the roles of parent and teacher.

We know of many parents who wish they had the time to home-school, but don't. We think that many parents might enjoy a compromise. For example, they might take a summer off and treat it like a "home schooling" summer on subjects of interest. Or they might purchase home schooling materials or join an e-mail chatroom to get ideas. Some home schooling newsletters and magazines are filled with wonderful and inspirational stories. It is a heroic task, but one that has clearly met the needs of many families and children.

If you are interested, by all means explore home schooling. At the very least, you may gain a greater respect for what teachers do every day, and for the responsibility a teacher has for cultivating the mind and well-being of a young child each year.

CHAPTER 8

EDUCATIONAL APPROACHES

How we got to where we are: Some great educators and educational theorists, past and present, and what they contributed. What parents can learn from them. How teachers and schools incorporate their ideas.

MOST SCHOOLS AND TEACHERS BASE THEIR CURRICULA AND TEACHING STYLES ON THE THEORIES AND PRACTICES OF A NUMBER OF LEADING EDUCATORS AND EDUCATIONAL PHILOSOPHERS. HOWEVER, SOME SCHOOLS, ESPECIALLY PRESCHOOLS, FAVOR ONE OR ANOTHER OF THESE APPROACHES, SUCH AS THE MONTESSORI METHOD OR A WALDORF SCHOOL BASED ON RUDOLF STEINER'S PHILOSOPHY.

When choosing a preschool, childcare center, or elementary school, it helps to know your options. Some teaching approaches may be particularly suited to your child's learning style, and others less so. In addition, understanding these approaches may be beneficial when you begin to help your child with homework assignments. This chapter provides a brief overview of the major educational theorists and practitioners whose works continue to influence modern education.

THE MANY THEORIES OF EARLY CHILDHOOD EDUCATION

There have been many pioneers during the last century who have helped us understand how children develop, and who have created innovative approaches to early childhood education. They include Maria Montessori, John Dewey, Jean Piaget, Rudolf Steiner, Jerome Bruner, and B. F. Skinner, among many others. Each provided unique perspectives and has inspired countless other teachers and scientists to find new ways to bring out the best in each child. We also introduce readers to the man who is widely credited as being the father of modern-day preschool and elementary education — Johann Heinrich Pestalozzi.

For a variety of reasons, we think that no one educational philosophy is best. Educators' ideas are often constrained or inspired by the time and circumstances under which they worked and the types of children and families they focused on. Yet their insights continue to be of great value.

The case for a well-informed, well-planned curriculum, effective teaching strategies, and a supportive teaching environment, is strong. All of these elements make a difference in the quality of a young child's early education — whether at home, or in a preschool or elementary school. Times change and so do the educational buzz words, but many of the ideas developed over a century ago are still valid.

We hope that parents will enjoy this brief excursion through educational history, reflecting on how modern education got to where it is and appreciating why so many teachers develop such a passion for their own "philosophy" of education.

JOHANN HEINRICH PESTALOZZI (1746-1827)

"LIFE ITSELF EDUCATES"

Swiss educator Johann Heinrich Pestalozzi was considered radical in his day. His contributions spanned five decades, from the 1770s to the 1820s. He strongly believed in a "back-to-nature" philosophy, influenced by the French philosopher Jean Jacques Rousseau. He emphasized individual differences, seeing the role of education as guiding and enhancing the child's own nature, rather than changing it or having all children develop in the same way.

Education's goal, according to Pestalozzi, was to strengthen each child's "faculties" so that he or she would be able to think independently. He had many years of experience, at first working with destitute children (war orphans) and later establishing his own school to experiment with his educational ideas. He was a great optimist about human nature, developing many practices which continue to this day as staples of preschool and elementary school education:

- **Group activities, including singing and recitation**
- **Vigorous physical exercise**
- **Field trips**
- **Collecting things**
- **Making models and maps**
- **Creating artwork**
- **Writing.**

His focus on children's individuality was considered revolutionary at the time. So was his belief that children learn through doing, starting with the familiar and moving into new territory. He believed that children needed to be actively engaged with a wide range of feelings and projects in order to learn. He opposed grouping children strictly on the basis of age, rather than ability and interests.

Another of his radical ideas was that teacher training was beneficial and needed. Pestalozzi's ideas were incorporated by Froebel, Montessori, Dewey, and Piaget, among others.

FRIEDRICH FROEBEL (1782-1852)

THE FAMILY AS THE ROOT OF EDUCATION

Froebel is widely known as the father of the modern kindergarten. His "infant school," originally named "The Child Nurture and Activity Institute," was later renamed "Kindergarten" — the world's first. Despite the fact that the Prussian government declared his techniques and the kindergarten subversive, he won worldwide acclaim for his "kindergarten movement."

He proposed that educating infants was an essential component of a comprehensive approach to education, and ultimately to social reform. In addition to his extensive writings, he created his own programs. These included a place to educate teachers and a publishing firm that created innovative play materials for preschoolers (sets of shapes, blocks, balls) and a mother–infant song book that was distributed internationally.

He was a passionate advocate of the family as the root of education. He endured a traumatic and neglectful early childhood. He was left motherless as an infant, painfully ignored by his father, and, as a young child, prevented from participating in school because of his difficult nature and slowness in learning to read. Later, when working as a tutor, he again saw the consequences of a father's disregard for young children. Happily, he stumbled into a teaching position at a school modeled upon Pestalozzi's educational philosophy.

Froebel realized the benefits from his own childhood when he could roam and observe nature closely, think, and experiment on his own. Based on these personal experiences and his observations of children, he ardently advocated the role of play and appropriate play materials to engage young children actively. He argued that self-initiation and control by the child were valuable, even essential for progress. This was a new idea at the time, since the prevailing convention was to treat children as passive objects whose only role was to absorb information and conform to the wishes of others.

His work foreshadowed what scientists today have affirmed in many ways — that all children are "ready to learn," and filled with curiosity and energy, and that efforts to judge a child's readiness to learn (that is, enter formal education) or his full range of later competencies by a common measuring stick are often in error.

JOHN DEWEY (1859-1952)

EXPERIENCE AND NATURE, ACTION AND THOUGHT

John Dewey was an original thinker, a great humanitarian, and a prolific writer of widespread influence on the philosophy of education and its practice. A native of Vermont, he grew up loving the outdoors. He began teaching high school, but soon found education woefully lacking — largely because the emphasis was on teaching students to fit into an industrialized society, rather than giving them a love of learning and a broader foundation for thinking. Dewey saw education as an integral part of life, not merely a tool to help a person obtain a job.

Dewey's own life was a testament to lifelong learning and contribution. He studied evolutionary biology and psychology, learning the basic principles of development that he later applied to the education of young children. He achieved national fame for his innovative approach to teaching young children. He emphasized the development of problem-solving skills, the incorporation of nature and personal experiences into the classroom, and the importance of the "here and now" in learning. His ideas and philosophy always incorporated the latest findings in psychology, a field that was in its infancy at the time.

Some of Dewey's revolutionary ideas are quite familiar today. He saw the school as a microcosm of society, allowing children to learn about the interdependencies and complexities of society as a whole. He emphasized coordinated thinking, rather than the dull and ineffective exercises that bored and constrained children's natural curiosity and intelligence. He also believed that education was more than the three "Rs," and should foster the development of a well-rounded, caring, and contributing person.

Dewey also established laboratory schools, where the newest thinking and scientific discoveries could be applied and tested rigorously, so that education would be grounded in empirical evidence rather than a marketplace of strongly-held opinions with no facts to back them up. His influence on "progressive education" and on the generations of educators that followed has been immeasurably positive.

RUDOLF STEINER (1861-1925)

INDIVIDUALITY, FREEDOM, AND CREATIVITY

Rudolf Steiner's ideas form the basis for the Waldorf School movement. In his words, "Our highest endeavor must be to develop free human beings, who are able of themselves to impart purpose and direction to their lives."

A central premise of the Waldorf approach is that each child has an essence or vital individuality that requires appropriate strategies to nurture it fully. Thus, Steiner's philosophy was one of the first to emphasize what is now described as "teaching to strengths." This educational philosophy also encourages children's fantasy, as well as the incorporation of music, poetry, dance, and drama into many parts of the curriculum. In Waldorf schools, children often function as partners in their own educational process, with many opportunities to engage in self-initiated and self-guided learning and productivity. Nature and the use of natural materials are evident in Waldorf classrooms.

Direct instruction of academic skills is de-emphasized in the early school years because Steiner recognized that this often imposes on children's natural development something that they are not ready for. Instead, he encouraged each child to flourish at what he is good at during each stage of development. He advocated learning in a home-like atmosphere. He also advocated learning through imitation, movement, and rhythm. Imaginative presentation of learning materials and natural beauty and order are considered invaluable in the Waldorf education of children.

In the U.S., Waldorf Schools typically start with preschools and sometimes extend through high school. The teachers and parents are committed and passionate in their love of children and their emphasis on discovery of the world, creativity, and learning through natural problem-solving and independent efforts.

MARIA MONTESSORI (1870-1952)

THE PREPARED ENVIRONMENT AND SELF-PACING

Maria Montessori was first educated as a physician. She then worked in a psychiatric clinic where she focused on the educational problems of children with mental retardation (a topic of particular interest to Rudolf Steiner as well). She studied widely in the fields of anthropology, psychology, and philosophy, all of which she incorporated into her prescription of how best to teach the young child. She was a professor in Rome and opened the first "children's house" ("Casa dei bambini") there in 1907. She moved to the Netherlands to escape Fascist rule. Over the next 40 years, she worked tirelessly to establish schools worldwide.

Montessori abhorred the conventional classrooms of the day, with their rows of desks and emphasis on group regimentation, which seemed to her to interrupt children's natural flow in the learning process and their undeniable need for movement and activity. She promoted teaching in an environment filled with appropriate physical materials and arrangements that invited learning through exploration and interaction. Some materials were incorporated into what she called the "prepared environment" — a highly organized or structured context to teach particular concepts. For example, a series of red rods of varying lengths could be used to teach visual discrimination. Other props included smelling jars with different aromas, rectangular pieces of wood that differ in their weight, tonal bells of different colors that can be matched by tone and color, et cetera. For many preschool teachers, the prepared environment offers excellent choices to encourage children to learn on their own. There are many special materials in Montessori classrooms, although similar products are now available in toy stores and schools everywhere.

Maria Montessori is widely credited with introducing the concept of "developmentally appropriate" education — identifying windows of opportunity or sensitive periods when children are ready to receive certain types of new information and to advance to new levels of understanding. This includes advances in motor and physical learning, academic learning, and sensory development.

Like many of her predecessors, Montessori advocated the value of self-direction in education, a cardinal feature of the Montessori method. She recognized the powerful links between biological and mental growth. She used the knowledge of the day to develop a detailed, systematic plan for teachers to foster children's learning, including specific techniques for particular concepts or skills. At the heart of this is a respect for the child's receptive or "absorbent mind." Like many other great educational philosophers, she saw that a child's education influences the child's inner being or psyche, not just a limited set of skills. She highly valued children's independence from adults, and defined what many today refer to as "child-centered education" and "active learning."

Her ability to inspire teachers is seen today in the dedication and high quality of many of the Montessori schools, both those in private and in public school settings (the first public school Montessori program started in Philadelphia in 1975).

Unlike the Waldorf approach, however, Montessori methods do not encourage (in fact, actually discourage) children from engaging in fantasy or make-believe activities, and there is less emphasis on aesthetics and artistic projects that have no specified educational goal. However, we have observed many modern-day Montessori schools that have incorporated elements of technology (including computers) and aspects of other educational approaches into a more eclectic method.

JEAN PIAGET (1896-1980)

UNRAVELING THE MYSTERIES OF CHILDREN'S THINKING AND REASONING

Early in his career in Paris, Swiss educator Jean Piaget devised techniques for testing school children's reading abilities. He was fascinated by the types of errors children made — which did not appear to result from random guessing — and wanted to understand why. In more than 50 books and monographs, he explored children's inner reasoning and how they advanced from one stage to the next.

He launched hundreds of studies and experiments creating a vast body of knowledge about children's stages of cognitive development, and the factors that influence growth in children's reasoning. Piaget identified four major stages representing how children think about the world and act upon it. These are:

- **Sensory-motor stage.** Visible in infancy and the toddler years when a child becomes aware of physical independence from others and discovers that objects have a separate, permanent existence with some qualities that don't change.
- **Preoperational stage.** Roughly from ages two to seven, when the child manipulates the environment through inner images and mental manipulations, including language. Physical activities are guided more by thought and experimentation.
- **Concrete operational stage.** Approximately from seven through 11 or 12 years, includes early forms of logic and extensive classification of objects and activities by similarities and differences. Children make tremendous gains in their understanding of numbers and time.
- **Formal operations.** Beginning in the pre-adolescence years and extending through adulthood, when children manipulate abstract ideas, form logical connections, generate hypotheses, and see the implications of their own thinking and the thinking of others.

Many activities in the three- to eight-year-old period lay the foundations for remarkable cognitive achievements later, even though the direct linkages may not be fully understood. Identification of these stages, however, has been useful to early childhood educators, who today are much more skilled in offering explanations and lessons to children that better match a child's level or stage of understanding. This means that the instructional approaches can build upon how a child experiences and thinks about the world. This "getting inside a child's head" was what Piaget did more masterfully than any other educator at that time.

Piaget's close observations of the early growth and development of his own children, recorded in revealing daily diaries, have inspired many developmental scientists and early childhood educators to continue this valuable technique of watching and asking children about what they are thinking.

There is no single program for Piagetian education. But most preschool and elementary school teachers are trained in the importance of the ways in which children's cognitive development and biological growth and experience combine to influence what children can grasp and how they learn. From a Piagetian perspective, practice and reinforcement aren't enough to guide and instruct a child. Instead, a teacher must build upon a child's readiness.

BURRHUS FREDERICK SKINNER (1904–1990)

PRINCIPLES OF PROGRAMMED LEARNING AND THEIR APPLICATION TO CHILDREN'S EDUCATION

B. F. Skinner has had a pervasive influence on what teachers do and don't do in the classroom, although today he is often critiqued (unfairly, we think) for being overly mechanical or precise in his approach to teaching children. Nonetheless, he discovered an original way to observe the learning process and to show that rates and types of learning could be affected by the conditions of a child's educational experience.

Every introductory psychology and education textbook reviews these principles. The idea of incentives and reinforcement (rewards) and the power they exert has been extraordinarily helpful to teachers. Notions of the immediacy of feedback, that behavior has consequences, and that withholding of rewards or withdrawing a child from a desirable setting could change the child's behavior in positive ways are part and parcel of what preschool and elementary school teachers apply today.

Skinner also helped adults identify the contradictory and ineffective strategies they were using, often unknowingly, in educating young children. Some of his writings now seem a bit cold. Yet Skinnerian principles of learning are at the heart of today's best child-oriented computer programs as well as learning contracts and other incentive plans to promote good behavior and learning.

His notions of individuality and the importance of individualizing the learning experience concentrate on such issues as self-paced learning, rather than standard group instruction, and the use of incentives that take individual preferences into account. While reward and punishment are important in shaping and controlling behavior, he recognized that the same rewards and punishments won't work for all children.

He also showed that a system based entirely upon rewards is not the best way to get children to learn. Varying the timing and types of reinforcement works best. He helped show how children can take new skills and knowledge and apply them to other situations and settings. Skinner is strongly associated with the traditions of "behavior modification," "programmed instruction," "positive reinforcement," "contingency contracting," "token systems," and "time out." Each can be tailored effectively at home and school.

JEROME BRUNER (1915B.)

CHALLENGE THE CHILD AT THE RIGHT LEVEL IN THE RIGHT WAY

Jerome Bruner has had a great influence on the education of young children through his own studies and his translations of the work of other scientists. Many of his findings about how children perceive and think about things are now basic to early childhood educational materials and programs.

Scientists' understanding of children's stages of growth and the best ways to attract and hold a child's interest in learning new materials has expanded exponentially in the past few decades. Teachers are now expected to stay informed about new findings on child development so that education can continue to improve.

Bruner deserves a great deal of credit for helping the field of education to incorporate and put into practice new scientific findings about children, and for identifying which educational strategies are best for different types of children at different times in their lives. Interestingly, Bruner demonstrated that children's perceptions (and ultimately what they learn) are directly influenced by children's own values.

OTHER INFLUENTIAL THINKERS AND SCIENTISTS

Our understanding of how children grow and learn is changing by the hour with contributions from many branches of research. Collectively, these findings continue to shape our appreciation of the enormous capacities of young children — and the great potential of parents and teachers to guide their fulfillment. Who are the educational gurus or great philosophers of our time? There are many, we think.

We have described some, but by no means all, of the educational leaders who have had a tremendous impact on what is happening in today's preschool and early childhood education. Many other original thinkers have worked diligently to improve learning opportunities for young children. These include: A. S. Neill, Lev Vygotsky, and Erik Erikson, as well as modern-day early childhood educators, including Sue Bredekamp, David Weikart, Sharon Lynn Kagan, Ed Zigler, Bettye Caldwell, Joseph Sparling,

Barbara Bowman, Lillian Katz, Reggio Emilia, Constance Kammi, and Isabelle Lewis, to name just a few. They have affirmed some fundamental beliefs:

- **Very young children are eager to learn.**
- **Young children thrive when they are in positive learning environments.**
- **Skillful educators using techniques adapted to the young child are highly effective in supporting children's growth and emerging competencies.**
- **Active learning and child-initiated activities are exceptionally valuable.**
- **Responsive, caring education that blends with a child's everyday life fosters the development of the total child.**
- **Children are individuals with a zest or life energy that is special and should be recognized and respected.**

The original works by the great educational philosophers provide parents and educators with a grand vision and inspiration to help with the everyday tasks that can obscure the significance they hold in a child's life.

THE MANY VALUES OF PLAY

One of the most important contributions of early childhood educators has been their understanding of the role of play in learning. Children's play helps them learn. Here are some of the things play is known to promote:

- **Learning basic relations and concepts**
- **Developing social skills**
- **Developing physical skills**
- **Mastering life situations**
- **Practicing language processes**
- **Developing literacy skills**
- **Enhancing self-esteem**
- **Preparing for adult life and roles.**

Almost every great theorist in early childhood education also stresses that education is not only to prepare for the future, and that the child's life today is important. We concur wholeheartedly. Life is not just about tomorrow, whether you are a young child or a mature adult. Positive experiences almost always contribute to opportunities in the future. This joy and zest for life can be sensed the moment a parent walks in the door of a great preschool.

We repeat: This joy and zest for life itself is what fills the air of a first-rate learning center, home, school, or any place you would want your child to spend time, where you and others would want to visit and participate, and where you might dream that, in an ideal world, all children could be.

THE SPECIALIZED FIELD OF EARLY CHILDHOOD EDUCATION

The creation of the field of "early childhood education" is relatively recent. It has its origins in a national organization begun in the 1920s known as the National Committee on Nursery Schools, which, in 1964, became the National Association for the Education of Young Children (NAEYC). The mid-1960s saw the beginning of vigorous research about infants and young children. At the same time, schools of education began offering instruction that emphasized the special needs of preschool-age children. Today, many schools of education offer both undergraduate and graduate degrees (master's and doctoral levels) in early childhood education.

A leading textbook, *Early Childhood Education Today,* written by George Morrison at the University of North Texas and now in its seventh edition (1998, Prentice-Hall, Inc.), is packed with information to help early childhood educators learn about developmentally appropriate programs and practices. For ages three to five, Morrison emphasizes how preschoolers learn through play, the value of a preschool curriculum, and the general characteristics of good preschool programs. An especially interesting aspect of this textbook is its coverage of the different approaches to early child development.

The most influential movement in early childhood education can be summed up in three words: *developmentally appropriate practices.* These practices are reviewed and endorsed by a committee of early childhood experts. At the heart of the concept of developmentally appropriate practices is a recognition that children's teachers need to know a lot about the development of very young children, both in general and as individual learners.

The individuality of each child is recognized and valued, and all children are understood to have strengths and weaknesses. Developmentally appropriate practices are grounded in the importance of educators knowing about the social and cultural contexts in which children live. Such knowledge about children's lives helps to ensure that the types of learning experiences children have are meaningful, relevant, and respectful of differences.

There are 12 central principles that guide NAEYC's recommendations for developmentally appropriate practices. These principles state what early childhood educators expect from children, what they do in the classroom, and how they interpret young children's progress. We think it is important that parents know these 12 principles because they represent a summary of a large body of scientific and professional knowledge.

Parents who will be selecting a center for their preschooler should ask questions that concern the five guidelines, listed below, that early childhood educators are taught to use in their professional practice. They can be used to gather information, to observe what

PRINCIPLES OF DEVELOPMENTALLY-APPROPRIATE PRACTICE

1. Children's development in different domains, such as cognitive, physical, social, and emotional, are closely linked and exert mutual influence on one another.

2. There is a relatively well-ordered sequence for children's development reflecting a cumulative building of knowledge and skills.

3. Development typically shows unevenness across domains from child to child and even within the same child.

4. Early experiences significantly influence development, showing cumulative effects and delayed effects in some areas. Further, there are particular times – "windows of opportunity" – when learning is easier or more difficult.

5. Growth proceeds in predictable ways, generally moving toward greater complexity and higher levels of organization.

6. Learning and development occur within, and are influenced by, multiple social contexts and cultures.

7. Children learn through activity, depending on their own direct social and physical experiences along with knowledge that is culturally conveyed. Children actively construct meaning about the world in which they live.

8. Both biological maturation and the environment influence learning and development.

9. Play is vital for children's social, cognitive, and emotional development; play also reflects their level of development in these areas.

10. Practicing newly acquired skills and being challenged just beyond a child's level of current mastery are two important means to promote further development.

11. Children show many different ways of expressing their knowledge, in different modes and different forms of representation.

12. The best growth and learning take place within a community that affords children their basic needs: safety, love, a sense of being valued, and psychological security.

happens in programs, and to make informed decisions about early childhood education. Parents should be able to conclude that there is ample evidence that the preschool program or school they select for their child does, in fact, do the following:

- **Create a caring community of learners**
- **Teach to enhance development and learning**
- **Construct an appropriate curriculum (integrated plan for education)**
- **Assess individual children's learning and development**
- **Establish reciprocal relationships with families.**

Clearly, an ideal setting for a preschool-age child does more than provide opportunities for play with other children. At the same time, it does not focus narrowly on pre-academic skills and getting ready for school.

CHAPTER 9

THE ACADEMIC SIDE OF SCHOOL

What teachers and schools expect of young children today.
Defining, measuring, and monitoring academic success.
What you should know about standardized tests, grades, and report cards.
What to do if your child does not like school.
Summer and special programs to extend learning.

NOT LONG AGO, ACADEMICS WOULD HAVE BEEN THE ONLY SUBJECT IN A BOOK ABOUT SCHOOL. WE HAVE CERTAINLY EXPANDED OUR APPRECIATION FOR THE BREADTH OF ADVANTAGES SCHOOLS OFFER. TODAY, LEARNING THE BASICS IN SCHOOL OCCURS IN A SOCIAL AND CULTURAL CONTEXT WITH MANY EXTRAS, FROM SPORTS AND PERFORMING ARTS TO SOCIAL GROUPS AND STUDENT GOVERNMENT. BUT ACADEMIC PROGRESS IS STILL THE CENTRAL CONCERN FOR PARENTS, AS IT SHOULD BE.

The term "academic" derives from "academy," the old-fashioned name for a school. It comes from the Greek, *Akademeia,* the name of the grove near Athens where Plato taught and which eventually became the name of his school. Today the term "academic" has an additional, less lofty meaning — something that is not practical or worldly. But the academic basics that young children learn are eminently practical and worldly, not to mention interesting.

The education of young children has long been an art and a passion. Only recently has it become a scientific or precise endeavor. Much of what happens in schools is a combination of historical influences, practical realities, and the best professional consensus. Professional consensus changes frequently, but should be based on advances in knowledge and proof of effective educational approaches. This does not mean that today's education is free of fads and passing fancies. However, to a greater degree than ever before, there is a sound basis for many of the educational strategies in use.

WHAT YOU NEED TO KNOW

In preparing your child (and yourself) for school, there are many things you need to know. For example, you should know what your child will be taught, who decides what gets taught, when and how your child will be instructed, and why certain things are included (or excluded) from the curriculum. As you look into these and other issues, you will probably be struck by the changes in early education since you were a child. Today's schools teach and expect more from students at a far earlier age than they did just a generation ago.

In the following exhibit of Academic Achievement Goals, several things are apparent:

- **Accomplishment:** Children are expected to learn a lot and to be able to demonstrate their skills through a wide variety of accomplishments.
- **Thinking:** In the three traditional basic subjects, even very young children are expected to become active thinkers and doers, not just memorizers or rote performers. Children are expected to use simpler skills or components to do more complex or higher-order tasks of reasoning and problem-solving. In this way, children's efforts to make reasonable guesses are worth something, even if their final answer or product has some errors. For example, a good story is not discounted because a few words are spelled incorrectly, nor is a math problem that is almost solved given no credit.
- **Incremental growth:** Children's skills are built incrementally in multiple areas at the same time. As a result, children benefit from being able to apply skills learned in one area to other areas.

While all of these complex cognitive skills are developing, what will likely impress you the most is the sheer volume of factual information your child will learn. In the first three years of elementary school, your child will master thousands of new facts that he will memorize, enjoy, use, and creatively rearrange and manipulate. In a short period your young child will become a walking encyclopedia.

ACADEMIC ACHIEVEMENT GOALS

Leading college textbooks used in training elementary education teachers give ample evidence of high expectations for student achievement in the first few years of school. These expectations also are reflected in written standards and approved curricula of many school districts. The following goals give examples of such standards for reading, writing, and mathematics by the end of the second grade. Note: school districts may vary in these specific skills, but the partial list below is fairly representative.

Reading Skills for Spring of Second Grade

Word recognition skills:

- Recognize, pronounce, and understand a sight vocabulary of approximately 500 words.
- Pronounce appropriate sounds of single consonants, consonant clusters, digraphs, vowels, and diphthongs.
- Blend letters' sounds into words.
- Break words into their syllables.
- Be able to identify unknown words through use of clues from phonics, structural analysis, and context.
- Separate roots from prefixes and suffixes.

Comprehension of second grade–level reading material:

- Understand the meaning of sentences and paragraphs.
- Grasp the central idea of a paragraph or short passage.
- Find important details in a passage or a paragraph.
- Recognize cause and effect in what was read.
- Identify time intervals (sequence; past, present, and future tense).
- Make predictions from what is known.
- Follow simple directions from reading material.
- Differentiate fact from fiction.

Writing Skills for Spring of Second Grade

Spelling:

- Use reasonable phonetic spelling when the precise spelling is not known.
- Learn almost all assigned spelling words (usually weekly lists that expand vocabulary as well).
- Pick up accurate spelling for many words through reading.

Handwriting:

- Have legible handwriting (age and individual differences have a strong influence on this skill, especially in the early grades).

Writing to communicate:

- Understand different forms of writing (stories, lists, letters, reporting).
- Write stories that have beginning, middle, and end.
- Revise writing to improve clarity, details, sequence, etc.

Mathematics Skills for Spring of Second Grade

Numbers and numeration:

- Count all the way to 1,000.
- Read and write numbers from 0 to 1,000.
- Interval-count (by 1s, 2s, 3s, 4s, and 5s, forward and backward).
- Read place values for 1s, 10s, and 100s, and comprehend what place values are.

Operations with whole numbers:

- Add three-digit numbers without regrouping, two-digit numbers with regrouping (adding and borrowing).
- Subtract three-digit numbers without regrouping, two-digit numbers with regrouping.
- Recognize that the order of numbers does not matter for addition or multiplication, but does for subtraction and division (non-commutative versus commutative, respectively).
- Understand that multiplication is repeated addition.
- Be able to multiply and divide.

Operations with fractions:

- Understand and manipulate fractions of ½, ⅓, ¼, ⅕, ⅛, and ⅒.

Probability and statistics:

- Collect data (information) and graph this for two or more categories simultaneously.
- Place data into meaningful graphs and tables.
- From larger sets of objects, be able to group into two or three categories.

Measurement and geometry:

- Can estimate and make approximate measurements.
- Understand different measurement systems (time, distance, weight, temperature).
- Can use different systems to measure and conduct operations (for example, can measure length in inches, feet, yards; weight in ounces and pounds, in grams and kilograms; capacity in ounces, pints, and quarts).
- Make comparisons within measurement systems.
- Can read and make calculations related to time (clock time in analog and digital versions, dates including days, weeks, months, and years).
- Know about many properties of two- and three-dimensional shapes and objects.

Math problem-solving:

- Can solve a wide range of math problems that come from written problems, oral problems, or problems the child creates. Problem-solving typically involves use of four steps:
  - Grasping the problem and its elements.
  - Making a plan for solving (such as sorting and classifying, making a graph or table, doing particular numerical operations or comparisons).
  - Following through on the plan (trying it out by making specific computations).
  - Checking the answer for reasonableness and then for accuracy (and, if necessary, correcting or trying another plan if the answer does not seem reasonable or accurate).

This is exciting and typical of what the best schools accomplish. Ideally, schools have high standards, but also are able to adjust standards to the progress of individual students, going beyond the basic levels when necessary and offering alternative ways of learning for children with special needs or learning differences.

In this chapter, we start with the essential questions almost every parent wants answered: How will I know if my child is learning as much and as well as possible? What indicators and whose judgment should I trust? Then we cover topics such as the essentials of good teaching, the many subject areas that complement and expand the three basics — "reading, writing, and arithmetic" — and what to do when things are not going so well. Parent involvement is crucial in many situations, although sometimes your child will be the one who can best fix things or learn to view things from a different perspective.

This chapter will help you in all of these related topics, so that your child's love of learning and repertoire of academic skills will grow. Because learning the basics of academics also involves social and emotional factors — even if you are home-schooling your child — how these intertwine with and contribute to academic success are discussed as well.

ACADEMIC SUCCESS

WHAT IT IS, HOW TO RECOGNIZE IT, WHEN TO EVALUATE IT.

Academic success is something that all teachers measure regularly, formally or informally. Parents do, too, through their daily interactions with their children and through their observations of the papers, products, and "things" that children bring home.

Our definition of academic success is grounded in the child's perspective, because this is what will really count in the long run. A child's sense of making progress (continuously getting better) and of learning a lot about a lot (acquiring knowledge) are important motivators and necessary ingredients to later

"ACADEMIC SUCCESS" - A DEFINITION

Our working definition of academic success has been widely endorsed by early childhood educators and parents. Even children understand and agree with this definition. It is given from the child's perspective — which, after all, is where the learning is occurring.

- **Learning a lot in many areas.**
- **Being able to show what I have learned to other people I trust and respect.**
- **Being able to use what I have learned to help understand other things.**
- **Using my learning to get better at making things, fixing things, using clues and hints, solving problems, playing games, and getting to do new things.**
- **Learning everything my teacher wants me to know (sometimes even more) by paying attention, working hard, and asking for help when I do not understand.**
- **Trusting that my teachers and parents will let me know if I need to work harder on something or if I am confused or making mistakes that I don't realize.**
- **Knowing that my success this year will help me in the future in school and in doing things I like.**

academic accomplishments. Social and emotional factors are included in this definition of academic progress, because all forms of learning depend on others, at least to some extent. This is just as true for home-schooled children as for children in traditional schools. A good education and good academic performance should contribute to children feeling good about their competencies.

Most kindergarten through third-grade teachers use a combination of approaches to measure children's individual progress, including:

- **Their observations of the child's progress in completing classroom assignments and participating in classroom activities.**
- **Portfolio assessments, which involve reviewing a child's "work products," the things she makes in class (drawings, stories, entries into the child's daily journal, science projects).**

- **Individualized tests in which the teacher reviews a child's level of understanding or skills in performing specific tasks.**

Based on the recommendations by the National Association for the Education of Young Children (NAEYC) that schools *not* use standardized, group-administered tests before third (or ideally, fourth) grade, the vast majority of schools have dropped this form of evaluation. The results were not trustworthy enough. Moreover, the anxiety and problems they created were viewed as distracting or negative for many children.

We define academic success in a way that allows every child to succeed if the mix of good learning opportunities and the child's interest and effort are well-matched. We have documented tremendous academic progress in children of all abilities and age levels. More importantly, we have seen children exceed any educator's wildest dreams, given where the child began.

ASSESSING YOUR CHILD'S ACADEMIC PROGRESS

What do you know about your own child? Important questions to ask about your child's adjustment to the academic side of school include:

- Does your child talk about learning things at school related to reading, writing, and math?
- If so, does your child show interest and report new facts or show you new skills?
- Is your child bringing home examples of work that reflect new learning?
- Does your child spontaneously ask questions related to the skills or topics taught in the classroom (indicating continued interest in, or thinking about, these topics)?
- Has your child shown pride in accomplishment and perhaps signs of self-critiquing and wanting to do better?
- In everyday activities, do you see your child:
  - Starting to pay closer attention to print materials, numbers, and writing (signs, looking at newspapers or magazines at home)?
  - Following words more closely when you read?
  - Wanting to read independently?

The same child-oriented focus is as useful for gifted children as for those with developmental delays or disabilities. In the final analysis, academic success is something a child wants and can achieve, when many people and conditions come into play in the right way and at the right time.

ASSESSING YOUR CHILD

It's helpful to know in advance what indicators you will have about your child's academic progress. Below is a list of questions to consider and a way to organize the answers you will get. The questions begin with your own observations of your child. They move to the many forms of teacher appraisal and evaluation strategies used by schools or districts. Finally, we describe the options for outside, independent assessment of your child's academic strengths and weaknesses.

- Counting things or using math skills on objects, such as adding money or dividing portions of food?
- Trying to write notes to you or others and looking at things you write?

What does your child's teacher tell you?

- In notes from school, what does the teacher say about your child's progress? Good teachers encourage parents to comment on report cards (if they are used), to ask questions, and to come in if they would like additional information.

Schools have widely differing policies about formal written communications with parents. Written progress reports or report cards typically are given at regular intervals throughout the year. Copies go into your child's record, where they may stay for years. Similarly, notes about serious incidents often go into children's records. In the early years of school, however, the majority of schools do not use a formal system of numerical or letter grades. In fact, many schools have adopted guidelines that prohibit teachers from making any comparative statements about the children's academic progress. This means that

continued

ASSESSING YOUR CHILD'S ACADEMIC PROGRESS (CONTINUED)

children who are exceptionally advanced in particular areas will not be identified as such *in any written report.* Instead, for the first few years in school, your child's report card is likely to place children into:

- **Two categories,** such as "satisfactory" versus "needs improvement," or "at grade level" versus "not at grade level;" or
- **Three categories,** such as "meets grade expectations," "emerging skills" (to indicate progress but not yet at grade level), and "starting skills" (to designate only a minimal level at this time).

These ratings often are provided for academic subjects as well as conduct, effort, and work habits in the classroom. Schools increasingly provide a lot of specific information about a child's mastery of specific component skills. These skills usually correspond to the school's standards for measuring the achievement of curriculum goals for that grade level. These ratings help parents know what is expected and what is being emphasized in their child's daily work.

Why are schools not grading very young children? There are two reasons. First, most early childhood educators recognize that children differ a lot in their rate of progress in the first few years of school when they are acquiring very fundamental skills for later academic achievement. Thus, teachers do not want children to be discouraged or distracted by formal grades or judgments. Rather, they want all children to feel pride in their accomplishments and to be encouraged to continue to do their best. Second, parents often place way too much weight on formal "report cards" or grades and then put pressure on their children. Some parents whose children are academically skilled pressure teachers to tell them how "gifted" or "accomplished" their very young child is. Such efforts are misguided. Schools help parents and children alike avoid inappropriate comparison and unproductive competition by not giving formal grades.

This is why parent–teacher conferences are so important to understand your child's progress, to appreciate his true strengths and areas of excellence, and to learn of areas that might be of concern. This is when parents learn more about activities outside the classroom that can help their children's progress to soar. Yes, *all* children can soar when they are in the right educational environment!

- In informal conversations when you come to school (typically at least two per year in the early elementary school years), the appraisals your child's teachers make matter a great deal, because your child will be receiving these evaluations in the classroom through formal and informal messages, and because this will affect the school's impressions of your child's academic progress. Teachers often are highly skilled in their assessments of individual children. But there are many exceptions, and sometimes even celebrated teachers make mistakes.

You must decide whether the teacher's comments match your impressions of your own child. If your child is doing well, be sure that both you and the teacher are thinking of ways to stimulate continued learning to prevent boredom. If your child is progressing only moderately well or not well, consider what obstacles might be preventing greater progress, and plan with the teacher how to improve things.

Remember, the teacher will rely on multiple approaches to monitor your child's progress. These include: classroom observations, work samples, specific challenges or tests, and individual appraisal that may follow a prescribed method or one the teacher has developed for the curriculum. In classrooms with an open educational arrangement, a child's social interactions with peers may contribute to a teacher's impressions of your child's academic progress, especially when group learning and cooperative projects are involved. These social factors may influence your child's performance and academic reputation considerably. Later on, children can show or apply newly learned skills in individual or group situations. However, for young children, this often is not true.

Pay attention to the teacher's tone and enthusiasm when talking about your child's academic progress. These are probably reliable indicators of how the teacher thinks about and treats your child.

What does the school or school district tell you?

As mentioned earlier, few schools administer standardized achievement tests in the first few years of elementary school. In many places, laws have been passed or policies adopted to prevent early achievement testing of children. This is based on beliefs and evidence that these scores may not be that useful and that they sometimes are harmful to children, inaccurate or incomplete, or a major deterrent to effective early childhood teaching practices.

Some public and private schools, however, continue to use these tests, albeit with increasing sensitivity and precautions to maximize responsible use and interpretation. If your child's school uses these in kindergarten through second grade, find out as much as you can about what they are, when they are given, and how the information is used.

Because this has been such a controversial subject, we repeat that the National Association for the Education of Young Children has adopted a strong position against the routine use of standardized tests in the early grades. NAEYC strictly cautions against using only one test or type of assessment in any educational placement decisions.

GUIDELINES FOR ASSESSING ACADEMIC PROGRESS OF YOUNG CHILDREN

The National Association for the Education of Young Children has adopted the following guidelines for assessing a child's academic progress:

1. **A child's progress should be assessed through a process that is ongoing, meaningful, and strategic.**
2. **What is assessed in terms of content should reflect progress toward important learning and educational goals.**
3. **Assessments should be gathered only for particular and clearly understood purposes, and then used only for the purposes for which they yield reliable and valid information.**
4. **The methods used to assess young children should be appropriate to their age and experiences.**
5. **Individual differences or variation in learners – their style and rate of learning, as well as initial ability levels – should be taken into account in the assessments and the interpretation of these assessments.**
6. **Important decisions about a child's placement or participation in learning activities should never be based on the use of only one assessment, test, or screening device. Rather, if there is an indication of a concern, then additional and alternative forms of assessment should be used so that teachers and parents have confidence that they are reaching an accurate, fair, and useful appraisal of a child's progress and current level of performance.**

ABOUT STANDARDIZED TESTS FOR CHILDREN

Some background may help you understand the debate about using formal tests or other criteria to measure educational progress in very young children, and why the debate has been so hard to resolve.

History: Development of methods to test young children's intelligence, or their "potential for learning," began in the early 20th century. The purpose was to identify early those children who were not capable of benefitting from traditional schooling of that era. Therefore, it was considered humane to spare these children the humiliation and frustration of failing in school. It was also considered prudent to save society the costs of trying and failing to educate them.

The phrase "standardized test" or "standardized assessment" refers to uniform methods of testing in which tests are given and scored the same way. The goal is to provide results about children's performance that are not influenced by how the test was given, or how the scores were interpreted by the test-giver.

Types of tests: There are two categories of tests your child might take. It is important for you to understand the differences to know how to evaluate your child's scores. Standardized tests are "norm-referenced," "criterion-referenced," or a blend of the two.

- **Norm-referenced tests** compare the scores of one group of children to another group of children called the norming group. All children are the same age and grade, and they take the same test in the same way. The norming group should be a representative sample of children from different parts of the country, different ethnic and cultural backgrounds, and different socioeconomic groups. The scores of the children in this norming group form the basis for giving rankings or percentiles to your child. Norm-referenced tests are inherently comparative and place children in their relative standing to others.

  If your child scores at the 50th percentile, this means your child's performance on this test is comparable to that of children right in the middle of the norming group. (Some parents incorrectly think a 50th percentile ranking means their child failed half of the test and earned a score of 50 percent. They incorrectly interpret this score to mean that their child is extremely deficient when, in fact, the child is typical or average.)

  Two important facts you must know about norm-referenced tests are:

  - *Norms can change greatly up or down,* making it difficult to know exactly what these norms or percentile scores mean in terms of your child's academic skills and knowledge.

- *This method of scoring is like "grading on the curve,"* since not everyone can do well, even if every child learned all that was expected. Moreover, the scores that create percentile rankings are uneven. For example, 20 correct answers might separate a 90th percentile ranking from an 80th percentile ranking, but only five correct answers might separate an 80th percentile ranking from a 70th percentile ranking. In other words, the children with scores of 70 and 80 may function at almost the same level in everyday classroom situations, even though their standardized scores would suggest that they are very different.

 Another caution: Some schools create their own method of giving percentile rankings to children. For example, they might use other children in the school district rather than the national norming group. Imagine how different a child's percentile score might be if a child attended a school in a district with many high achievers versus a district with many low achievers. Children who pass the same number of items and have equal levels of academic achievement could be given very different percentile scores if this method of local scoring is used. Therefore, *be sure you know what comparison or norming group is used.*

 Percentiles do tell parents if their child is above or below other children in their grouping. However, the numbers fail to convey much useful information about how capable the child is in terms of specific competencies.

- **Criterion-referenced tests** provide information about specific competencies in particular subjects. The scores show what children know and the skills they can demonstrate. In this type of scoring, there is no limit on how many children can earn very high or very low scores. Some criterion-referenced test scores are converted to terms that indicate a child's grade-equivalency. They also may indicate whether a child's achievement is below, at, or above grade level.

Many people want to know whether children are learning what is being taught and demonstrating the proficiencies expected at a given grade level. Establishing these criteria is challenging and hotly debated. Over the years the consensus has shifted on what children should learn and when certain material should be taught and mastered.

Overall, the well-known standardized tests are pretty good at measuring a broad array of skills in reading, language, and mathematics.

Alternative methods are increasingly used to assess children's writing skills. These methods usually involve a timed writing test in which writing samples are scored in a standardized way for organization of story, number of supporting details, spelling, grammar, length of sentences, originality, etc. Schools can request that writing be analyzed by experts.

Testing companies are trying to create useful new assessment strategies. However, developing a new test that proves accurate and sensitive is arduous and expensive. Gathering up-to-date national norms on a representative sample of children is also complicated and costly. Many states and school districts are commissioning new tests. Others continue to rely on the "old-timers," recognizing these tests' limitations, but using their scores as rough proxies of how the school's children are progressing and how well they stack up against children elsewhere.

ADVICE TO PARENTS ABOUT STANDARDIZED TESTS

Rely mostly on the information that comes home to you every day — your child's self-report and evidence of skills — tempered by your informed impression and those of the teacher. We see no necessity or benefit from knowing scores on most group-administered tests.

When a child does really well on standardized tests, parents understandably feel good. However, such scores can be misleading. For children who entered school at an older age and who were advanced in their academic skills, the scores provide little helpful information about whether the child's education is promoting academic achievement at the best possible rate. In such cases, academically bright children can continue to receive high scores compared to national norms and will usually show above–grade level competencies on criterion-referenced tests — *even when they are receiving a mediocre education.*

For children with special needs, or who start behind grade level, standardized tests may continually provide discouraging scores that fail to capture the child's academic progress. Parents of these children are encouraged to look at their child's actual performance and get individualized help that fosters their child's strengths.

If your child will be taking standardized tests, ask:

- **Do teachers use the group-administered tests to help them with their teaching? If so, how?**
- **Do teachers use these tests to help them in their judgments of an individual child's progress?**

The answers are likely to depend on when the tests are given, whether the teacher can have timely results back within the school year (historically, this has not been possible), and whether the teacher thinks the standardized tests assess subjects that are emphasized in the curriculum. Good elementary-school teachers typically rely on their own assessment procedures. They request additional tests only when there are questions about some aspect of a specific child's academic progress.

GOOD USES OF STANDARDIZED TESTS

We advocate a "parent–beware" stance for results from routinely administered tests. However, there is ample evidence of two excellent uses of standardized tests:

- **General indicator of the achievement level** of students in the school or school district. It is important to pay attention to the full distribution of scores as well as numerical averages or mean test scores. For example, some first-rate school systems may attract a large number of children at both ends of the academic continuum because of their support programs and talented teaching staff. This may result in average or mean scores that are misleading unless read alongside the range of scores of all students who were tested. Schools usually provide information about averages to parents. You might want to encourage your school to share this and other useful information.

- **Adjunct source of new information** about an individual child. Children may be assessed individually by professionals with advanced training in the use of special standardized tests. These are used to reveal specific strengths and deficiencies or differences in how a child learns, processes information, performs, or perceives the world in terms of vision and hearing, spatial relationships, sequence, and manipulations of objects, etc. Schools may seek such assessments, but only with parents' permission. If your school requests such tests for your child, get as much information as you can to help you appreciate the purpose of such tests and the uses of the results.

  If you want to obtain such assessments on your own, we recommend that you discuss the matter with your child's teacher or pediatrician, or the school's counselor or psychologist. They can help you determine whether such assessments are likely to be helpful, and, if so, they can provide referrals.

If you are especially interested or concerned about the use of standardized tests in your child's school, consider joining a committee or parent group that deals with the school's assessment program.

SOME THINGS HAVEN'T CHANGED

Your child's curriculum is unlikely to look just like yours or your parents'. But there will be some familiar elements:

- **Show-and-tell:** Children still have show-and-tell because it helps them learn to present things clearly and allows others with a different perspective to understand something new.
- **The "classics":** Many of your favorite childhood books are used today in classrooms, media centers, and libraries because they are as interesting, lively, and educational today as when you were a child.

- **Handwriting:** Children still practice handwriting, even though they probably will use typed letters or voice-recognition software almost exclusively by the time they are in high school, and certainly when they are in college. They begin as you did, by first printing letters and then, by the second or third grade, learning cursive letters. They still use sheets with lines and dashes in the middle to help them make "perfectly" shaped letters.
- **Spelling and vocabulary lists:** Children learn to spell lists of words (beginning in the first or second grade). They also expand their vocabulary with word lists.
- **Practice:** Repetition still makes perfect. Some children just love these activities, while others find them drudgery. Apparently, early interest in math activities is not all that highly predictive of children's later interest in more advanced forms of mathematics and mathematical reasoning.

Above all, the elements of good teaching are very much what they always have been — caring, enthusiasm, good preparation, love of children, genuine curiosity, interest in the world, respect for the progress each child makes, and the ability to interest children in a wide array of topics and activities. Good teachers, just like good parents, make all children feel special and capable. Such teachers are responsive, and they have high expectations for the children in their classroom.

MANY THINGS ARE NEW

There have been significant changes in teaching since you were in elementary school. Many of these changes are the result of extensive research that has proved some techniques and approaches to be more effective than others. Good teachers today are trained in:

- **Teaching strategies for reading, writing, and mathematics that have been proven to be highly effective.**
- **Good classroom management skills.**

- **Incorporating multi-cultural activities in the classroom curriculum.**
- **Meeting specialized needs of children with significant learning and behavioral differences (mainstreaming for special education students).**
- **Communicating with parents about classroom activities, each child's progress, and how parents can be involved in their child's education.**
- **Using technology in the classroom – teaching students to use computers and other high-tech equipment, and using such equipment as a teaching aid.**

From this partial list, you can see how expectations for teaching have risen sharply in recent years. You also can appreciate how important it is that schools invest in continuing training for teachers to keep them up-to-date with new techniques and knowledge that will help your child.

MANY FACETS OF SCHOOL ADJUSTMENT

We know of no adequate means to measure a school's performance in the role of building competence, responsibility, innovation, leadership, and cooperation in students. Similarly, assessing a single student is just as complex. As you look for ways to make sure your child is doing well, remember that the goals of education are long-term and extend well beyond grades or standardized test scores. A happy child who is eager to learn, who looks forward to new challenges, and who is willing to try new solutions is worth much more than a straight-A report card or a 99th percentile score on a standardized test. Trust your own judgment and intuition, and allow your child's strengths to flourish and be celebrated.

Academic achievement is only a partial indicator of your child's adjustment to school. There always have been late bloomers and children who show delayed achievement in some areas but not others. Early starters may slow down in some areas and then catch up or surge ahead. These variations are more common than most parents realize.

IQ TESTS

Many people believe children have a "true potential" (or "innate ability"), and they either perform at this predicted level or they don't. If a child's performance differs from the estimated "potential," the child is classified as an under- or overachiever.

We believe this approach is misguided. It persists for three reasons: We have a long tradition of testing in our culture; many people hang on to old notions that "intelligence" can be separated from the experiences of life; and many people believe "intelligence" is largely inherited.

Our increasingly sophisticated understanding of human cognitive development has debunked these older approaches, but confusion and misinformation abound.

The intelligence tests on which so many people still rely were developed to measure mostly those aspects of intelligent behavior that remain stable from year to year. As such, these IQ tests measure only a small portion of human thinking and reasoning capacities. Research has not been adequately conducted on whether ability (potential) can be separated from performance (achievement).

Clearly some children seem not to try their best. Others diligently persevere and make great progress in learning. Because factors such as a child's motivation, attention span, and interest influence learning and achievement, the idea has persevered that the child has two selves or two separate dimensions — the potential self and the proven or realized self.

We think this dichotomy should be abandoned. IQ tests provide some clues about important aspects of a child's behavior and general store of knowledge. But the questions on IQ tests are never "content-free." The test-taker's ability to answer correctly is invariably affected by experience and practice. Of course, biology and genetics influence the course of human

GRADES AND REPORT CARDS

There are supporters and critics of report cards. However, as we indicated earlier, most schools don't formally grade students in the first year or two for three reasons:

- **Many educators believe early grading can be harmful.**
- **Early grading is rarely a motivator or source of useful information to young children.**

development. But many other factors count as well. For example, it has now been proven that experience itself can turn some genes on and off.

There are better indicators than IQ tests of a child's capabilities and progress. If a child is doing very well, it is impossible to be "overachieving." The very idea puts the child down, rather than calling into question the accuracy of IQ test results. Moreover, it suggests that the child's performance may be an aberration and may disappear without extreme effort — a terrible message to give a child or parent! In our judgment, success is success is success.

As for children who do not do their best under some situations or at some times in their lives, it is much more productive to understand why and to correct the problem, rather than labeling the child an "underachiever." The cause is usually one or more factors such as the child's biomedical or personal circumstances, changes in the family, a mismatch between the child's needs and the quality and quantity of instruction, peer influences, transitory periods of fears or anxieties, or disorganization at home or in the classroom.

There are no quick and certain answers to what is reasonable to expect of your child's performance. Predicting a very young child's later school success or lifetime achievements is rather like trying to predict the economy in 20 years. Certain forces will affect it, and these are not total unknowns. But a precise prediction is highly unlikely.

In your daily observations, you will be able to gauge your child's competencies to a great extent. What your child can do and understand today are real and trustworthy indicators. They set the stage for what happens tomorrow and in the years ahead. So forget predictions. Instead, invest in maximizing what you and your child have as assets today.

There is evidence that some early differences associated with chronological age or physical maturation tend to level out by the third or fourth grade.

In any event, grades in and of themselves offer no guidance on what needs to be done to improve a child's learning or to maintain it at a desirable level. More detailed interpretations and assessments are needed. As a parent, you need to feel confident that you understand the cause of any difficulties your child may have, and know what you can do — with the teacher cooperation — to correct the problem.

MONITORING YOUR CHILD'S ACADEMIC PROGRESS

The best ways to keep tabs on your child's progress are to trust your everyday observations and to listen to your child's opinions. Our research has produced a very surprising finding. Children often self-report academic difficulties or school-related learning problems earlier than their parents do. This suggests that parents may discount their young children's complaints and concerns. Perhaps these parents see their child's progress through rose-colored glasses, or they deny early problems. Or teachers may paint an unduly positive picture of a child's progress in the early years.

But children are in the classroom every day with numerous opportunities to judge how they compare to classmates. What better position to be "in the know"? Based on our findings, we think parents should pay close attention to what their child says about school, and investigate if their child says that things are not going well.

The sooner you detect a problem, the sooner you can start correcting it. Or you may find that negative reports are a result of your child's failure to meet self-imposed, overly strict standards. If so, you can help your child to set more realistic expectations.

At the other extreme, a child who never reports any concerns or difficulties may not be paying attention to the things that show academic progress. Alternatively, the child may not be challenged enough. Some researchers have found that children in schools with low academic achievement have very high opinions of their performance — opinions which are not confirmed by standardized tests or teachers' ratings.

SELF-ESTEEM

Regardless of your child's accuracy in evaluating his progress, his feelings toward school and his sense of self-worth are important. Self-worth or self-esteem should be generally positive but not inflated. It certainly should not be based on the assumption that everybody is equally great and smart. True self-esteem is a natural by-product of genuine achievement, not pointless praise or self-congratulation.

Young children's self-evaluation should be tied to direct, concrete examples of things they can and cannot do, their improvement in certain skills, and their increased knowledge. We know of recent examples where public schools have tried to boost children's performances on year-end standardized achievement tests by taking children to the gymnasium and leading cheers, as if the children were about to enter a sports competition! We were disappointed at this approach, even though we appreciate that the educators were hoping to encourage children to try their best.

VARIATIONS IN ACHIEVEMENT

In different settings, children are likely to show different competencies and even different levels in the same competencies. This is normal, but why does it happen?

From early on, children are sensitive to expectations and to opportunities and ways of doing things. Like adults, children are influenced by what is going on around them and what their typical habits are in different places. This means that certain environments can bring out or thwart aspects of their behavior.

We have observed this dramatically in children with disabilities. These children may appear skilled, self-guided, or efficient in learning in one setting, but may appear incompetent, withdrawn, slow, and error-prone in another. *These differences correspond clearly to the expectations and to the active supports children have in one versus the other setting.* In studies, scientists have found that typically developing children use different techniques to solve the same problem, depending on whether they are in a classroom or at home. This also affirms the conclusion that a child's competency level is not absolute, or something that is "inside" the child. Instead it reflects a combination of expectations, opportunities, and the importance of being "competent" in different places and at different times.

These findings are important to parents who suspect that their child's school setting is less than ideal. We know of many children who made big gains in school achievement in relatively short periods of time once they were placed in a better situation. This does not mean that every child should be relocated the minute something goes awry. But it is an option when there is a pattern of difficulty, insufficient progress, and lack of interest in school.

Another approach when there is difficulty is to reassess your home environment. What could you do to promote learning? Children benefit from having an adequate place to do schoolwork, as well as enough time and good materials readily at hand. Parental expectations and support, including guidance, assistance, modeling, and answering questions, are important components of good home environment.

For many families, this means reassessing priorities and allocating time to valued and constructive activities. Not every minute must be planned or programmed. But children must have enough time to do schoolwork without being rushed, stressed, or distracted. Recognize that your home setting can influence your child's behavior. Use this knowledge to good advantage.

WHAT IF YOUR CHILD DOES NOT LIKE SCHOOL?

Very few children dislike school in the first year or two. In a recent study, fewer than 10 percent of children in kindergarten and first grade reported not liking school. Those who reported not liking school and who also felt they were not doing well had further difficulties later on and showed less progress in learning.

Therefore, we generally favor an activist stance rather than taking a "wait-and-see" attitude or assuming that the school will handle the problem. Parent involvement really counts here, because this is one area in which parents are likely to find the least help or agreement about how to solve the problem. If your child does not like school, you will likely encounter many reasons why, conflicting opinions about how long to wait before you act, and disagreement on what to do.

Clearly, however, children who are only five to seven years old are not well-equipped to evaluate their situation or make things better on their own. They are still just getting used to being in school. By resolving the problem, you are not coddling your child. You are doing what's needed. It is the only way to be sure that your child's learning opportunities are the best ones, and that there are no external factors that may do lasting harm.

If your child dislikes school, here are four important things you can do:

- **Understand the situation.** How did you find out that your child does not like school? How serious is the dislike? When did it begin? Was it gradual or triggered by a particular event or incident? Try to determine the cause. Is this dislike associated with changes in your child, such as being unhappy, irritable, withdrawn, physically ill, frustrated, socially inappropriate, extra needy, or academically disengaged and nonproductive? Even one of these signs – if it persists for more than a short time – warrants further investigation. Check out factors such as an undiagnosed disability or illness.

  Listen to what your child has to say. How you talk with your child about this issue will depend on her age and understanding of the situation. Have a good grasp of what "not liking school" means for your child and understand the factors contributing to it.

- **Find out what the teacher and others at school think.** What do the teacher and school know or think is the cause of your child's unhappiness? How helpful their answers will be depends on the circumstances. Neither discount nor fully trust the teacher's and school's appraisals until you determine whether their opinions match, add new information to, or are at odds with your understanding. Ask the teacher and others at school for suggestions to improve the situation. Good schools will be responsive, have ideas, and take needed steps, even when the problem seems relatively minor.

  Remember, *you are your child's primary advocate.* You also know your child better than anyone else. You may not always be right, but your hunches, ideas, and concerns are grounded in experience. Moreover, no one else will be as committed to your child's well-being as you are.

- **Find out what the alternatives are.** Consider the following:
  - Assess whether the problem is likely to resolve itself shortly without any action, other than reassurance that things will get better (which is not, however, an easy concept for young children to grasp). Such a resolution might be in the offing if, for example, the dislike resulted because your child was embarrassed in the classroom on a single occasion for reasons not related to inappropriate teacher behavior or poor classroom management. Or perhaps a squabble with a classmate made the child suddenly not like school.
  - Request a meeting with key school personnel, including the principal, to discuss solutions.
  - Check with other parents to see if their children have similar feelings and whether there are contributing factors you might not be aware of.
  - If there is evidence of teacher maltreatment or unresponsiveness from the school, go to the superintendent or the school board to identify corrective strategies.
  - Consider placing your child in another classroom if the cause appears related to factors that cannot be changed within the classroom, especially a mismatch of styles between the teacher and your child.
  - Consider placing your child in another school if the difficulties appear related to the overall school climate. For example, are expectations too high or too low for your child? Is the environment too structured or too free for your child?
  - In extremely serious matters, seek help from attorneys knowledgeable about school law and parental rights. If the problem is taking a toll on your child, check with child development experts. For the latter, get referrals from a trusted pediatrician or educator who knows your child and family.

As you explore these options, keep a folder of information you have gathered. Document all calls and meetings. This need not lead to litigation or even unpleasantness. The documentation is important for you to keep the facts straight so you can help solve the problem.

- **Take action.** Develop a plan and take action based on the options that meet your priorities and look most promising. Monitor changes or progress. Encourage your child to let you know about feelings, good and bad, concerning your actions. Your child's active participation and cooperation are needed.

  If the actions succeed, thank the key people who have helped. Let them know things have improved and that their ideas or actions have made a difference.

We know of too many families who waited too long before moving their child from an unfavorable situation to a better one. The most common explanation for the delay is that the first school was considered good, and the parents just thought things would turn around in time. When they see their previously unhappy and unchallenged or unaccomplished child "come to life" and look forward to going to school, they invariably ask, "Why did we wait so long?"

We pass this advice along because there are occasional mismatches in elementary school, just as there are in college. Some students thrive in smaller colleges, others feel thwarted; some love a big, anonymous university, others feel lost and dehumanized; some do their best in a highly competitive or conventional school setting, others need an ungraded and self-initiated form of learning. Research findings clearly show that no one style of education fits all children. Unfortunately, there is no research basis to guide parents about when, why, and how to find a new teacher or new school when their child does not like school.

A final note: Don't worry about children's normal responses, especially when friends are around, or when they answer adult's generic queries, such as, "Do you like school?" It's common for children to respond that recess, gym, or lunch is their favorite subject (which may be true) or that they "hate" homework, especially when they would rather be doing something else.

LEARNING MORE ABOUT ACADEMICS YOURSELF

Children learn more than the basics in the first years of school. They also are introduced to other cultures and countries, geography, history, civics, famous people, nature, and the communities in which they live.

Your child's studies are a great opportunity for you to learn more about topics that have long interested you. Showing an interest in topics your child is learning about can lead to great dinner table conversation. Don't overwhelm your child with your interest. You don't want to be seen as doing the teacher's job. Instead, be an active parent-learner, showing curiosity and commitment to lifelong learning.

If you discover good sources of information along the way — from books to videos to displays at local museums — that complement classroom teaching, pass the information on to the teacher. Good teachers welcome such information, and they appreciate parents' interest in what is happening in the classroom.

Biographies are a special source of enjoyment for parents and children. They are fascinating stories, and they usually teach valuable lessons about such things as overcoming adversity, the value of perseverance, and discovering and using one's talents. There has been a recent explosion of new biographies suitable for reading with a young child. More sophisticated biographies can be read if you interpret big words or skip sections that are too complicated or inappropriate.

TUTORING AND SPECIAL BOOSTS FOR "SCHOOL SMARTS"

Tutoring used to be a form of compensatory education reserved for children who were failing. Tutors were typically used only for specialized topics, and they were rarely employed to help children in the elementary grades. Sometimes teachers tutored in their "off-duty hours." Other times parents had to find tutors from among high school and college or university students.

Another older notion of tutoring came from elite families whose children were educated by tutors. These teachers were the school-age version of a nanny or governess, but with a focus on the child's education. These tutors often became special allies and mentors of children of rich and powerful families whose parents often were preoccupied by busy social, business, or political lives.

Today, however, tutoring has new meanings which vary from one part of the country to another. For example, in New York City, many talented writers and teachers tutor children. While some tutors help with identified problems, many are employed to give children a "competitive edge." These tutors enrich the children's educational experiences and help prepare them for school entrance exams. In fact, many cities have commercial learning centers or special programs that are costly, well-advertised, and offer guaranteed results to give children an academic boost.

Is this a good idea? Or are children being pressured too early or too much in terms of their academic development? In our experience, children are being pressured more often than they should be. Knowing your child's needs, talents, and interests is important. Knowing your own motives is also important. There often is undue pressure on parents to "keep up with the Joneses" when it comes to providing tutors and special programs for their children, even if the children are thriving without them or don't want them.

Of course, there are times when parents are too busy to provide the needed hours of patient review, encouragement, and home-based teaching to supplement school learning when their children need extra help. Dedicated, well-prepared tutors may offer enthusiasm, skills, and an emotional distance from children that parents or other relatives can't provide. They also can help children pursue a subject they especially love, such as writing or science.

In any event, tutoring for children as an enrichment technique (rather than remedial tutoring) has not been subjected to rigorous evaluation. In general, schools do not encourage families to enlist their own teachers, largely because it isn't needed. Children who are busy all day in school and who are making satisfactory progress are probably better off spending their free time in play, rest, and being with friends and family.

We have heard of families who paid large fees for tutoring or extra assistance that did not deliver on its promises. Sometimes well-meaning relatives will sign your child up for a prepackaged support program that you don't want. Whenever possible, try to coordinate outside professional help in advance with your child's teacher to make sure you will not confuse or tire your child. Good schools usually have suggestions about how parents can get extra help, including referrals of qualified tutors.

SUMMER ACTIVITIES AND PROGRAMS

What happens when your child is not in school can make a big difference in overall school achievement. This is particularly true for the long break in summer.

The breaks from formal schooling offer a much-needed diversion and a fresh daily schedule. However, children continue to learn and show academic progress during these breaks if they are engaged in interesting, challenging, organized activities, and if they continue reading.

Nevertheless, don't overdo. Part-time day camp, free activities at public libraries or schools, and family vacations can broaden children's interests without pressuring them. Kids need unstructured time to play, think, and dream. If you live in a pleasant, safe neighborhood with plenty of kids, be sure your child has lots of time for having fun.

You also can use summers and other extended breaks to enhance your child's education. Children's minds are active, and they learn a great deal from play and recreation at camps or programs that emphasize subjects of interest to your child, such as sports, arts and crafts, science, and nature. Summer vacations and other family learning activities are valuable, too.

Research confirms that children who are not occupied in meaningful activities in the summer and who receive little adult supervision do not continue to grow in their intellectual and academic abilities, while children who are so engaged, do. This additional growth over the elementary school years can amount to a large difference in a child's academic outcome. So balance the "rest and relaxation" with some planned and organized activities. The time and money you invest in these will be well-spent.

Playing and having fun, including unplanned days or hours, are needed and can be constructive. Overall the emphasis should be on creating opportunities for natural learning and skill-building, for creative expression, and for pursuing interests in the context of a well-rounded life. Have fun — and take some time off yourself.

CHAPTER 10

THE LANGUAGE ARTS

The art and science of listening, speaking, reading, and writing. How to encourage your child's language skills. Proven ways to promote learning to read. Common causes of reading difficulties and what to do about them.

LEARNING OCCURS IN MANY WAYS — SUCH AS THROUGH SIGHT, SMELL, AND TOUCH. BUT IN SCHOOL, ALMOST EVERYTHING THAT COUNTS INVOLVES LANGUAGE.

The three most obvious reasons why language is central to academic success are:

- **Most teacher instruction to children is given through words — primarily speech with elaboration or reinforcement in writing.**
- **Children seek information and often show their understanding through speech.**
- **Learning about most subjects involves reading. Written materials reinforce what is learned in other ways.**

Reading is central to learning. Children who can't read with ease, speed, and comprehension are at risk for failure in many areas.

THE POWER OF WORDS

The power of words goes beyond their individual meanings. Streams of words can convey more than the sum of the individual words. And language is more than streams of words. Patterns and forms of speaking and writing convey feelings and meaning. How things are said, written, or read can add immensely to the literal meaning of words. This is a lesson children learn early.

Think of what a five- or six-year-old already knows about the nuances of language:

- **Timing what you say can influence its outcome, such as waiting for the right moment to make a request, confess a wrongdoing, or offer thanks.**

- **The tone and volume of voice matter a lot.**
- **A person's facial expression and gestures can increase understanding. For example, they show the difference between a gentle tease and a serious expression.**
- **Using new, big words can sometimes impress people. More important, new words can open up new conversations and learning.**

Beyond its importance for school, reading is part of almost everything we do. Through reading, people improve skills in other activities. Beyond this, the information age has elevated reading and writing to even greater importance for on-line communication. Many adults who struggled to learn to read, later discovered the joy of reading. Their enthusiasm is phenomenal and contagious! We hope fewer children today will struggle with learning to read, and that the joy of reading will be part of all children's everyday life right from the first years of school. In this chapter, we tour the world of language arts.

NEW WAYS OF TEACHING LANGUAGE ARTS

Today we know a great deal about language development and the skills needed to learn to read. This has revolutionized the ways teachers are taught to teach reading.

In the first few years of elementary school, your child will spend the majority of each day thinking about and using one or more of the language arts. There will be extensive and direct instruction about them, as well as the informal use of language for social exchange. Creative expression and imaginative interpretation will be encouraged, as will memorization and rote rehearsal of the basic elements of reading and writing.

Your child will quickly become a skilled reader who first learns to read, then reads to learn, and then reads for many reasons, including pleasure. The appearance of reading skills is as exciting to most parents as their child's first steps or first words. As children learn to read, their ear-to-ear grins are special rewards that parents never forget.

If your child is slower in learning to read or has reading difficulties, you will need to provide extra time, patience, encouragement, and skill-building. Rest assured, things will fall into place, and the world of print will be open to your child, too. As in all other areas of human competence, the rate and style in which children progress are individual. Today, early childhood educators are improving their own skills. Armed with the latest research, they are using new learn-to-read programs that have been proven effective. Reading enhancement programs are gaining widespread use, and with good reason. Parents can be effective partners in teaching reading at home.

LISTENING: THE MOST BASIC OF THE LANGUAGE ARTS

Listening is where language learning begins. Right from birth, your child was exposed to the nuances, complexities, and practical uses of language when you cooed, sang, read books, and talked. By about one year of age, most babies' word-like sounds become real words that parents can understand. By 18 months, most children are using word combinations and even phrases. From then until school entry, children add hundreds of new words to their vocabulary.

Children acquire impressive uses of language in this period, including for humor, social and emotional expression, and internal behavioral guidance. They also begin to acquire grammatical understanding and appreciation for the structure of language, as in stories and songs.

Children also have the opportunity to listen to people and to recorded and transmitted sounds. But the most important form of language learning takes place in interactive exchanges in which the child listens and speaks.

As with social interactions, the give-and-take of language is filled with rules, order, surprises, and subtleties. Children whose parents talk to them more and use more complex forms of language, richer vocabulary, longer sentences, and labeling show more advanced language development.

- **Listening problems:** Early problems in listening usually are due to hearing loss or phonemic processing difficulties. (A phoneme is the sound made by one or more letters.) Hearing loss now is detected early with clear benefits to children and their families. Unfortunately, very bright infants with profound hearing loss often "fool" their parents and pediatricians for up to eight months, because they rely on non-auditory cues associated with sound. Universal hearing tests for all newborns are now being proposed to prevent delays in detection.

  Much of children's hearing loss is not present at birth, but is acquired from chronic ear infections. This form of loss is often milder. Therefore, it is less likely to be detected or treated appropriately, often not until the first few years in school.

- **Promoting good listening:** In school, the demands on children to listen, comprehend, and act upon what they hear are greater than in the preschool years. In preparing your child for school, consider the following activities:

  - Tell longer stories if your child seems interested.
  - Give multi-part instructions: first two, then three, then four things to do.
  - Name things in books, magazines, your home, or outdoors.
  - Play games with words that sound alike, rhyme, or start with the same sound, or use very short or long words.
  - Teach songs and add verses.
  - Read, especially books that expand your child's understanding of language and that contain enjoyable uses of language.

As your child gets older, discuss the importance of listening attentively or with interest and respect. Be sure that your child understands why making sounds, jumping around, or talking while someone else is talking are unacceptable ways of listening in most places. Teach your child about turn-taking in conversation, but take into account your child's maturity and your family's conversation style. Some families notice seemingly minor interruptions during even casual social exchanges. In other families, a child might never get to speak if he waited for a pause in the conversation!

Since listening is a lifelong necessity and an art, set an example with the way you listen to your child. Attending movies, plays, concerts, and other performances also can encourage extended listening. Use the telephone with your child. Don't forget the radio. From talk shows to storytelling, there is a lot on radio that will appeal to you and your child. Many child experts think that having opportunities to listen without seeing *images* may be useful in helping a child to visualize or imagine words.

Wonderful books on tape and delightful collections of songs can be found at bookstores, children's specialty shops, and libraries. You and your child can even make your own tapes.

We know of no courses in listening skills taught to elementary school teachers. But any experienced early elementary school teacher knows that capturing and holding children's attention are vital to teaching. Such teachers also know that children must focus their attention on what teachers and others say.

SPEAKING: THE BASICS FOR INTERACTIVE LEARNING

Speaking involves brain activity and muscular control to generate complex sequences of sounds and memory for words and their use. A young child often wants to say something that she cannot adequately convey. Patience helps. So does good intuition in guessing or elaborating on the child's efforts. However, some frustration in early speaking is inevitable.

By school age, children are generally pretty adept in speaking. There are a number of common problems with speech production that may plague children throughout the elementary school years. Most children have difficulty with a few sounds. Typical problems include sound reversals and mild lisps. Most of these problems are minor and subside or disappear with time.

Parents often are concerned about these early problems and seek professional advice because they know that speech is an important way that we present ourselves to others. Think of how spoken words help or hinder the work of world leaders. Think of some expressions we use to describe people's speaking skills:

- **soft-spoken**
- **well-spoken**
- **has a way with words**
- **can really turn a phrase**
- **silver tongue**
- **win anyone over with words**
- **persuasive**
- **a real talker!**

Schools actively promote language skills. Language arts take up the majority of time from first grade through third grade, including oral presentations, talking, and asking and answering questions.

At home, parents can encourage children's speaking skills through storytelling, asking questions, and elaborating on things their child shares with them. Encourage your child to share what he is learning with others outside the family. Teach your child to do this in appropriate ways — not too much or in too forward a manner, and at the right times.

WRITING: NEW WAYS OF TEACHING

There has been a revolution in teaching writing skills to very young children. A few generations ago, writing was divided into three phases. First, mastering the art of printing the letters. Next, spelling. Finally, combining these skills to communicate in writing.

Today, most kindergarten teachers have children "writing" and even creating their own journals. Many also allow children to invent their own spelling and to scribble what look like words or sentences, even though they would be indecipherable to an adult. Why this emphasis on early writing and tolerance for mistakes?

The answer is that educators have learned that many children love to write. Writing is a version of talking for them, allowing them to capture on paper things that are meaningful. Children will show remarkable progress over the years in their journals and other written projects. Sometimes they pick up accurate spelling by seeing the words in books or around the room. But mostly they learn to feel comfortable with the writing process. Their love of writing is not hampered by the self-consciousness of making errors.

While this early, integrated approach to teaching language arts has a great deal of support, there are some controversies. Disagreement among parents and teachers on the goals of this approach can cause tension between school and home. Even top educators do not agree on the best way to implement this approach. Many teachers continue to experiment and fine-tune the ways they encourage children to write.

The jury is still out on whether this new approach to writing will improve writing skills to levels above those of previous generations. But the evidence shows that young children seem to like writing more when taught this way, and they are not seriously delayed by the shifting rules and expectations as they progress to later grades. They understand that teachers and parents overlooked minor mistakes in their early efforts, and with practice they are expected to improve.

Nonetheless, most educators today see writing skills as a part of the larger picture of integrated language arts. The earlier widespread dislike or fear of writing that some children experience can be reduced when children have successful, early experiences with writing. They will be able to understand the goal (and the joy) of transforming thought and speech into a written product. They soon see how words and their proper sequencing convey meaning. They also learn how certain words are especially delightful or effective in communicating.

When teaching methods help children see this big picture, they are more likely to be enthusiastic about learning and using new skills. The old-fashioned way of teaching language arts often did not convey this message early or well enough to some children. As a result, they tended to disengage from writing and feel lost or intimidated by writing assignments.

Promoting writing: You will likely delight in deciphering your child's notes and letters to you. You also will be reminded how arbitrary our rules of spelling are! And you will certainly empathize with your child's struggles in learning to write. You also will get a refresher course in reading as you try to decode these notes by sounding out and making wild guesses. English is a demanding language with all of its irregularities. You may vividly recall your efforts with words that sound alike but have different spellings — weather and whether, hear and here, there and their, which and witch.

Then, of course, there are words that should be pronounced differently, but often aren't — picture and pitcher; Mary, marry, and merry; sense and cents. Or words with letter combinations that can be hard to pronounce — spaghetti, library, pneumonia. No wonder that parents' complaints about the complexities of English often are directly related to their child's stage in learning language arts. English is not a consistent language. Share these realities with your child.

The language arts don't necessarily progress evenly. Most children have writing strengths and weaknesses early on. For example, children who are good spellers may not be good storytellers, and vice versa. Good storytellers may not be as skilled in fictional writing as in their descriptive writing.

If you were or still are not a perfect speller, be especially supportive of your child's efforts. Some tendencies appear to run in families.

Children enjoy looking over their earlier journals and work forms, finding mistakes, and seeing their growth. This is what *active learning* is all about — giving children opportunities for discovery, self-correction, and seeking adult help. This approach has clearly accelerated learning in many areas. You may be amazed that many kindergartners can use a dictionary.

Keep an assortment of dictionaries at home that are appropriate for your child's level. These will be fun to use together, and they provide a great prop for expanding vocabulary and teaching spelling and word usage.

Remember that your child's writing reflects a combination of skills that may be developing at different rates. Also, he may have practiced the various skills of writing to different degrees. Your child's fine motor abilities may be behind others in the class. This seems to be maturational, and may also reflect how much a child enjoys seeing perfectly formed letters. And girls typically have better penmanship earlier than boys.

Your child's growing worldliness and vocabulary will make writing more interesting, but may also lead to more spelling and grammatical errors. If your child loves drawing and seeing lots of colors, his writing may have fewer words and more pictures. This is great. Don't worry about it.

There are many ways you can encourage writing at home, including thank-you notes, holiday cards, reminder notes, diaries, journals, spelling games, and writing poems, jokes, or jingles. You also can ask an older family member to work with your child to record a special part of family history, write down a beloved recipe, or draw a family tree. As adoptive parents, we know this is just as important an exercise for adopted children as for birth children.

Save many of your child's early writings. You and your child will cherish them for years to come.

READING: THE MOST IMPORTANT SCHOOL SKILL

Whether reading is the culmination of the language arts or an independent skill is an interesting academic question. But the answer doesn't affect how you can help your child. Scientific studies show that all components of the language arts complement the others. The two major findings about reading are:

- **Children who are introduced to reading and books early, in natural and enjoyable ways, are much more likely to become good, enthusiastic readers.**
- **Children's overall language skills, which are stimulated and promoted at home, are of immense help in the reading process.**

Promoting reading. We repeat: early parental reading and family literacy activities, as well as a rich family environment of spoken language, are *strongly* associated with children's reading success.

However, there are some qualifications to this important conclusion. Simply reading a lot to your infant, then toddler and preschooler, does not guarantee that your child will learn to read early, rapidly, or without struggle. Every child is unique. Also, the benefits of your child's cumulative reading and language experiences will show up by about third grade.

Experts disagree on how parents can best encourage their child's language skills. There is as much debate about these issues as there is about how much to read, what types of books to use, which skills to emphasize, and whether to practice the alphabet or phonics before kindergarten. However, the general consensus among reading experts and teachers is to incorporate these activities as much as you can into your family life.

Whatever you do, be creative. Don't limit reading with your child to books. Read newspaper and magazine stories. Comics are OK, too. Read aloud letters and e-mail from friends. Read instructions for toys and games and household projects. Read recipes, labels on clothes, and signs when you are on excursions. Decipher the components of written messages, such as identifying words and parts of words that are alike or different, picking out certain letters and sounds, and making rhymes.

There has been excellent recent research on reading problems as well as what promotes good early reading. Here are some answers to questions parents most frequently ask:

- **How likely is my child to have or develop a reading disability?** Reading difficulties are not uncommon. Depending on the definition of "reading disability," the best estimates are that about one in five children have such a difficulty.
- **Why do boys have so much difficulty learning to read?** Boys and girls actually have about equal difficulty in learning to read. However, schools identify boys' reading problems much more often. Teachers refer boys for placement as

"learning disabled" based on their reading problems about four times more than girls. Why? This is probably because of boys' classroom behavior that accompanies their reading difficulties.

- **What causes reading problems? Are all children who have reading problems dyslexic?** Most children with a serious reading disability have problems in word recognition – deciphering individual words. We don't know what causes it. Research indicates that there may be value in using brain imaging technologies to study the process of learning to read. As yet, however, there are no adequate studies of young children who differ in their reading acquisition skills. Reading problems tend to run in families, but this is not always the case.

  The term *dyslexic* encompasses a wide range of specific problems. The word comes from the Greek roots of "dys," meaning "trouble," and "lexia," meaning "word." The term describes the person's reading-related skills, but does not indicate the cause. Not all children or adults diagnosed as dyslexic are the same. Dyslexia refers to difficulties in letter and word recognition, and usually includes difficulties with spelling, writing, and reading. Some well-known features of dyslexia, such as letter reversals (for example, where b's and d's are confused) typically occur briefly in children who are developing normally. Yet not all people labeled dyslexic have this problem.

- **Will reading difficulties prevent my child from doing well in school?** This is hard to answer. In general, children with severe reading disabilities and those who lag in their reading skills encounter more problems in academic achievement and overall adjustment to school. However, many "academically gifted" children have early reading delays. They also can have significant difficulties, such as with spelling, that persist into adulthood.

Reading, spelling, or writing problems and their impact on other subjects can be minimized when children receive good reading instruction and individualized help at school and home. There are many success stories. National organizations advocating for individuals with dyslexia and learning disabilities remind us that many highly accomplished individuals were or are dyslexic.

Poor instruction is another suspected cause, often unrecognized, of many reading difficulties. Reading instruction is still largely teacher-controlled in the classroom. It is not routinely supported or monitored in most schools. A teacher's enthusiasm for teaching reading, love of literature, or even time spent on reading activities in the classroom do not necessarily guarantee that children are receiving the "best practices" in reading instruction. This often happens because teachers were taught sub-optimal reading instruction methods in college.

Most children can learn to read with even mediocre or poor instruction, although perhaps not as well. Educators suspect that substandard instruction negatively affects all children, but children "at risk" or those with reading disabilities, of course, are harmed most. Therefore, there is no justification for continued use of inadequate teaching approaches.

National studies are underway to test the effectiveness of the best reading instruction methods. These studies include children with delays in language development and those at risk for dyslexia. Early results are so promising that many states are adopting programs to help retrain teachers on the newest advances in reading instruction techniques. Based on programs that have proven beneficial to children with reading disabilities or "at risk" children,

GREAT PEOPLE WITH READING DIFFICULTIES

Here's a short list of some historical greats who had dyslexia or major reading difficulties: *Hans Christian Andersen, John James Audubon, Lewis Carroll, Agatha Christie, Winston Churchill, Charles Darwin, Thomas Alva Edison, Albert Einstein, Michelangelo, General George Patton, Auguste Rodin, Leonardo da Vinci,* and *Woodrow Wilson.* Notice that many of these individuals are renowned for their writing ability, their speaking ability, and original contributions to the sciences and arts. There also are very long lists of nationally prominent individuals in all walks of life, including entertainment, politics, arts, writing, sciences, and sports, who willingly let others know that they are dyslexic. Whatever the causes — and there probably are many — dyslexia need not doom a child or obscure the child's talent.

below are important factors that make a measurable difference in children's reading progress:

- **Intensity must be sufficient:** Children who receive more time in good reading instruction and activities benefit more. Many remedial or individualized reading instruction programs (including tutoring) that did not produce good results may not have had enough time each day, enough days each week, for enough weeks to produce optimal and lasting benefits.
- **Direct instruction is necessary:** Children who receive more explicit instruction related to letter and word recognition, decoding, phonemic awareness, and other literacy skills do better than those who spend equal amounts of time in reading programs that do not directly teach children these skills.
- **Comprehensive, combined approaches work best:** Such approaches include teaching reading and spelling at the same time, not separately. They also balance the use of literature and an emphasis on comprehension with the type of direct instruction described above.
- **Social and emotional support are very important for learning to read:** When children encounter reading difficulties, there is much frustration and confusion. Children need extra patience, encouragement, reinforcement for their efforts, and recognition and celebration of their advances. They need reassurance from both parents and teachers that they are capable and intelligent, and that reading – important as it is – is not the only measure of their learning ability or their school success.
- **Practice, practice, practice!:** All children need to practice their reading skills. This is especially true for children with reading difficulties. However, there is an additional challenge for children with difficulties. When children perceive they are not good at something or that it is more difficult for them than for their classmates, they are usually less inclined to spend lots of time in that activity. The key is finding ways to make reading enjoyable and rewarding, so that practice can occur. Let your child find books that are especially appealing. Try writing your own books. Play reading games, including board games, computer games, and games you invent. Be sure you have comfortable places to practice reading. Practice when you and your child are well-rested, and -nourished, and able to focus on reading.

LEARNING TO READ AND HELPING CHILDREN OVERCOME READING DIFFICULTIES

Two of our nation's leading experts in the field of learning disabilities and reading interventions, Dr. Jack M. Fletcher of the University of Texas–Houston Medical School and Dr. G. Reid Lyon, Chief of the Child Development and Behavior Branch at the National Institute of Child Health and Human Development, have provided an informative summary of what we know about early reading. Here are their major conclusions of interest to parents:

- **Learning to read** is a lengthy and difficult process for many children.
- **Much of the success** in learning to read is based on language and literacy skills that are developed very early in life.
- **Reading failure** represents the lower end of reading proficiency – not a set of qualitative characteristics that distinguish the poor reader from the good reader.
- **Vigorous efforts** are needed to inform parents, educators, and health care practitioners of the importance of involving children in reading from the first days of life; of playing with language through nursery rhymes, storybooks, and writing activities; and of helping children understand as early as possible the purpose, wonder, and joy of reading.
- **Parents must be aware** of the importance of vocabulary development and verbal interactions with their children to enhance grammar, syntax, and verbal reasoning.
- **Preschool children** should be encouraged to learn the letters of the alphabet, to discriminate letters from one another, to print letters, and to attempt to spell words that they hear.
- **Reading aloud to children** is an important activity for language development. Yet, reading to children is not a necessary or sufficient means to teaching reading skills.
- **The ability to read** requires different types of skills that, for many children, must be acquired through direct and informed instruction provided by properly trained teachers.

AN INTEGRATED APPROACH TO LANGUAGE ARTS AS A WAY OF LIFE

Language is always singled out as the most distinctively *human* activity, one that simultaneously is social, intelligent, complex, and emotional. It is our most multi-purpose tool for civilization and human learning. Language exists in all cultures.

Dr. E. Boyer, in a landmark report published by the Carnegie Foundation, concluded that the research evidence is compelling that language may be the single most important factor in children's success in school. He stated unequivocally that language is the key to learning. For those children who fail to develop adequate speech and language skills in the first years of life, the risk of reading difficulties is increased up to sixfold. In a national survey, kindergarten teachers reported that "deficiency in language" most restricted children's school readiness.

Numerous studies document the centrality of the home language environment to children's language learning and development. Research confirms that parents who encourage their children's verbal expression and comprehension and stimulate their children's language skills through their own speech, explanations, verbal prompts and queries, and elaboration of what their children say have children whose language is more advanced. Their language ability is not simply attributable to "good genes." Rather, parents who receive professional instruction and guidance in improving their language interactions with their young children show improvements in their parenting behavior. This directly benefits their children, whose language growth is significantly improved. These findings hold true even for children who are already delayed or who are at risk for delay because of family circumstances.

Listening, speaking, reading, and writing will open many doors for your child. These skills will provide you and your child with countless hours of enjoyment and learning together. Enrich your family's life, your child's development, and your own lifelong learning by bringing the language arts into your everyday life.

CHAPTER 11

THE SOCIAL SIDE OF SCHOOL

How social skills complement academic achievement. Teaching your child good behavior. Helping your child choose and make good friends. Fostering social success in school. Independence and respect for authority. The importance of parents' social skills in school.

WE KNOW OF NO ASPECT OF A CHILD'S DEVELOPMENT THAT MATTERS MORE IN THE LONG RUN THAN SOCIAL SKILLS. BEING ADEPT IN EVERYDAY SITUATIONS WITH OTHERS LEADS TO OPPORTUNITIES AND ENJOYMENT IN LIFE, AND IS THE FOUNDATION FOR THE CONNECTEDNESS THAT DEFINES OUR SOCIETY. FROM OUR FRIENDSHIPS AND LIFELONG PARTNERSHIPS TO RELATIONSHIPS WITH CO-WORKERS AND THE COMMUNITY, SOCIAL SKILLS MATTER ENORMOUSLY.

The transition-to-school period — from ages three to eight — is one of remarkable progress in social competence, social understanding, and independence. During this time adults work vigorously to "socialize" young children by guiding and encouraging them in the social ways of the world.

Thinking and reasoning are part of social development, as are good emotional self-regulation, politeness, and belief in one's self-worth. In school, your child will acquire and practice these social skills.

Children's temperament influences their social behavior, but their temperament is not set in stone. A great deal of social and emotional competence is learned. How you encourage and teach your child about the social and emotional side of school will make a big difference. It will influence your child's school adjustment and academic progress as well as his adaptation to all life situations.

NEW TIMES, NEW FOCUS

What constitutes socially engaging and well-mannered behavior in children has shifted over time. So has what parents teach young children about behavior.

In past generations, much of parents' socialization efforts focused on preventing or eliminating negative behavior in their young children. They focused less on teaching positive social behavior, social reasoning, and social problem-solving. Today, more teachers and parents recognize that young children can be successfully encouraged to use their thinking, feeling, and planning skills to great advantage in the social arena.

Even today there is great variation in how and what children are taught. Not all families and teachers encourage the same social behaviors from children at a given age because of cultural, geographic, or inter-generational differences, as well as personal values and beliefs. Families vary in their emphasis on such things as sensitivity to others, competitiveness, leadership, social conformity, good manners, and the balance of social interdependence and personal independence.

Studies also show that parents often repeat what their parents did, with some modifications to reflect "the changing times." As a result, a great deal of social teaching may occur without conscious thought or planning.

Finally, the usefulness of social skills depends on the child's situation. "Acceptable" behavior varies based on such factors as the safety of a child's neighborhood and whether the child travels, goes to concerts, or attends religious services.

There is no neat chart of what to expect in the growth of children's social competence. However, the scientific literature identifies typical stages in children's social development. This is especially true of children's understanding of moral or ethical reasoning — knowing the difference between right and wrong and acting on that knowledge.

WHAT IS SOCIAL INTELLIGENCE?

The concept of "social intelligence" is not new. There has long been widespread recognition of differences in people's social abilities. But recent books on "emotional intelligence" — a term made popular by Daniel Goleman in his books on the subject— have captured widespread public attention about the importance of social and emotional skills in life.

Clearly the quality of our lives is related to other people. Many of the world's most serious troubles reflect an inability to anticipate and resolve conflicts. Ending the harm and destruction wrought by human divisiveness, territoriality, stereotyping, extreme competition, and social control is paramount.

On the positive side, social and emotional skills greatly enhance the chances for success in almost every sphere of life. But what are the components of social and emotional intelligence?

Despite differences in what constitutes optimal social behavior, some widely held values are at the heart of a democracy. These include acceptance, tolerance, cooperation, and striving for the common good. Our country's diverse religious heritage has contributed to these values. That so many people attend regular worship services or participate in some form of ethical endeavor shows a strong desire to be uplifted and to live a life that fulfills our ideals.

The following social qualities are central to most religious and humanitarian belief systems. These also are emphasized in several major new initiatives in the elementary school grades to promote positive social behavior:

- **Concern for the safety and well-being of others (not just oneself)**
- **Accepting responsibility for one's own behavior**
- **Being helpful to others, especially those in need**
- **Understanding others and their feelings**

- **Being able to resolve conflicts effectively**
- **Sharing**
- **Having strong social connections to family and to school**
- **Willingness to make amends and strive for social harmony.**

The limited social skills of young children often hinder their ability to anticipate, avoid, or remedy social problems. Yet growth in these skills is essential for children to choose good friends, to build lasting, enjoyable relationships, and to get along well with teachers.

TEACHING YOUR CHILD SOCIAL BEHAVIOR

Parents are children's primary teachers of socially acceptable behavior. Children learn a lot through observation, imitation, and role-playing. Every great philosophy and religion teaches compassion and patience. Good advice for parents. They also emphasize that we "practice what we preach" to set an example. This, too, is sound advice. Allow your children to see your acts of kindness, respect, and generosity.

Children's social learning through observation extends to the media, not just to their direct personal experiences. Hence the intense national concern about children's TV viewing, which exposes them to violence, rudeness, exploitation, greed, and crude language. Science again backs popular opinion. The more TV children watch, the more their social behavior is negatively affected. Therefore, it is surprising that so many parents allow young children to watch so much television unsupervised. Do you monitor what your child sees? Do you watch shows together? When your child sees behavior on TV that you would find unacceptable, how does your child learn your views?

Children also learn about social behavior in books. Reading to children accomplishes more than teaching them to read. They learn valuable lessons in stories, biographies, poems, and songs. Heroes can be role models. Many books for young children deal with acceptance, caring, giving, and cooperation. These include children's classics and new books that make these themes relevant to young children's everyday lives. Choose books that help you teach good values and behavior to your child.

EVERYONE CAN HELP WITH SOCIAL BEHAVIOR

Children count on their parents to be "there for them" when they are in school. In the early years parents may not think to help their children connect to others regarding school work or learning. Given the increased demands on parents to be involved in their children's education, parents should consider taking advantage of the talents and experience of relatives and friends. They can play key roles in helping your child to learn and succeed in school. For example:

- **Special topics**: If your child is studying a special topic, invite others to talk or to read to her about it. This helps her realize that others know about and can help with the subjects she learns in school. Your child is likely to share something impressive with others that she has learned, giving her a sense of mastery over information, and an understanding that she is not always "way behind" adults in her knowledge. Teaching is a wonderful activity for children, too.
- **Information games:** Play information games, such as the children's version of Trivial Pursuit. You may be surprised at how much your child already knows about dinosaurs, cartoons, fairy tales, the planets, American history, and the weather. Such games also can be a fun way to "teach" without worksheets or lectures. Invite friends and relatives to join in. Helpful hint: To level the playing field, make adults give two correct answers in a row instead of one.
- **Special events:** Include relatives and friends in special school events. Most parents turn to these people for school fund-raising to buy gift wrap, candy, magazines, or raffle tickets. But remember to include them in special school performances, fairs, open houses, holiday parties, field trips, and other events. With school permission, consider inviting friends or relatives to visit the class-

room to read or speak about their work or hobby, especially if the topic is relevant to something being taught:

- Your mother, the surgeon, to do a demonstration when the class studies the human body.
- Your uncle to teach about a traditional or ethnic food when the class is studying the appropriate culture.
- Your next-door neighbor, who illustrates children's books, to talk about how books are made, from the author's idea to final printing.
- The local pet-shop owner may be willing to give a presentation on "prehistoric" reptiles that are alive today.

- **Religious and ethical teaching:** These can be important forces to promote your child's well-being, and they need to be considered in school and social choices. Children need nurturing that is compatible with the family's core values.

  Some families choose home schooling or religious-based instruction to ensure that schooling and values work together. Other families may choose a religious-affiliated school for academic or other excellence, even if the school's denomination differs from the family's beliefs. Most families choose secular schools, confident that they can provide the appropriate religious or spiritual values to complement their child's schooling.

  Consider the many ways that social and personal well-being can be strengthened. Ideally your child will be well-grounded in what represents "good" and will strive comfortably toward that goal.

- **The "good old school days."** Stories of school when you or your parents were students are a natural way to connect your child with others about going to school. Encourage relatives and friends to tell about their school experiences. It's reassuring to children to hear that happy, well-adjusted adults had their ups and downs as students. Most adults like to remember their early years in school – a wonderful or horrid teacher, or something they loved or hated learning, or what embarrassed or delighted them. These memories can make for enjoyable and revealing dinner conversations, ones that a young child will want to join.

By connecting your child to the community, you open up the learning process. Your child won't see school as a closed or isolated system. Moreover, when your relatives and friends have a personal connection to what is happening in your child's school, they will likely get more than the perfunctory "OK" that children give to the routine query, "So how's school going?"

CONFORMITY: THE PROS AND CONS

Like it or not, school will make conformity an issue. Children will make social comparisons in school. They will notice what other children do, say, wear, eat, and play with.

Most children want a certain amount of social conformity. Yet they also take pride in some individuality. For many years, your child will feel the tension of wanting to conform versus wanting to be distinctive.

Parents vary greatly on the continuum from highly conforming to non-conforming. Wide variations in degree of conformity work fine. However, the extremes can lead to social disarray. Totalitarian rule has led to untold human suffering. Total disregard for others can lead to chaos and intolerable incivility.

In the early elementary school years, conformity is not likely to be a serious issue. Children's increasing self-consciousness might make them reluctant to stand out. For example, the day after losing two front teeth, a child may not want to go to school or smile. Similarly, when there is a new fad for a certain type of pencil, T-shirt, backpack, or music, your child is almost certain to want it.

Parents can commiserate with other parents, but fads have always been a part of social life. Before condemning your child's impressionability, check out how much you continue to be influenced by new fads. Even counter-culture and non-conforming individuals have been proven to have their version of conformity — it's just not to the mainstream!

By the middle school years, a child's moral reasoning is more sophisticated and complex, but peer pressure mounts. There will be many opportunities to teach the importance of making independent choices guided by one's own values.

Most parents need to adjust their own standards about their children's social behavior. Some new words or mannerisms may at first seem questionable. Some will be innocent and not worth trying to change. Others will warrant a vigorous effort to curtail. The best advice: remember your own childhood and the flux of conformity. Overly strict parents can contribute to backlash; overly lax parents can allow children to acquire harmful habits.

Teachers also differ in the level of classroom conformity they want. In the event of extremes, be pro-active. Don't assume things will get better, particularly if the teacher's requirements are seriously at odds with your priorities.

Otherwise, talk with your child about why the teacher wants children to be so much alike or doesn't care if children do things differently. Examples of differences in teacher expectations your child may encounter from year to year:

- **All children must use the same manner of address when speaking to the teacher OR there is no prescribed manner of teacher address as long as children speak considerately.**
- **Children always must raise their hands and be called on before speaking OR only in some situations.**
- **When waiting in line, children must be quiet and orderly OR just reasonably well-behaved.**

Many schools have adopted common expectations, particularly for behavior in public places, such as the lunchroom, auditorium, hallways, and the playground. Some schools have a "hands to yourself" policy at all times. Others do not. Some strictly enforce quiet rules. Others are more casual. Some emphasize cooperative learning and group projects. Overall, the variety of different social expectations and opportunities will be a plus. But your child may need help adjusting to different teachers and rules, especially in the first few years.

FRIENDS: MAKING, KEEPING, AND SOMETIMES GETTING RID OF THEM

In the early years of elementary school, your child's friendship skills will grow tremendously. This reflects his advances in thinking and reasoning as well as increased opportunities for making friends.

Children are aware of the social skills and social differences among classmates. They notice who is good at leading activities, who has good ideas for fun things to do, who is agreeable and cooperative, who is shy, who has trouble controlling anger or frustration, and who is good at talking and explaining. In the early elementary school years, there is much fluidity in who plays with whom and the nature of friendships. Recent scientific findings about young children's friendship patterns and skills include:

- **What makes a friend:** Even four- to seven-year-olds have their own ideas about what things help turn children into friends. These include engaging in common activities, showing affection, sharing, helping, and being supportive. They also know that propinquity makes a difference. Physical features, such as attractiveness and size, are more influential in younger children's choices of friends. As children become older, emotional understanding and caring are considered more important qualities for a friendship.

- **Shyness and aggression:** Children who are not overly shy or overly aggressive are preferred most as friends.

- **Attraction:** The most important behaviors that attract young children to others are smiling and laughing a lot, sharing, and taking turns.

- **Language skills:** Children who make and have good friends in these early years tend to have good speaking skills, enabling them to tell others what they like and dislike.

- **Reciprocity:** Children with positive friendships are especially likely to show reciprocity. They can lead and follow (not just one or the other), and they can take turns without adult prompting.

- **Popular children:** Children who are good at making friends and who become socially popular tend to come from families with:
  - Warm, secure early mother–child attachment.
  - Warm and supportive fathers.
  - Parents who use reason to guide their children's behavior.
  - Parents who offer frequent praise for good behavior.
- **Less popular children:** Children who have difficulty making and keeping friends are more likely to come from authoritarian families that use physical punishment and withdrawal of privileges as strategies to guide and control their children's behavior. These children tend to use aggression and overly assertive behavior, to understand less about the reasons for certain social behavior, and not to understand the feelings of others. Their reliance on external control, rather than internal self-regulation, takes a social toll on their competencies in situations that require ongoing judgment, monitoring, and cooperation.
- **Play behavior:** Children's play behavior includes many components, some solitary, some parallel or compatible with others, and some indicative of joint endeavor. Children's play evolves in a typical pattern:
  - ***Stage 1:*** More solitary, independent play with objects.
  - ***Stage 2:*** Engaging in associative and parallel play with some joint use of the same toys or doing the same things alongside another child.
  - ***Stage 3:*** Cooperative, organized play involving understanding the rules, taking different roles, and negotiating and resolving deviations from the rules or the group. These skills will not be perfected in an eight-year-old, but you will see remarkable advances in the first few years in school. In school-based activities, such as physical education, music, and art, as well as in the primary classroom, there are many chances to practice and refine group participation under responsible adult supervision. Organized sports and backyard or park-based play are other great ways to provide group activities important for children's social development.

Parents are important social negotiators for their young children. The opportunities to play safely and constructively in the yard or street are fewer than a generation ago. Further, some families live where there are not many age mates nearby. Think of ways to maximize your child's opportunities for developing friendships outside the school day. Also help your child cultivate several friendships with children in the same classroom. This gives them a common base for shared experiences, and it reinforces continuities between school and home life.

Friendships need time and in-person experiences. But even young children can use the telephone, e-mail, and regular mail to stay in touch with friends.

In different communities, parents follow somewhat different age guidelines about when to have friends spend the night or join them on family forays into the community. To some extent, these are arbitrary. However, younger children require closer adult supervision and more assistance with the everyday negotiations. Trust your judgment and experiment slowly with how much time friends should spend together. A general rule of thumb: shorter periods with lots of positive exchanges, and not much time for children to get tired, hungry, or irritable is best. You may need to be prepared for children fussing that they want to be together longer — from begging "please, just a little longer!" to resistance at being separated — but this is better than being together too long.

By first grade, children strongly prefer playing with children of the same gender. This will last for a long time. There will be exceptions, of course. Children will confess, often to parents, that there is a child of the opposite gender who is really different and who is "nice" or "OK," usually adding "not like all the other boys [or girls]!" This gender preference appears to emerge even among children whose parents avoided stereotyping boys and girls. While there are many activities enjoyed by both genders, boys and girls often differ in some activities that they prefer and in the vigor of their play.

Most of your child's experiences with friends and classmates are likely to be positive. Nonetheless, some cases may require your guidance or intervention:

- **Over-eager friends:** Popular children can attract too much attention from some children. A good response from the popular child is to explain that "I like spending time with you, but I also like to be with lots of my other friends, too." The over-eager child should be encouraged through teaching and play dates to make lots of friends and not to concentrate on just one or two children.

- **Questionable friends:** If your child is spending time with children whose behavior differs from your standards, guide your child into new relationships through play dates and special events. It's OK to mention the behavior you don't like in a questionable friend, or to ask your child how she feels about that behavior. Be careful not to condemn the child or strictly forbid any contact, however.
- **Problems at school:** Bullying behavior in some children can emerge as early as the first or second grade. Such behavior is readily apparent at school, and teachers and other school staff are usually vigorous in addressing it. They may meet with the child's parents to develop a plan to prevent bullying or other unacceptable behavior. Sometimes parents of children who are "victims" may be contacted as well. If problems persist outside school, talk with other parents and be sure to prevent your child from continued exposure to unacceptable behavior or abuse from another child.

RESPECT AND APPRECIATION FOR AUTHORITY

Do children need to look up to their teachers? Emphatically, yes! Do they need to respect their teachers? When the teacher's behavior has earned this, yes! Fortunately, most teachers do not want authoritarian respect devoid of content. Teachers work in the classroom to create a mutual respect, especially for the different roles that students and teachers fulfill.

In the classroom, there is no doubt that the teacher is in charge. But teachers often turn over part of the day to the children when they can initiate and guide their activities. Only part of the day is spent in whole-class activities led by a teacher.

Many classrooms have learning and activity centers designed for independent activity. These are found from kindergarten through third grade classrooms. This type of classroom environment is new to many parents. It certainly isn't the desks-in-a-row arrangement they may have had.

Have the rules for respecting authority also changed along with classroom arrangement? In some ways they have, because a flexible arrangement affords more types of teacher–student interaction than does a highly structured classroom. Thus, very young students need to become skilled in approaching their teacher, not just in responding to what a teacher asks. They also need to show respect for the teacher in more ways than before.

For instance, when children are instructed to work cooperatively in small groups not under the teacher's immediate supervision, they show their respect by staying with the task and helping classmates accomplish the goal at hand. This form of respect looks quite different from just saying, "Yes, ma'am," and sitting quietly for as long as possible.

Classroom guidelines for good social behavior emphasize respect for other students as well as the teacher. The word "respect" may or may not be used. What counts is that children know that their behavior reflects important feelings and values.

Most children show the best type of respect spontaneously when *they* are treated respectfully. Polite teachers usually have the most polite students. Children learn from their teacher's behavior, just as they do from their parents' behavior.

Parents may wonder whether they need to teach their child to show respect in the classroom for the teacher, or to show respect to other personnel at the school. In general, yes. But the advice to former generations to comply *without question* with whatever a teacher or principal asks is no longer considered sound advice. Even young children are expected to be active thinkers. They should ask for clarification rather than blindly follow instructions they do not understand. And they certainly should be taught to refuse to do anything that would compromise their physical well-being, especially involving inappropriate physical or sexual contact.

Instead, parents should encourage children to show respect in the following ways:

- **Be attentive when teachers or other adults speak to them.**

- **Ask questions if they do not understand an instruction.**
- **Follow the classroom rules with good cheer.**
- **Answer teacher questions with a polite form of address (such as "Yes, Mr. Smith" or "No, Ms. Mary") that is consistent with the local practices (using titles, first or last names, and ma'am or sir).**
- **Express thanks and enjoyment, including "thank you" or complimenting the teacher.**
- **Offer to help the teacher in appropriate ways.**

Collectively, your child's behavior reflects respect. Make sure he knows that it is important to tell teachers when they are doing a good job, and that considerate behavior extends to everyone in the classroom, not just the teacher. If your child is having difficulty, be sure the classroom rules are clear and that your child is not using a form of respect that differs from the teacher's expectations.

A word to parents who were brought up in a family that emphasized immediate, rigid forms of expressing respect for authority: many of today's teachers expect give-and-take in their social exchanges with even young students. If a child appears overly eager to comply, conform, or please all the time, the teacher may be concerned that he is not thinking on his own. Asking questions, as long as they are not excessive, intrusive, or rude, is not considered a challenge or threat to a teacher's authority. Rather, teachers value children's questions and opinions, even when these differ from their own.

PARENTAL SOCIAL SKILLS
(NOT JUST PARENTING SKILLS)

School will greatly expand your child's social network and opportunities to see different ways of coping with social situations — not just your way. This poses some interesting challenges. Parents differ in their social adeptness and tendencies to be shy or outgoing, a leader or a follower, talkative or quiet, and a loner versus a joiner. Parents often become more aware of their tendencies, including strengths and weaknesses, during this period of active socialization on their child's behalf.

School necessitates social skill in negotiating your child's activities. As a result, you will be in more frequent contact with other parents and adults. If you are a loner, or a shy or domineering person, you may find some challenges. Fortunately, your enjoyment of your child's activities is likely to help you deal effectively with the new social demands.

Your warmth, consideration, social creativity, and ability to solve social dilemmas will be closely watched by your child, especially when it affects her life. Your behavior will be on public display, as is your child's for most of the day.

Parents' own social skills may influence who wants to be friends with your child. Children much prefer to spend time with friends who have positive, fun, and understanding parents. They may avoid becoming friends with a child whose parents are disinterested, or unpleasant. You don't need to abdicate your parent role around your child's friends. Rather, use your best parenting skills and explain things to your child's friends and their parents so you can agree ahead of time about important matters that are likely to arise.

Taking time to be extra nice or extra fun can be useful with a special activity in a social context. Indeed, your social skills are likely to be noticed most.

THE LASTING REWARDS OF GOOD SOCIALIZATION

The rewards of good social skills last a lifetime, but they have tangible benefits right from the start. The more your child and other children enjoy one another, the more pleasurable their school experience is likely to be. The more your child enjoys school, the more likely that she will succeed in school. Notice and cherish your child's emerging social competencies as much as you do the academic ones. Social giftedness, like academic giftedness, is not simply a genetic or innate quality unrelated to life experiences. To the contrary, many of your child's social skills will be learned, practiced, and refined over the months and years ahead. The quantity and quality of your child's social learning will make a big difference. Your teaching and examples over these transition-to-school years will make a great deal of difference to your child's success in school and in the years to come.

CHAPTER 12

YOUR UNIQUE CHILD

Nurturing your child's individuality. Identifying learning and other disorders as well as special interests and talents. The importance of teaching to your child's strengths. Encouraging your child's resilience. Taking advantage of opportunities for typically-developing children. Getting support for special needs and talents in the school setting.

EACH CHILD IS UNIQUE. THE GREAT EDUCATIONAL PHILOSOPHERS ALL AGREE ON THIS POINT. WHAT WORKS BEST FOR ONE CHILD MAY NOT WORK AS WELL FOR ANOTHER. MOREOVER, YOUR CHILD CHANGES FROM YEAR TO YEAR, EVEN HOUR TO HOUR.

A great education involves continuing adjustment in give-and-take, trial and error, excitement and patience, novelty and repetition, encouragement and discouragement, praise and criticism, creativity and conformity. A good teacher adjusts to each child's individuality, just as a good student adjusts to the teacher's style.

In the early elementary school years, children are closely observed by teachers and eager parents. Most children understand the new demands for learning in school. They recognize that opportunities for failure abound, even when teachers and parents focus on the positive. They also know that they are in a fish bowl where their performance will be compared to that of others.

Many children who enter school with no diagnosed learning, behavioral, sensory, motor, or emotional problems will behave in a way that raises suspicions about the possibility of some "exceptionality," such as attention deficit disorders, learning disabilities, giftedness. These are detected, in part, because of the new demands for evidence of increasingly mature social and emotional behavior, as well as growing demand for proof of academic achievement. This is a tall order.

If questions are raised about your child, do not take this as a sign of failure or of doom. Checking into the factors that may account for your child's differences in school adjustment does not mean that your child will not or cannot be successful in school. In fact, some children's exceptionalities reflect very high levels of performance. Just as often, there are modest differences, and adjustments can be made to improve a child's learning.

This chapter is about individuality — not just problems. Even the so-called "average" or "in between" child is now described by some as representing a special type of school child, one who is neither highly talented nor seriously challenged! We are not endorsing a problem-oriented or pathological view of young students. Instead, we see early identification of problems as evidence that no two children are alike. Our philosophy, briefly stated, is this:

Strategic investments to minimize problems and maximize talents is an effective way to celebrate individuality and to enhance the next generation. Probably all children have very real biological and behavioral propensities that make certain things easier or harder for them to do or grasp compared to other children. The more parents and educators know about and can use an individual child's strengths in the educational process, the better. Many problems will not become bigger problems if they are detected and acted upon early. Indeed, they may lessen or disappear. Just as important, early detection of each child's strengths, talents, and interests warrants attention – at least comparable to the time and effort spent diagnosing and treating problems.

EARLY DIAGNOSIS AND TREATMENT

Most problems related to school are detected by teachers. They notice something that falls outside the normal range. Or, parents may realize in talking and working with their child that something is thwarting their child's progress or enthusiasm. Hopefully, parents and teachers talk or exchange notes and agree on a next step. If the problem is not resolved, additional consultation is sought.

This process is effective for the vast majority of young children. Many early adjustment problems are brief, mild, and easy to resolve with collaboration among the teacher, the parents, and the child.

However, a small percentage of children have significant, unanticipated difficulties in their early years of schooling. There can be many reasons. For these more serious challenges, there are useful lessons in the experiences of other families.

The four most important lessons revealed to us in our 30 years of conducting research, designing and evaluating education and treatment programs, and providing consultation and guidance to parents and schools:

1. **Parent perseverance and advocacy on behalf of their children can accomplish wonders!** Children with significant differences in their development or early adjustment to school often have very positive outcomes because of the dedication, investigative ability, intuition, and support of parents who were convinced that things could get a lot better.

2. **Diagnosis and treatment of children's exceptionalities continues to evolve; often there is more than one opinion or approach.** There is substantial professional difference of opinion regarding diagnosis and treatment of children's exceptionalities. This means that many children with serious problems may receive different diagnoses, different recommendations for clinical and educational interventions, and different prognoses for success. This is due to the evolving knowledge about child development and to differences among professionals about the causes of many childhood difficulties.

   Differences of opinion among "experts" can be upsetting to parents. But they also may be an advantage, especially when differing views offer multiple avenues for treatment. Do not hesitate to seek multiple opinions when it comes to understanding your child's individuality. This applies to choosing strategies or interventions to improve your child's education. Select the most promising, monitor your child's progress, and adjust accordingly. If progress is not optimal, consider other options, including a combination of approaches. Be sure to share the results with all key players so they may learn from your child's experience.

3. **Children's resilience to adversity is important and can be enhanced by caring adults.** Children whose development places them at extremes (such as being very high or low in scholastic skills, very mature or immature socially or physically, developmentally disabled, or chronically ill) are more likely to encounter difficulties in their school adjustment. In the process, they may acquire a "resilience" or "survival skills" that will help them immensely.

   Children are not born with or without this quality of resilience. Rather, resilience develops over time and adults can actively promote coping skills in children so that they can deal better with difficulties, including frustration, fears, disappointment, rejection, boredom, insensitivity of others, or personality conflicts.

4. **Adults other than parents can have a powerful effect in enhancing a child's life course.** Time and again, we have observed how one committed person can step up and fulfill a much-needed benefactor role, altering the course of a child's life, or the family's, when school-related problems arise. Most often, these are talented, dedicated, and effective teachers. There also may be a physical education coach, music teacher, principal, school librarian, or counselor who really cares about your child. Adults outside the school, such as a Sunday School teacher, classroom volunteer, relative, family friend, or neighbor, can also provide valuable insights or solutions.

The success stories of many children who start school under strained conditions are a tribute to human adaptability. A remarkable number of children have succeeded far beyond what anyone thought possible. When each child's individuality is accepted, understood, valued, and treated, amazing outcomes have been realized.

WHAT IS INDIVIDUALITY?

Individuality represents the summary profile of a child at any point in time — the combination of traits, abilities, propensities, styles, interests, and motivations that makes each of us unique. Individuality is apparent at birth. But it is shaped by life's experiences. As such, it reflects the past and contributes to the future. Everyone has it, yet we also share many similarities. Individuality can be the source of grief or confusion when a child does not fit easily into conventional modes, but it also is responsible for great joys, achievements, and contributions.

Over the years, there have been vigorous efforts to measure and explain individual differences among children. None totally has achieved this. The task may be too monumental. Or perhaps individuality transcends classification.

Educators and child specialists too often categorize children by twos — normal or abnormal, healthy or sick, well-adjusted or poorly adjusted, fit for regular education or needing special education. Yet we know of no child who does not have some exceptionalities worthy of note and action. Further, we know of no child who does not periodically encounter some ups and downs at school.

Responsible adults need to keep things in perspective. But telling a child "It's not that important" is seldom any consolation to children who feel terrible about something.

FEDERAL MANDATES AND SPECIAL EDUCATION

Many parents are surprised to learn that about 10 percent of all children nationwide are in special education. In kindergarten, however, these numbers are much lower and vary depending on where a family lives.

Federal law now mandates that schools decide which children need special education. Detailed guidelines govern determination of need, classification, and decisions about educational interventions and supports. For very young children with problems detected before the age of five, free and appropriate educational services must be available starting at age three. Most states provide such services even earlier, from birth through age two.

What about our country's most talented and capable children? Are they included in special education, too? It varies. There is no federal assistance for children who are academic high achievers, much less for children who show extraordinary talent in music, dance, sports, or leadership. Many schools offer some locally funded academic enrichment or accelerated learning programs. Specialists in these areas of education cite ample research evidence showing that scholastically gifted children perform much better when they are appropriately challenged rather than left in typical classrooms without extra supports.

Some children who enter school with a diagnosed problem may have it disappear in later years; for others, a trouble-free start in school may be jolted later when certain types of academic or social demands are made, or when there is a poor fit between a child's learning style or expression and that of the teachers or school.

PARENTS WHO SUCCEED AGAINST THE ODDS

This section could become a book in its own right. The number of children and families we have seen who were transformed through parents' heroic efforts is astounding. Such success stories are not new. There have always been exceptional parents. But we think the number of parents who take things into their own hands and forge educational partnerships with teachers and clinicians is higher than ever. What these success stories have in common is parents' certainty that things had to be improved for their child to have a good outcome in school and in life.

There is no formula for success. Perseverance is not enough by itself, but it is essential. We have seen numerous instances of parents who took charge of the situation, often providing extra supports to their child, even as they were trying to figure out what to do. Sometimes these parents encountered cruel criticisms from other parents and educators, who implied that they evidenced an unwillingness to accept their child or were in denial about realistic options.

The parents we know who accomplished their "Mission: Impossible" also have been excellent problem-solvers. They started by learning all they could about their child's condition. Some childhood conditions that lead parents to become active information-seekers are:

- **Childhood autism or autistic-like disorders**
- **Learning disabilities that manifest themselves when a child shows tremendous unevenness in performance in different areas**
- **Attention deficit problems (including the older labels of hyperactivity and minimal brain dysfunction)**

- **Mild mental retardation or "borderline intelligence" with no known cause**
- **Social-emotional disturbances, especially those that erupt in school but are not apparent at home.**

Some parents take up the cause when they suspect that their "just average" child could learn at higher levels. For these parents, there are hundreds of articles in scientific and clinical journals, and a staggering array of books that offer help. Chatrooms on the Internet can be useful to parents who seek advice and support from others as well.

Opportunities for idea-sharing are great, but so are the pitfalls, especially when a child's symptoms do not fit the typical pattern for a given disorder. What works for one person may not for others. Further, many parents become vulnerable in their hope or desperation to find solutions. They may get sidetracked by promises of "quick fixes," such as unproven therapies using nutrition, mysticism, and expensive specialized treatments.

Sorting through it all is just part of parents' detective work. Parents who are successful bring a healthy dose of skepticism to their search. If they already have read much, they know that many promising treatments have not proven effective for most children. They also quickly learn that the experts don't agree on the basics, such as the signs that differentiate children with one condition from those with a closely related one. The most effective parent advocates we have known remain open in their search for solutions, yet they do not fail to act simply because there is no agreed-upon solution.

Besides this vigorous hunt for information, many parents show a remarkable acceptance of their child, even as they strive to minimize problems and to accentuate their child's strengths. Their attitude serves as a buffer for the child. It also is conveyed to teachers and other specialists, who may become more dedicated in their efforts on the child's behalf.

Parents' good social skills come into play here, as well. Before giving up on a teacher, school, or school system, parents need to be as diplomatic as possible in enlisting the support of those who are instrumental in their child's well-being. Frustrated, disappointed, or angry parents can drive away the very people who can help. Persistence, eagerness, and conviction are acceptable qualities. Rage, attacks, accusations, and unwillingness to listen are not helpful. Above all, many solutions reflect a parent's strong intuition that something was awry and could be changed. Dramatic examples we have seen include:

- **Artistic strengths.** A mother who knew her bright six-year-old would learn to read "in her own time" and thus home-schooled her until she became interested in reading. This child had spent a few weeks in a first-grade classroom in "one of the best public elementary schools." But the classroom was very large (more than 30 students), had a teacher fresh out of college who was highly regimented, not child-oriented, and placed a huge emphasis on learning to read. During the year of home schooling, this mother taught to her daughter's strengths: her love of music and the arts. Throughout the year they took two field trips each week (their city was filled with cultural opportunities as well as lots of natural wonders). The mother played phonics games and read a lot to her daughter. But she did not push independent reading. Instead, she remained patient until her daughter showed an interest in reading at age eight. At that time, the family moved to another city where an ideal school option was found – a private school with no more than eight children per class. During the early years when this student was not ready to read, her love of music and the arts was cultivated by her mother and eventually at a specialized high school for the performing arts. Today she is earning high marks in college and pursuing a career in the performing arts.
- **Slow or not?** Parents who refused to allow their nine-year-old son – their only child – to be tested by the school for suspected "mild mental retardation," because they did not want their son to have this label even if he did have a below-average IQ score. They moved their child to a fairly structured, but very warm parochial school and did not bring their child's prior school records to the new school. They asked the sisters to allow them to help their son with extra "at-home" materials. They purchased a duplicate set of textbooks and invested many hours helping their son succeed in the new school environment. His early problems with fine motor coordination disappeared by adolescence, when he became an accomplished athlete. They made a deal that he keep good grades to play sports – and he did. He has since graduated from a well-known, competitive college and is a very successful, well-adjusted adult. (To this day, he has never been told this story.)

- **Autism.** Parents who were highly knowledgeable about their son's condition of autism, but who would not settle for the types of support that one public school offered. These supports were not negligible, but they fell below what the parents thought was possible and necessary to improve their son's learning and overall adjustment. After they exhausted all possibilities with the first school system, they moved to another school district. Their son now spends time in a mainstreamed classroom, receives ample individualized support, and has a home-based program, partly paid for by Medicaid. The child and his parents are happier than they've ever been.

- **Advanced learner.** Parents of an academically advanced child were concerned by her persistent ailments, from stomach aches to headaches. The child's pediatrician diagnosed the ailments as stress-related, but the parents were unable to identify a source of stress at home or school. The child was attending an excellent private school with an outstanding program for advanced children, and her grades were superior. However, the parents' concern over her discomfort led them reluctantly to move her to the local public school. The parents gave the new school no indication of their daughter's advanced learning capabilities. The results were astonishing. Their daughter's physical ailments ceased immediately. She soared to the top of the class. The school subsequently identified her as advanced and provided additional supports to keep her challenged.

- **A better fit.** A stepmother who initiated the search for a school where her stepson could feel better socially and academically. This was difficult at first because he was not failing and had no serious problems. Also, their suburban school district was tops in the state; the school thought the parents were being "pushy"; and teachers officially rated the student as progressing well, even though the student knew he was not, and the teacher confirmed this "off the record." The most pressing problem was a steady decline in the child's self-esteem, happiness, and friendships. When the stepmother found a private school with very small classes, high academic expectations, and experience with children who "fell between the cracks," the parents agreed to give it a try. Within less than a year at the new school, this student was transformed. He became interested in reading, even for pleasure (reading had never been a favorite subject before). He earned straight As (meaningful, not inflated grades), made new friends, and resumed smiling and laughing.

- **Exceptional intelligence.** Highly accomplished parents who had already raised three academically bright children faced an unexpected challenge with their fourth child, whose accelerated intellectual development was truly "off the charts." She did not adjust well to the school where her siblings had thrived, and no one knew why. When the parents suggested to the school that their daughter was not being adequately stimulated intellectually, the school resisted and gave a variety of other reasons for her unremarkable progress and increasing detachment from school. These parents, too, began a search for a school that would meet their child's needs. Within the first week at a new school with all high achievers, their young daughter came home filled with glee and excitement: "I never knew there were other children like me!" In this new social situation, with true peers, her learning and her social-emotional adjustment flourished, immediately. She later entered college very early (at the age of 14), earned a Ph.D. eight years later, subsequently has held several very different, interesting jobs, and is the mother of two children herself.

All of these examples of parental determination have a common theme. Their children were in school systems considered among the best. Yet the schools did not recognize or could not accommodate the parents' requests for individualization. In each case, the solutions involved finding the right school, including home schooling. None of these families were wealthy, but all had incomes and education above the national average. In all of these families, at least one parent had been trained as a teacher or was in a specialty field related to child development. Further, their solutions required much thought and deliberation, as well as time to enact. In the process, the parents were perceived as overly concerned, even neurotic, demanding, or highly critical. In the end, each family benefitted immensely from its choice and strategic investment in the child's education. One wonders what might have happened had they settled for what their child's "good" school had offered!

Are all successful solutions this costly and time-consuming? Not always. However, in our experience, easier solutions typically concern issues that are more restricted in scope. Many involve switching to another teacher's classroom, even in the middle of the year (something schools do reluctantly and usually only under parental pressure). For the families described above, a poor education would have taken a pervasive, negative toll on their child — improper labeling as "reading disordered," "dull," or "mentally retarded"; social isolation and out-of-control behavior; depression and withdrawal from academic challenges due to low self-esteem; and boredom and a sense of being so different that social-emotional consequences were likely.

Sadly, we know scores of parents and students who survived one or two really bad years and now regret the periods of unhappiness they endured. We encourage parents to be vigilant in observing their eager-to-learn child and what happens during these first few years in school.

When schools will not or cannot change quickly to help your child, be brave and consider finding a good match elsewhere. This is not spoiling or babying your child. A five- to eight-year-old cannot endure or ignore a year or more of a poorly matched education, a difficult or incompetent teacher, or a school environment that does not readily accommodate the child's individuality. The risk of negative consequences is simply too high. Your child will lose much valuable learning time, which is difficult to make up later, and may suffer in terms of emotional well-being, friendship patterns, and a distrust or dislike of teachers, schools, and themselves.

TEACHING TO STRENGTHS

Teaching to strengths is a philosophical approach using optimism and awareness of children's individuality. It is not a formal program or instructional method — at least not yet. There is no one way to do this, but there are many examples of teachers and schools that emphasize this as a theme.

What does "teach to strengths" mean and how can you promote it? Three important ingredients are:

- **Your child's strengths be identified by parents and teachers.**
- **Classroom activities be identified that allow your child's strengths to contribute to progress.**

- **Your child spends more of each day engaged in active, enjoyable learning than in activities that engender repeated failure, boredom, or frustration.**

Many parents and educators recognize that not every person needs to be very good at all subjects taught in schools. Many successful, well-adjusted adults are not good in handwriting, spelling, creative writing, drawing, initiating imaginary play, public speaking, listening attentively to others, or being quiet in hallways! All of these skills are emphasized in the first few years of school.

Highly skilled teachers let children know that everyone will not be equally good at all of these things. If a teacher emphasizes an area excessively, and if your child is not progressing well in that area, talk with the teacher about how this is being handled in the classroom. In the "teach-to-strengths" classroom, some children may be allowed to complete tasks in a different way or to spend more time in certain types of learning activities.

Great teachers have an impressive repertoire of ways to teach the same thing. This repertoire means that children with different learning styles and different strengths will:

- **Become interested and stay attentive most of the time**
- **Learn the lesson for knowledge and skills**
- **Be able to express their advances, possibly in different ways.**

Undoubtedly, this is demanding on the teacher. It certainly requires preparation and sensitivity. Furthermore, teachers who receive formal instruction in teaching to strengths become more skilled in this aspect of teaching and classroom management. But the benefits are so obvious that this becomes "a way of life" for good teachers (and for good parents, too).

Examples of adaptations in teaching to children's strengths include:

- **Use of different methods to convey the same information, such as storytelling, demonstration, reasoning, pictorial representation, personalization of the material, and analysis.**

- **Multiple opportunities for children to show signs of how much they are comprehending.**
- **Different ways for children to learn actively, including questioning, direct experience, thinking, reviewing, applying the new skill or information in another situation, imagining, and watching other students before they try something on their own.**
- **Multiple ways of evaluating children's progress in an area, and giving children credit for correctly grasping components of a lesson or activity even if they make mistakes. For example, the math reasoning is correct but the numerical computation was in error, or vice versa; the story had a great beginning, even if some sentences were incomplete; or the show-and-tell was well-organized even if the child giggled a lot or forgot to tell everything.**
- **Having many types of props and materials related to the topic or skill, so that children have different ways of interacting with and reviewing what is being learned. Such materials include pictures, books, music, games that use the skill, computer activities, and physical materials for manipulation.**

All of these examples are useful for parents to consider for children's learning at home. As you work with your child on school-related activities and review the work products she brings home, develop your own "theory" of how she learns best and what her strengths are. Do some experimenting at home with different ways of advancing skills or teaching something new. Does your child learn better, faster, or with more pleasure when you just talk, just do, or just read? Does a combination of techniques work best? How does your child tell you about the new things she has learned at school? By showing you? By telling you? By incorporating new information in a make-believe game or a drawing? As you continue to observe your child's individuality in action and talk with her teacher about her "strengths," you will become more skilled in your home-based teaching.

What if your child has an obvious weakness or disability related to spelling, reading, or handwriting? Should you ignore it and wait patiently until your child shows a greater interest in it? Find ways to compensate for it? The answer: there is no best way for all children. Help your child to recognize these weaknesses or differences and ask what ideas he might have about how to improve things.

For example, an older child may do most or all of his creative and expository writing on the computer, thus compensating for handwriting and spelling problems. In the process, he will learn typing skills and enough about spelling words to get "close" so that the computer's "spell-check" works. Should children with speech impediments be excused from all public speaking? Again, individuality prevails. See what works. Engage your child in finding a solution.

Teaching to strengths does not mean that children do not try to progress in areas that are not their strong suits. Rather, it is a way to ensure that each child's intelligence develops fully and is not thwarted by spending large amounts of time and effort mismatched to the child's strengths. Conventional schooling has disproportionately focused on intellectual activities characterized by analytical reasoning, use of abstract signs and symbols, and memorization. Such an education often ignores or excludes creative and practical areas of competence, and frequently fails to take into account the emerging and

THE MULTI-FACETED NATURE OF INTELLIGENCE: NEW THEORETICAL PERSPECTIVES

Dr. Robert Sternberg of Yale University is an innovative thinker who has challenged conventional, one-dimensional theories of intelligence. He has developed a Triarchic Abilities Test that measures (1) analytical, (2) creative, and (3) practical abilities. In contrast, more conventional IQ tests focus on analytical abilities.

Recent research on individuals who have distinctively different profiles in terms of these three intellectual abilities confirms what many educators have suspected for a long time — that different teaching styles really do work better for certain students. When different teaching and testing styles were used with college students, for instance, Sternberg proved that students who were taught in ways that "matched" their ability profile — emphasizing their strengths in either analytical, creative, or practical thinking — performed markedly better compared to similar students who were in classrooms "mismatched" to their intellectual strengths. Sternberg strongly affirms that students of all ages should be able to learn in ways that:

- **Build directly upon their strengths**
- **Allow for compensation for, and remediation of, weaknesses**
- **Use multiple evaluation techniques that allow each learner to demonstrate what has been mastered or accomplished.**

important social skills of children. In a balanced approach to education, children can succeed through many different routes, not just one.

Teaching to strengths must become the norm if children and society are to realize the full potential of education. Parents can promote this actively at home and in their parent involvement at school. One freedom that adult learners have is that they get to select what they want to learn and do in life, when and where they will learn it, and how they will use their new knowledge. Moreover, they can quit if they don't like something or are not making satisfying progress. Many adults build their lives on their strengths and minimize or hide their weaknesses. In our diversified society, there is ample opportunity for people to excel in different ways.

The start your child gets on the path of lifelong learning is precious, irreplaceable, and vital to success. Make sure your child has every chance to develop and build on his strengths.

HELPING TO DEVELOP CHILDREN'S RESILIENCE

Most children are remarkably adaptable, able to bounce back, and resourceful enough to think of different ways to do things. However, some children may be less flexible, accommodating, and easy-going.

All children encounter disappointments, failures, frustrations, losses, and unfairness. To weather these inevitables, children acquire resilience.

A number of years ago, two prominent child specialists, Dr. Norman Garmezy of the University of Minnesota and Dr. Emmy Werner of the University of California at Davis, observed that some children in extremely challenging life circumstances did far better than expected. They postulated that some children were more "resilient" than others or were "vulnerable but invincible." Why some children do well in the face of adversity is a fascinating and important question.

What is it about those children who do so well against the odds? Are these children smarter, more attractive, less aware of the negative aspects of their lives? Or have they encountered people who have helped to offset tragic circumstances or inadequate resources? Many scientists and clinicians worldwide are studying what accounts for such resilience.

Over the past decade, Dr. Edith Grotberg of the University of Alabama at Birmingham has launched a monumental study of more than 1,200 families, and children in over 20 countries. Collaboration with colleagues at colleges and universities around the world has produced a great deal of information about children's resilience and how adults promote it. This project is focusing on understanding the *sources of resilience.*

One key finding that has emerged so far is this: for younger children, resilience is promoted largely by parents and other adults. Older children, on the other hand, more actively take responsibility for resilience, including seeking help from peers and others.

There is much inspiration to be gained from realizing how well many children and families worldwide survive tragic circumstances. Do not think that resilience is only for times of war, natural disaster, or other extreme conditions. Resilience can be put to good use regularly by all families. In fact, resilience is vital for coping with the inevitable ups and downs that are part of all of our lives.

Do not worry about whether your child has enough adversity in her life. You will not need to create extreme or artificial conditions to have a resilient child. Life will afford adequate opportunities.

A final word of clarification: even though children can learn from adversity, subjecting your child to poor schooling is not an advisable way to achieve this. Resilience requires being able to solve problems, trust others, and to evaluate situations in a timely and accurate way. A good education helps promote resilience. A poor education or a poor schooling experience does not foster resilience. It hinders it, especially in the early years when children aren't particularly self-reliant and resourceful.

FIFTEEN ELEMENTS OF RESILIENCE

While extreme conditions affecting children in some parts of the world may not seem relevant to your family, some valuable lessons have been learned that may apply to your child. In summarizing what parents and adult caregivers throughout the world shared, Dr. Grotberg identified 15 features of children's evolving resilience. These are not to be expected in their full form in a three- or four-year-old, or even an eight-year-old. But study this list and consider the ways that you and your child's teacher can encourage these qualities and provide the context for optimizing resilience.

To overcome adversities, children, youth, and adults draw from three sources of resilience: I HAVE, I AM, and I CAN.*

I HAVE

1. **People around me I trust and who love me, no matter what**
2. **People who set limits for me so I know when to stop before there is danger or trouble**
3. **People who show me how to do things right by the way they do things**
4. **People who want me to learn to do things on my own**
5. **People who help me when I am sick, in danger, or need to learn.**

I AM

6. **A person people can like and love**
7. **Glad to do nice things for others and show my concern**
8. **Respectful of myself and others**
9. **Willing to be responsible for what I do**
10. **Sure things will be all right.**

I CAN

11. **Talk to others about things that frighten me or bother me**
12. **Find ways to solve problems that I face**
13. **Control myself when I feel like doing something not right or dangerous**
14. **Figure out when it is a good time to talk to someone or take action**
15. **Find someone to help me when I need it.**

*"I Am, I Have, I Can: What Families Worldwide Taught Us About Resilience" by Edith Grotberg, Ph.D. Reprinted from *Reaching Today's Youth: The Community Circle of Caring Journal,* Vol. 2, Issue 3. Copyright 1998 by the National Educational Service, 800-733-6786.

LEARNING AND ATTENTIONAL PROBLEMS IN CHILDHOOD

Attentional disorders and learning disabilities are the most common "serious" school difficulties that receive outside professional consultation, diagnosis, and treatment. They usually are not detected until the first or second grade. All parents should know some basic information about these common disorders:

- **When and how often such problems are diagnosed varies among countries and cultures.**
- **There are many unresolved issues and controversies about accurate, responsible diagnosis and treatment for the most common childhood problems.**
- **Parents and teachers often see a child in a very different light. They may have different standards for judging what behavior is acceptable or ideal at a given age or in particular situations.**
- **All children show large differences in their attention and learning abilities as they grow.**

The effects of labeling a child as having a learning or attention problem are not fully known. Negative and positive effects have been reported. The consequences probably depend on when and how the situation is handled.

Too often, labeling a child's difficulties has led to inadequate, short-term solutions, such as medicating or transferring the child to special education with no plan for improving the situation. This is especially unfortunate because there is ample evidence that multi-faceted approaches yield the best outcomes.

When such difficulties are identified, vigorous efforts should be made to understand all possible causes — biological or maturational, family-related, school-related, or individual differences in learning style. Then parents, teachers, and specialists can develop a treatment plan tailored to the child. Such a plan may include changing things at home and/or at school, specialized therapies, or medication.

Any proposed plan must take into account the rapid developmental changes and phenomenal amounts of learning that all children experience in these early school years. The child's strong need to be continuously engaged in learning and advancing is often neglected as frustrated educators and parents seek to "end" problem behavior or create a compliant and conforming child.

The history books are replete with examples of famous and highly productive individuals who did not fit into the schools of their day. Thomas Edison's and Albert Einstein's early school failures are well-known (teachers thought both men were dull and slow). Can anyone imagine Wolfgang Mozart *not* having been home-schooled and privately tutored to "teach to his strengths"? Even Nobel Prize-winners such as Dr. James Watson, who helped solve the mysteries of DNA, were judged by some to have very ordinary or even low intelligence. Dr. Watson proudly tells of his rejection from one prominent graduate school that advised him to seek another career, since it thought he clearly lacked the mental capacities to succeed as a biologist! For these and many other accomplished individuals, can we fathom what their lives might have become if they had been evaluated, diagnosed, and treated as having an attention disorder or a learning disability? They might well have qualified for such diagnoses by the fluctuating standards and practices in use throughout our country. And who knows what forms of treatment intervention they might have been given using today's standards?

We are not against efforts to find out why children have adjustment problems, or having qualified specialists diagnose and recommend treatment. We also are not opposed to the use of medication or behavioral control programs. Many children and families have benefitted from such efforts.

However, we are acutely aware of far too many situations where the right level and quality of supports and expertise were not available or used. Study after study documents the biases that can result when children's problems are labeled, when children are placed unnecessarily in special education (or denied such placement when it might be beneficial), and when the focus is on the problem rather than on the child's total development and education.

We strongly advocate:

- **Seeking early and high-quality assessment of suspected problems.**
- **Obtaining at least two assessments or professional opinions, even if the first seems satisfactory.**
- **Including interdisciplinary perspectives, rather than relying on one field of expertise. This is especially true for such problems as persistent headaches that do not respond to standard treatment or for reading delays in an otherwise bright child. Experts from several fields – nutritionists, psychologists, occupational therapists, neurologists, optometrists, ophthalmologists, audiologists, pediatricians, reading specialists, and nurse practitioners – may contribute to an effective solution.**
- **Reading extensively from the most recent scientific and professional journals from leading universities.**
- **Talking with other families with similar recent experiences.**
- **Providing extra supports and encouragement for your child, especially during the early efforts to understand and resolve the problem.**
- **Not blaming your child or anyone else until you have "the big picture."**
- **Being wary about any person or company promising something that works for most or all children and costs a lot.**
- **Supporting expanded research on learning in regard to all types of children with and without exceptionalities and with different learning styles.**

We now know a great deal about the many conditions that contribute to developmental problems in children. Many discoveries concern rare childhood disorders, but our knowledge is growing. We advise parents to be optimistic and cautious in applying new research findings to a child's life!

THE MOST COMMON CHILDHOOD "DIFFICULTIES"

It is beyond the scope of this book to cover children's disorders in depth. Thought and observation are certainly valuable if your child is having difficulties. But we strongly admonish parents not to diagnose on their own.

Three types of childhood difficulty may be encountered by readers:

- **Problems related to language arts, especially reading failure or delays. These are discussed in Chapter 10.**
- **Academic capabilities that are not fully recognized or nurtured in typical classroom environments.**
- **Suspicion of problems related to paying attention and conforming to classroom expectations for behavior.**

FOR CHILDREN WITH ADVANCED DEVELOPMENT

NANCY M. ROBINSON, PH.D.

Dr. Nancy M. Robinson is a world-renowned child psychologist and scientist who has nurtured academically advanced young children and their families for many decades. She is Director of the Halbert B. Robinson Center for Capable Youth at the University of Washington in Seattle.

You may have noticed that in some ways, your child's development is ahead of agemates in her preschool or those you've seen on the playground. Perhaps her conversation is more complex. Perhaps her interests and even her fears are more like those of older children. She may be reading independently (although many bright children are not early readers). She may have a remarkable memory for details or for events long ago. Maybe she comments on numerical relationships, asks questions about big numbers, and sees patterns readily. Maybe she does many-piece puzzles quickly, draws more complex pictures, uses pencils and scissors with skill. Your child is unlikely to be equally skilled in all areas — hardly any children are — and may or may not be gifted in academic skills. But her advancement is worth your attention.

As "real school" approaches, you may wonder whether the school is as ready for your child as she is for school! You're probably wise to keep an eye on how things go, because your child — who has been so eagerly anticipating kindergarten — may be disappointed that the pace seems slow, or that what is presented as "new" is really "old" to her. Of course, at the beginning of school, some of this is likely to happen for most children, as teachers assess what new students already know and where they need help to move on.

For the latter two topics, the following materials come from leading experts. For further information, use as many sources as you can, including your child's teacher and other school personnel, pediatricians, local experts, other parents, libraries, bookstores, and your child. Some parents are amazed to learn that their child knows a lot about what's happening and can provide valuable clues to help improve the situation.

But if the situation persists for more than six weeks, it is probably time to ask for a special conference with the teacher to brainstorm what sorts of adaptations might be useful and doable in the school context. For example, your child might be excused from exercises designed to teach what she already knows and given different work, preferably more advanced or complex, to do instead. When other children are writing a sentence, your child might be expected to write a paragraph. If your child is a reader, you can make sure to tuck a book in the backpack that he could read when class work is completed early. (After first grade, the book should probably be nonfiction so it looks like "work.") The situation is likely to be more acute in first grade than kindergarten for children who are already fluent readers, because in first grade, reading receives the primary emphasis.

In addition to establishing a partnership with your child's teacher, be sure to acquaint yourself with the special services your school district may offer highly capable children. Some districts offer self-contained (full-time) classes; some have "pull-out" enrichment classes a few hours a week; some cluster the brighter children within a single, regular classroom; some have consultants who work with teachers; some offer after-school activities. Seldom do these begin at kindergarten, and many do not begin until third grade or so, by which time many highly capable children have endured a good deal of disappointment.

Be sure you know about application deadlines for special services. If you think your child is seriously mismatched with the school setting, you may want to seek testing from a qualified psychologist to further your understanding of your child's abilities and academic skills, and to clarify matters for the school. There's no reason to seek testing if things are going well or if such information won't be used in the near future.

Continued

FOR CHILDREN WITH ADVANCED DEVELOPMENT (CONTINUED)

The main way you'll know whether your child is thriving at school is by watching and listening, even though your young child isn't likely to say much when you ask directly, "What did you do in school today?" Is your child eager for school in the morning? Are the stories he tells you casually about school positive or negative? Do you see new skills emerging and being refined? Does your child pop out with unexpected information about new topics? Does he approach new situations with the confidence of one who has met challenges and mastered them?

In a healthy situation, these things should be happening for every child. If they are not happening for your child, it's time to approach the teacher to discuss the situation so that you can problem-solve together. Try some experiments to see what works. Yet even the best-hearted teacher is unlikely to be able to differentiate more than a portion of your child's school assignments from the rest of the class. Remember that the teacher has a whole room full of children. Be reasonable in your expectations. Remember also that a good deal of what children learn comes from home. Keep on enriching your child's experience outside of school with interesting extra-curricular lessons and family activities. If your child is good at math, engage her in the numerical side of family activities such as cooking, gardening, vacation-planning, even going out for dinner. And – above all – keep reading, reading, reading to your child even after he can read well.

What if you have one of those rare children who is remarkably ahead in one or several aspects of development, one of the "profoundly gifted?" If the talents lie in school domains, there are a number of ways your child's education might be accelerated. Some children with fall birthdays may enter school a year early. In the early grades, acceleration may mean going to a higher class for part of the day or even skipping a grade. Some parents these days even turn to home schooling as a solution for all or part of the day, though this solution obviously has many pitfalls.

What if your child shows a special talent in some skill that is not emphasized at school, such as music, dance, art, or creative writing? During the early school years, it's usually best to find a tutor or mentor who is pretty good at the skill but mainly loves to teach and understands young children. If your child progresses rapidly and continues to show unusual talent, after a few years you probably will need to switch to a more specialized teacher and "go for it." But at the beginning, the most important goal is to help your child love the activity and learn to weather what it takes to get better at it. It's important not to outpace your child's motivation and desire.

HELPFUL HINTS

- **Don't be overwhelmed** by a gifted child who can argue you out of any rule you lay down or needs four new reasons to take a bath! Your child needs structure and predictability in life as much as any other child does!
- **Some reasonably bright** children learn to read before they go to school. Some very bright children learn to read when everybody else does. It's true that early readers do tend to stay ahead of average readers (trading reading comprehension for pure and simple decoding), but bright students who learn to read at the ordinary age are likely to become good readers very quickly and advance just as well in the long run.
- **Being "gifted"** doesn't make your child immune from other disorders of childhood – learning disabilities, behavior problems, attention deficit disorders, or any other childhood disability except slow learning. Sometimes, though, it is hard to separate hyperactivity and/or inattention from the energy, curiosity, intensity, and restlessness of a gifted child for whom school is moving too slowly.
- **Just because children** are bright, don't expect them to be perfect, and don't let them expect it of themselves.

As a final note, at the University of Washington's Halbert B. Robinson Center for Capable Youth, the following is shared with parents who request information on how to engage children who are advanced:

> *"There are some popular books by such authors as Doman, White, Engleman, and Beck which assert that, by following their planned program of activities, a child can be made more intelligent. Most have some useful ideas for stimulating activities, but the intensive programs advocated by these writers (particularly Doman) are not in the best interests of children or parents, and no scientific evidence exists for IQ-raising in young children already living in supportive families."*

ATTENTION DEFICIT DISORDER (ADD) AND ATTENTION DEFICIT/HYPERACTIVITY DISORDER (ADHD)

The disorders now referred to as Attention Deficit Disorder (ADD) and Attention Deficit/Hyperactivity Disorder (ADHD) are the most commonly diagnosed neurobehavioral disorders in children. From three to five percent of the general population is estimated to have these disorders, although the rates during the school years are much higher — perhaps 10 to 20 percent. Boys are at least four times as likely as girls to be diagnosed with one of these conditions. There is mounting concern about the increasing numbers of children being diagnosed and the possible overuse or misuse of prescribed medications.

The key defining features of these disorders involve (1) multiple behavioral symptoms of inattention, which may occur with or without (2) multiple symptoms of hyperactivity and impulsivity. For school-age children, what is most noticeable is the tremendous difficulty they have with "cognitively effortful work." The clinical diagnosis of either ADD or ADHD relies on evidence of a strong, consistent behavioral pattern for at least six months that occurs in multiple settings (not just at school) and is associated with impairment in everyday activities.

Because preschool-age children are normally very active and not highly attentive in the everyday sense of the word, it is important to avoid giving very young children inaccurate labels. Children with true ADD are more prone to temper tantrums, noisy and unruly behavior, frequent arguing, aggression, and fearless actions that often cause injury. This early form of ADD often is the most troublesome and long-lasting.

ADD becomes apparent in elementary school much more often than in preschool. For children who are diagnosed in elementary school, common complicating factors include poor peer relationships and non-compliant behavior in the classroom. Also, learning disabilities, especially in reading, often occur in children diagnosed with ADD.

The most widespread form of treatment for ADD involves the use of drugs — mostly stimulants — to control behavior and improve concentration. Effectiveness in carefully diagnosed children is estimated at 70 percent or better. Schoolwork and social interactions typically show improvement immediately. Predicting which medication will work best for a child is still more an art than a precise science.

The best approach appears to be one that uses multiple methods involving home and school management programs, daily monitoring, and medication.

Many parents are unaware of the following important facts about these disorders:

- **There is no single diagnostic test for ADD or ADHD.** The diagnosis is a clinical judgment based on direct observation, clinical interviews, and other people's descriptions of the child's behavior.
- **The cause or causes of ADD are not known.** Specialists believe a combination of biological and psychosocial factors probably account for most cases.
- **Children with ADD or ADHD do not simply "outgrow" it** when they enter puberty, although the most pressing behavioral concerns are likely to change with age.
- **Despite the names, ADD and ADHD have not been proven to be caused by attentional processing problems.** Note that there is a lot of confusion in the technical versus common use of the word "attention."

There are a number of national support groups for families, including Children and Adults with Attention Deficit/Hyperactivity Disorder (CHADD) and National Attention Deficit Disorder Association (ADDA).

For excellent reviews of the scientific and treatment literature on these disorders, see Bennett Shaywitz, Jack Fletcher, and Sally Shaywitz, "Attention-Deficit/Hyperactivity Disorder" in *Advances in Pediatrics,* 1997, and Dennis Cantwell, "Attention Deficit Disorder: A Review of the Past 10 Years," *Journal of the American Academy of Child and Adolescent Psychiatry,* 1996.

INDIVIDUALITY DOES NOT MEAN WEIRDNESS OR GENIUS. IT JUST IS.

To end this chapter, we want to encourage parents to recognize, accept, and cherish their children's individuality. Your children will be like and unlike you. This is true in all types of families and all types of children.

Use your compassion and empathy from your experiences when your child's similarities to you are a source of challenge, distinction, or celebration for your child.

When facets of your child's individuality are foreign to you, get insights from others who have been there. Children invariably lack at least one trait that their parents value, such as neatness, logical planning, or patience. The child may not show it, and perhaps doesn't like or want that trait. Keep your senses of balance and humor. You will need them. So will your child. And everyone will benefit. There is no one prescription for being a great child or grownup, or having a wonderful education and life!

LOOKING TO THE FUTURE

YOUR CHILD'S FIRST FEW YEARS IN SCHOOL WILL BE TRANSFORMED INTO LIFETIME MEMORIES. SOME WILL FADE. BUT YOUR CHILD'S FEELINGS ABOUT SCHOOL AND HIS LOVE OF LEARNING WILL BE SHAPED BY THESE EARLY EXPERIENCES. SO WILL HIS SENSE OF COMPETENCY AND SELF-WORTH IN DEALING WITH INTELLECTUAL AND SOCIAL MATTERS.

Measure your child's success in school in many ways that relate to daily well-being and zest for life. Some struggles are inevitable. They are sources of learning and growth. Many early problems can be identified and addressed so they do not become major obstacles to later school adjustment.

Celebrate your child's accomplishments and strengths. Make sure she often experiences success. Her individuality will become increasingly apparent, probably with some surprises. Children, like adults, are not always consistent. Be slow to label your child as "not good" in something, especially in front of her.

We asked faculty, administrators, and graduates of the School of Education at Samford University, Birmingham, Alabama, what they would recommend to parents of children three to eight years old. Here is what they shared:

- **Turn off the television and video games on school nights.**
- **Read to your child nightly.**
- **Have lots of conversations with your child.**
- **Be a mentor to your child.**
- **Become an involved parent in many ways.**
- **Create a time and place for schoolwork and provide needed supervision.**

- **Give your child lots of interesting experiences and family outings.**
- **Let your child see you read.**
- **Provide learning games that promote skills, such as cards and Scrabble.**
- **Eat lunch with your child at school several times a year.**
- **Communicate your concerns early and often with teachers.**
- **Understand what the teacher and school expect from your child and you.**
- **Ask your child questions about school in a positive way.**
- **Buy lots of books for your child.**
- **Establish and keep a regular bedtime.**
- **Make and serve breakfast.**
- **Get to know your child's teacher.**
- **READ, READ, READ and talk about what has been read.**
- **Promote responsibility.**

There is much wisdom in these teachers' words. Given the amount of time parents and children spend together in the first five years, parents teach their children far more than teachers do. Your contributions to your child's understanding of life and to school subjects will not end when school begins. Most parents enjoy going to school a second time through their child's experiences. Have a great adventure as your family shares the experience of going to school, pursues lifelong learning, and celebrates human adaptability, ingenuity, intelligence, and love.

Sharon Landesman Ramey
Craig T. Ramey

Additional References

AND SOURCES OF INFORMATION FOR PARENTS

Early development, learning, and school adjustment: Some recent excellent books include:

Hall, Susan L. and Moats, Louisa C. (1999). *Straight Talk about Reading.* Chicago, IL: Contemporary Books

Levine, Karen (1997). *What to Do When Your Child Has Trouble at School.* Pleasantville, NY: Reader's Digest

Shelov, Steven P. (Ed.) (1998). The American Academy of Pediatrics' *Caring for Your Baby and Young Child, Birth to Age 5.* New York: Bantam Books

Shore, Rima (1997). *Rethinking the Brain: New Insights into Early Development.* New York: Families and Work Institute

Several leading textbooks on early childhood education and classroom management may also be of interest to parents:

Morrison, George S. (1998). *Early Childhood Education Today.* Upper Saddle River, NJ: Prentice Hall

Cunningham, Patricia M. and Allington, Richard L. (1999). *Classrooms that Work: They Can* All *Read and Write.* New York: Addison-Wesley

Seefeldt, Carol and Galper, Alice (Eds.) (1998). *Continuing Issues in Early Childhood Education.* Upper Saddle River, NJ: Prentice Hall

Bredekamp, Sue and Copple, Carol (Eds.) (1997). *Developmentally Appropriate Practice in Early Childhood Programs.* Washington, D.C.: National Association for the Education of Young Children

Specialty books and periodicals: There are many magazines for parents and families with young children. These are excellent sources of news about research findings and practical tips for parents. Periodicals on home computers often contain reliable reviews of software programs for young children. A number of books describe children's software programs, and include suggestions for appropriate use of computers with very young children. Finally, many books provide annotated lists of great children's books for parents and children, usually organized by children's ages and topics.

Children with special needs: There are many associations for parents whose children have special needs. These associations often are excellent sources of information and offer support, ideas, and encouragement to parents. Some parent advocacy organizations have endorsed treatment approaches or educational practices that professionals have judged to be ineffective or, more often, not yet proven. Yet parents' organizations have undeniably wielded tremendous political power in advancing research to improve the health, education, and quality of life for children whose development is not typical. We encourage parents to talk with other parents and professionals they trust about these organizations.

Professional associations: Major professional associations that are directly relevant to understanding children's early learning, development, and school success include:

- The Society for Research in Child Development
- The American Educational Research Association
- The National Association for the Education of Young Children
- The American Academy of Pediatrics

These professional associations all publish journals and special books or monographs for scientists and practitioners. Increasingly, these professional organizations also are reaching out to parents to share important advances in understanding children and what parents can do to promote positive development.

Educational philosophers: Finally, not everything old is out-of-date. Many great educational philosophers of this century have written extensively on education and young children. Their original words often are inspiring and fascinating treatises on the deliberations of their day about how to educate young children. Readers will find that not all current debates are new. There have always been differences of opinion and struggles about which educational approach works best for most children.

About the Authors

DRS. SHARON LANDESMAN RAMEY AND CRAIG T. RAMEY are two of the most highly regarded child development researchers in the country. They have extensive experience in successfully promoting early child development, school readiness, and success in school and life. They are co-authors of *Right from Birth: Building Your Child's Foundation for Life — Birth to 18 Months* (1999, Goddard Press).

The Drs. Ramey are the founding Directors of the Civitan International Research Center at the University of Alabama at Birmingham, an interdisciplinary center dedicated to research, training, and service about human development, focusing on preventing and treating learning and intellectual disabilities. The Rameys hold professorships in Psychology, Pediatrics, Psychiatry, Neurobiology, Sociology, Maternal and Child Health, and Nursing.

Dr. Sharon Landesman Ramey received her B.A. from New College in Sarasota, Florida, and her graduate education at the Institute of Child Development at the University of Minnesota and the University of Washington, where she received her Ph.D. in Developmental Psychology. Dr. Craig T. Ramey earned his B.A., M.A., and Ph.D. from West Virginia University and completed postdoctoral training at the University of California at Berkeley.

Collectively, the Rameys have published more than 350 scientific articles, chapters, commissioned reports, and books for professional and scientific audiences. They each serve as frequent consultants, advisors, reviewers, and keynote speakers on the topics of early child development, families, parenting, school readiness, children's disabilities, school adjustment, effective prevention and treatment programs, and public policy related to children and families.

The Rameys each have received numerous citations and awards for their many independent and joint research contributions. Dr. Craig Ramey received the American

Psychological Association Award for Exemplary Prevention Research and recently was designated as a University Professor by the Board of Trustees of the University of Alabama. Dr. Sharon Ramey is the recipient of the 1999 Award for Distinguished Research from the American Association on Mental Retardation and was elected to fellowship status in the American Psychological Association, the International Association for the Scientific Study of Intellectual Disabilities, and the American Association on Mental Retardation. The Rameys serve in leadership roles for many national and international professional organizations.

This year, the Rameys completed the largest study ever of children and families during their transition to school. Its purpose was to better understand the factors that contribute to children's early school success. This Congressionally-funded study followed over 10,000 children nationwide from kindergarten through the first four years in elementary school. It involved collaborative research with colleagues at more than 30 universities and colleges.

The Rameys also have completed major research on the following topics: changes in American family life and their implications for elementary school–age children; how early educational and family supports can enhance the school achievement and life success of children from families with multiple challenges; and how university–community partnerships can strengthen families, children, and schools. Their research has included children from all walks of life. These include children with developmental delays and those who are gifted; those from different ethnic, cultural, and geographic backgrounds; and those in school and community settings that offer varying levels of support.

The Rameys have three grown daughters, a young son still at home, and two granddaughters. They live in Birmingham, Alabama.

Also from Goddard Press:

★

Right From Birth

Building Your Child's Foundation for Life

Birth to 18 Months

Craig T. Ramey, Ph.D. ★ Sharon L. Ramey, Ph.D.

A comprehensive guide to raising happy, well-adjusted, successful children *Right From Birth.* In this landmark book the Rameys make sense of the wealth of new research that shows how everything — from personality to early learning ability — is being shaped for a lifetime *beginning in infancy.* They then translate their expertise into "Seven Essentials" — practical steps parents can use every day to raise good-natured, confident, caring, and accomplished children.

Me, Myself and I

How Children Build Their Sense of Self

18 to 36 Months

Kyle D. Pruett, M.D.

An indispensable guide to the phenomenal growth of competence, personality, and self-image in early childhood — and *how parents can guide the process and shape the outcome for life.* Richly illustrated with warm, humorous, "real life" case studies, *Me, Myself and I* is filled with proven strategies based on the best scientific, clinical, and child development knowledge.

KYLE PRUETT is a practicing child and family psychiatrist, clinical professor at the Yale Child Study Center, and president of Zero to Three — National Center for Infants, Toddlers and Families, the nation's leading "think tank" on early childhood development.